ITALIAN HORROR CINEMA

ITALIAN HORROR CINEMA

Edited by Stefano Baschiera and Russ Hunter

EDINBURGH
University Press

Edinburgh University Press is one of the leading university presses in the UK. We publish academic books and journals in our selected subject areas across the humanities and social sciences, combining cutting-edge scholarship with high editorial and production values to produce academic works of lasting importance. For more information visit our website: www.edinburghuniversitypress.com

Edinburgh University Press Ltd
The Tun – Holyrood Road
12 (2f) Jackson's Entry
Edinburgh EH8 8PJ

Typeset in 10/12.5 pt Sabon by
Servis Filmsetting Ltd, Stockport, Cheshire
and printed and bound in Great Britain by
CPI Group UK (Ltd), Croydon CR0 4YY

A CIP record for this book is available from the British Library

ISBN 978 0 7486 9352 8 (hardback)
ISBN 978 1 4744 1968 0 (paperback)
ISBN 978 0 7486 9353 5 (webready PDF)
ISBN 978 1 4744 0581 2 (epub)

CONTENTS

FIGURES

CONTRIBUTORS

Stefano Baschiera is Lecturer in Film Studies at Queen's University Belfast. His work on European cinema and film industries has been published in a variety of edited collections and journals including *Film International, Bianco e Nero, Italian Studies, New Review of Film and Television Studies*.

Mark Bernard is an Instructor of American Studies at the University of North Carolina at Charlotte. He is the author of *Selling the Splat Pack: The DVD Revolution and the American Horror Film* (Edinburgh University Press, 2014) and co-author (with Cynthia Baron and Diane Carson) of *Appetites and Anxieties: Food, Film, and the Politics of Representation* (2014). He has written about food in horror cinema and race in serial killer cinema, among other topics. He is currently writing about acting and stardom in horror cinema and television.

Francesco Di Chiara is Associate Professor of Film Studies at the eCampus University (Novedrate, Italy). He is part of the editorial board of the international journal of film studies *Cinéma & Cie*. His research interests include (but are not limited to) Italian genre cinema from the 1940s to the 1960s, the European film industry, and Italian film co-productions. He is the author of *I tre volti dell'orrore, Il cinema horror italiano 1947–1965* (2009), *Generi e industria cinematografica in Italia: il caso Titanus 1949–1964* (2013) and *Peplum: il cinema italiano alle prese con il mondo antico* (2016).

Austin Fisher is Senior Lecturer in Film and Television Studies at Bournemouth University, author of *Radical Frontiers in the Spaghetti Western*, editor of *Spaghetti Westerns at the Crossroads* (Edinburgh University Press) and founding co-editor of Bloomsbury's 'Global Exploitation Cinemas' book series. He is also founding Co-Chair of the SCMS 'Transnational Cinemas' Scholarly Interest Group, serves on the editorial boards of the *[in]Transition* and *Transnational Cinemas* journals, and is founder of the Spaghetti Cinema festival.

Craig Hatch is a PhD candidate specialising in film sound and Asian cinema at the University of Southampton. He currently runs www.horrorjapan.com, a project that aims to review and collate media from all aspects of Japanese horror culture.

Leon Hunt is Senior Lecturer in Screen Media at Brunel University. He is the author of *British Low Culture: From Safari Suits to Sexploitation* (1998), *Kung Fu Cult Masters: From Bruce Lee to Crouching Tiger* (2003), *The League of Gentlemen* (2008), *Cult British TV Comedy: From Reeves & Mortimer to Psychoville* (2013), and co-editor of *East Asian Cinemas: Exploring Transnational Connections on Film* (2008) and *Screening the Undead: Vampires and Zombies in Film and Television* (2014).

Russ Hunter is Senior Lecturer in Film & Television at the University of Northumbria. His research is focused upon Italian genre cinema, critical reception, European horror cinema and genre film festivals. His monograph, *A History of European Horror Cinema*, is due to be published with Edinburgh University Press in 2016.

Peter Hutchings is Professor of Film Studies at Northumbria University. He is the author of *Hammer and Beyond: The British Horror Film, Terence Fisher, The British Film Guide to Dracula, The Horror Film* and *The Historical Dictionary of Horror Cinema*, as well as co-editor of *The Film Studies Reader*. He has also published numerous journal articles and book chapters on horror cinema, British film and television, science fiction cinema and television, and the thriller.

Marcia Landy is Distinguished Professor Emerita in English/Film Studies with a Secondary appointment in French and Italian at the University of Pittsburgh. Her books include *Fascism in Film: The Italian Commercial Cinema 1931–1943* (1986); *Film Politics, and Gramsci* (1994); *Cinematic Uses of the Past* (1996); *The Folklore of Consensus: Theatricality in Italian Cinema* (1998); *Italian Cinema* (2000); *The Historical Film: History and Memory in Media* (2000); *Stardom Italian Style: in Italian Cinema* (2008) and *Cinema and Counter-History* (2015). Her essays appear in anthologies on Italian cinema, British cinema, history in and of film, film genres (Western, biopic, horror and comedy), melodrama, fascism and film.

Adam Lowenstein is Associate Professor of English and Film Studies at the University of Pittsburgh, where he also directs the Film Studies Program. He is the author of *Shocking Representation: Historical Trauma, National Cinema, and the Modern Horror Film* (2005) and *Dreaming of Cinema: Spectatorship, Surrealism, and the Age of Digital Media* (2015).

Paolo Noto is currently a fixed-term lecturer at the University of Bologna. His main research interests are Intertextuality and film, genre theory and history of post-war Italian. His publications include *Il cinema neorealista*, a reader on Italian neorealism co-edited with Francesco Pitassio (2010), and *Dal bozzetto ai generi* (2011), a monograph in which he challenged the most established examples of theory of film genres in the light of Italian popular films of the 1950s. His article '"Che credeva, che fossi Cenerentola!": Changes of Clothes, Guest Appearances, and Other Diva Performances in 1950s Cinema' was published in a recent issue of *Italian Studies*.

Karl Schoonover is Associate Professor (Reader) of Film and Television Studies at the University of Warwick. He is the author of *Brutal Vision: the Neorealist Body in Postwar Italian Cinema* (2012), co-author of *Queer Cinema in the World* (2016) and co-editor of *Global Art Cinema* (2010).

Johnny Walker is Lecturer in Media at Northumbria University. He is the author of *Contemporary British Horror Cinema: Industry, Genre and Society* (Edinburgh University Press, 2015), co-editor of *Snuff: Real Death and Screen Media* (2016), and is a founding editor of Bloomsbury's 'Global Exploitation Cinemas' book series. He is currently working on a book about the infancy of video rental culture in Britain.

ACKNOWLEDGEMENTS

Sincere thanks to all of our contributors for all of their hard work and for their enduring patience. Plus, a special thanks to Gillian Leslie, Eddie Clark and Richard Strachan of EUP for their unfailing support and encouragement.

Stefano Baschiera
I would like to thank Queen's University Belfast for funding a semester sabbatical which allowed me to work on this book. A particular acknowledgement goes to Daniel Martin for his 'matchmaker' role, as he made the suggestion of being in contact with Russ when I began to think of this endeavour. A thank you is also due to Francesco Di Chiara, Paolo Noto, Francesco Pitassio and Christopher Wagstaff for their support and advice on this research, and to Laura Rascaroli for the continued inspiration. Finally, I would like to thank Elena Caoduro for her uncanny ability to spot all my typos and because she still covers her eyes during the scary parts of horror films.

Russ Hunter
A very big thank you to my colleagues in the Department of Media & Communication Design at Northumbria University – as ever, their support was unfailing and is sincerely appreciated. But, most of all, thanks to my wife, Pamela Atzori, for her unflagging support and brave attempts at enthusiasm amid all this talk of gore and mayhem.

ACKNOWLEDGMENTS

INTRODUCTION

Stefano Baschiera and Russ Hunter

THE UNEXPECTED CONTEXTS OF ITALIAN HORROR CINEMA

When the esteemed English actor David Hemmings passed away at the end of 2003 his obituary quickly appeared in numerous newspapers. Naturally his long and varied career was widely celebrated. Few newspapers, however, gave much attention to his starring role in Italian horror film director Dario Argento's *Profondo rosso/Deep Red* (1975). One of the few exceptions here was *The Guardian*, which rather enigmatically noted that Hemmings sometimes turned up in 'unexpected contexts' (Pulleine, 2003). Over the course of its history from the late 1950s until at least the early 1980s, Italian horror was unique enough, strange enough and distinctive enough to be considered an 'unusual context'. The nature of Italian horror films varied greatly depending upon the director involved and the budget available. But a typical Italian horror might 'star' a partly or mildly well-known British or American actor, be directed by an Italian using an Anglo-Saxon pseudonym operating on a low budget, ape at least some of the central features of a previously successful film (perhaps copying the formula of its title), contain a large smattering of gore, and nudity, be scored with a pulsating (possibly synth-based) soundtrack and receive little or no critical praise.

In many ways *Profondo rosso* was atypical, as Dario Argento had access to higher budgets than his contemporaries, better distribution channels and was arguably the first Italian horror director with 'auteur' ambitions.[1] Instead, most Italian horror directors, working with low budgets and constricted schedules, were viewed more as popular cinema specialists rather than formally esteemed craftsmen. Regardless, David Hemmings' appearance in one of the most iconic of all Italian horror films was not really all that unexpected, at least not within the context of how Italian horror cinema functioned as a whole. The dynamics of how such films were conceived, produced, marketed and exhibited are exemplary of the way Italian low-budget genre production of the time worked. However, it is precisely these features that mean Italian horror cinema has, for most of its history, been viewed as a particularly lowbrow manifestation of genre cinema. As Leon Hunt (2000: 326) has noted, there is a long-standing orthodoxy among critics of the horror film that suggests '"good" horror movies do not show much actual horror (Universal, Lewton, Tourneur), but "bad" ones do (Hammer, the Italians) because they lack imagination, taste and restraint'. But more than just being viewed as 'bad' horror for their lack of coherence or for being too gory, Italian horror films have also been controversial. They have, at various points, been caught up in legal battles, and most notably were central players in the Video Nasties phenomenon in the UK in the early 1980s. Overall, Italian horror has been defined, understood and canonised internationally by its extreme content, arguably its only common feature in relation to the variegated production mechanisms that directly challenged its national belonging.

THE TRANSNATIONAL ROOTS OF ITALIAN HORROR CINEMA

Somewhat perversely defining the 'Italian' in Italian horror is not a straight-forward task. A tendency towards more extreme, visceral content aside, there are few easily recognisable 'Italian features' in the films produced. So many of the characteristics most notably recognised as informing and defining Italian horror films – from the international casts, the use of directorial pen-names, the often non-Italian settings, the international funding arrangements, to the intended final market, etc. – challenge a clear sense of national identification.

Generally, the development of genre film in Italy owes to the borrowing, imitation and adaptation of non-native models (in particular, American ones). With a few exceptions (like the comedy and *poliziottesco*), Italian genre production is characterised by a transnational dimension evident in the role played by foreign funding, stars and locations. This is due to a mode of production that relied on a system of distribution advances, state interventions, co-production agreements and, starting from the 1950s, the commercial possibilities offered by international markets. Indeed, the successful distribution in the US of *Le fatiche di Ercole/Hercules* (Pietro Francisci, 1958) made Italian producers particularly eager to conquer foreign markets and attract new interest and investment (Baschiera and Di Chiara, 2011).

While state interventions after the Second World War tried to protect and promote a national cinema, they created the basis for an international dimension to Italian productions, in particular in its popular products. In fact, the protectionist measures put in place by the government in order to limit the presence of foreign films on Italian screens eventually led, somewhat perversely, to a transnationally inclined industry. For instance, a special norm introduced in 1951 forbidding Hollywood productions from exporting a significant part of the gross made in Italy, forced them to invest in Italian films, generating the direct involvement of American companies in national film production. As Wagstaff points out:

> paradoxically, the internationalization of the cinema market which would so corrode the Italian-ness of the Italian cinema was not so much the result of abandoning nationalist attitudes as, on the contrary, a coherent commercial reaction to the intensification of nationalism within the industries of the various countries. (1995: 96)

Horror cinema was no different from other generic forms in Italian cinema developed mainly as imitations of successful foreign models. In contrast to other genres (such as the Spaghetti Western), however, Italian horror did not have a 'ready made' national audience and needed to rely on foreign markets in order to facilitate production. For instance, Mario Bava's *La maschera del demonio/The Mask of Satan*, which found American distribution thanks to American International Pictures (AIP) and the drive-in circuit, creating in the process a new important market for the genre's development.

For Italian producers the involvement of American distributors meant it was possible to make films by relying upon distribution advances, effectively minimising financial risk. For the American companies, investing in Italian horror cinema meant being able to take advantage of Italian state aid and to find cheap spin-offs (made with a quick turn-around) to meet grindhouse audience demands. Moreover, the production of Italian horror exploited the mechanisms of European co-production agreements in order to have access to different markets and to minimise the financial risks (see Baschiera and Di Chiara, 2011).

An example of the transnational dimension of Italian horror can be seen in the production history of *Sei donne per l'assassino/Blood and Black Lace* (Mario Bava, 1964). The film not only evinces some of the key stylistic features characteristic of the *giallo* in particular, but also demonstrates the production mechanics of Italian horror as a whole. The production pattern for the film was one that, with a little variation, was typical of Italian horror cinema. In the first instance, the film was a three-way co-production between Italy (50 per cent), West Germany (30 per cent) and France (20 per cent). That said, *Sei donne per l'assassino* was shot with an Italian crew and featured a multinational cast (including several Americans, Italians, a German, a Hungarian and a Spaniard) and was made with a budget of 141,755,000 lira.[2]

As was not uncommon for Italian genre films in this period, the film was made with the co-operation of three small production companies, none of which made films after the 1960s (see Baschiera, 2011). For the Italian company involved, Emmepi Cinematografica, *Sei donne per l'assassino* was to be its fourth and final production, and the only film in which it was involved as principal investor.[3] Active from 1958 to 1968, the French partner, Les Productions Georges de Beauregard, had produced *À bout de souffle/ Breathless* (Jean-Luc Godard, 1959) and other early Godard films such as the Italian/French co-productions *Le petit soldat* (1963) and *Pierrot le fou* (1965), as well as Rivette's *L'amour fou/Mad love* (1968). At the same time, the French company was involved in popular cinema with films such as *Goliath e la schiava ribelle/Goliath and the Rebel Slave* (Mario Caiano, 1963) and *Le vampire de Düsseldorf/The Secret Killer* (Robert Hossein, 1965), both shot in Italy and co-produced by Italian companies.

The West German production partner, Monachia Film Produktion (Munich), co-produced two films, *Zwei Bayern in Bonn* (Rudolf Lubowski, 1962) with the Swiss producer Urania, and the following year the West German/Italian/Spanish co-production *Marcia e crepa* (Frank Wisbar, 1963), although it is listed on the final print of *Sei donne per l'assassino* as Top Film.[4] Under this latter name, starting with *Sei donne per l'assassino*, Top Film featured in the production of thirteen films during the decade, mainly European co-productions of genre films. As was often the case with such co-production agreements, the market share was mainly based on the language of the country of distribution and with an option for the Italian distribution to expand to different markets (mainly in the US) upon the payment of a 15 per cent commission.

The small production company Monachia Film had the support of the West German film distributor Gloria. Considering that Gloria's activity during the 1950s and early 1960s was mainly characterised by *Heimatfilme*, women's melodrama and comedies (see Bergfelder, 2005), it is possible to see how Bava's film was symptomatic of the distributor's attempt to open its network to a diversified series of genres in order to aim at a wider target audience (see Baschiera 2011). From this perspective, *Sei donne per l'assassino* was, on the one hand, an occasion to compete with the Central Cinema Compagnie-Film GmbH (CCC Film) *Krimi* films and to target younger audiences thanks also to the use of colour. However, on the other hand, the film presents some elements of continuity with Gloria's production: from the bourgeois décor to the importance given to stardom over technical innovations. To this extent, it is noteworthy that during the production the German title for the film was *Mord in der Via Veneto* (literally 'Death on Via Veneto'), which would have indirectly linked Bava's film to the dissolute Rome depicted in Fellini's *La dolce vita* (1960), successfully distributed by Gloria a few years before.

According to Tim Lucas (2007: 547–58), while the film fared badly in Italy, making only 123 million lira – a sum that did not cover the production costs but which was sufficient to pay back Emmepi Cinematografica for the initial investment – it was well received in Germany, making the producers of *Krimi* films reconsider their reservations about abandoning its traditional black and white in order to experiment with colour.

From a production standpoint there were three features that characterised Italian horror cinema from the start. Firstly, the ability to make films with low budgets whereby the financial limitation of any given production was often evident (Della Casa, 2001; Pitassio, 2005). Secondly, what might be termed a fragmentary mode of production, with the participation of small production companies that were often involved only in the production of a limited number of films. In fact, the result of a production system which strongly relied on advances on distribution and bank loans was the proliferation of small short-lived companies, often involved in co-production agreements and able to quickly make low-budget (low-risk) films for the third- and second-run movie theatres. Finally, the frequent use of international actors and locations to appeal to a broader, more international market and to in some way disguise the (Italian) origin of the films.

The last feature, in particular, deserves some examination. In fact, Hemmings' appearance in an Italian horror, like that of so many other 'known faces', was driven by a desire to obtain crucial international box office receipts. The export market was where Italian horror films were truly aimed, at least in terms of commercial returns. In fact, Italian producers recognised quite early on that foreign markets were far more lucrative, and hence appealing, especially after the resurgence of horror cinema in both Britain and America in the late 1950s. The imperative to export to larger markets (ordinarily understood as being the US but also importantly encompassing a relatively large European market in Germany in particular) also saw producers turn to multinational casts in an attempt to promote both a distinctly non-Italian feel to the films and exploit the domestic star potential cast members might have. The idea here was both to make it *appear* as though these could be American films and that they were not Italian.

In practice this meant that the Italian film industry often employed American and British stars who were either well past their prime (as they were likely to be cheaper) or who were on the rise (who were also likely to be inexpensive). Since the advent of sound it had been standard practice in the Italian film industry to post-synch dialogue rather than record 'in the camera'. This meant that international casts – with little or no linguistic similarities – could be gathered together and overdubbed (if necessary) at a later stage. Crucially, the adoption of post-synching and the practice of dubbing Italian movies for cinematic release meant that casts could – theoretically – come from anywhere. The effect of this was two-fold. On the one hand many genre stars established themselves by working within the Italian film industry (such as Barbara Steele and John Saxon), while for those whose careers were in the doldrums or who were not selective it offered the opportunity of work. Others owed their fame to and spent much of their career working within the Italian horror/thriller industry (Ian McCulloch, David Warbeck). The latter offered little in terms of box office based on reputations gained in Hollywood, but rather their North American 'look' afforded films they appeared in the illusion that they *might be*.

A VERY ITALIAN FORM OF EXPLOITATION

As director Luigi Cozzi has observed, the Italian film industry during these years was mostly a form of exploitation cinema in that 'movie producers . . . [didn't] . . . ask what your film is like, they ask what film your film is like'.[5] The name of the game was repetition with only minor variation. Christopher Frayling (1981: 70–1) has noted that Italy's popular genre films 'tended toward a cyclic, rapid production mode after the war . . . [evidencing] such major cycles as the "film fumetto" (tear-jerkers, 1948–54), farcical comedies (1958– 64), the peplum films (1958–64), horror (1959–63), the sexy documentaries spawned by *Mondo Cane* (1961–4), and series of sub-James Bonds (1964–7)'. These production cycles tended to chime with whatever genre was performing well at both the domestic and international box office. It was a growing aware-ness of – and dependency upon – this market that would eventually lead Italian horror to the kind of onscreen excesses that would see it become exploitation cinema.

Given the dynamics of the Italian film industry as a whole, it is no surprise that filmmakers such as Lucio Fulci, Joe D'Amato or Ruggero Deodato drifted into making horror films. Previous to their involvement in the horror genre they had variously worked on the sex film, Spaghetti Westerns, sci-fi and police thrillers, among others. An understanding of the Italian concept of the *filone* is crucial, relating as it does the Italian conception of genre. Literally translating as vein (or thread), it is best conceptualised as a trend or a current. In filmic terms, a keen awareness of commercially popular *filone* meant that producers would look to see what genre was current and try to exploit its popularity. The concept of the *filone* is a particularly Italian notion that lies close to, but is not the same as, Anglo-American ideas surrounding exploitation cinema.

But Italian filmmakers not only imitated American or British films and formats, they also copied each other. The box office success of Argento's Animal trilogy of *L'uccello dalle piume di cristallo/The Bird with the Crystal Plumage* (1970), *Il gatto a nove code/The Cat o' Nine Tails* (1971) and *Quattro mosche di velluto grigio/Four Flies on Grey Velvet* (1971) led to a rash of films attempting to copy the animal motif of their titles. In this way films with titles like *Una farfalla con le ali insanguinate/The Bloodstained Butterfly* (Duccio Tessari, 1971), *Una lucertola con la pelle di donna/Lizard in a Woman's Skin* (Lucio Fulci, 1971), *L'iguana dalla lingua di fuoco/The Iguana with a Tongue of Fire* (Riccardo Freda, 1971) and *Non si servizia un paperino/Don't Torture a Duckling* (Lucio Fulci, 1972) rapidly appeared.

The most iconic symbol of Italy's exploitation film culture came in relation to George Romero's *Dawn of the Dead* (1978). The commercial success of Romero's film in Italy – where it was released as *Zombi* – led to a succession of quickly produced spin-offs. Notably here its initial success on the European and Italian market led to the Lucio Fulci release *Zombi 2/Zombie Flesh Eaters*, a film that was not connected with Romero's film in any way other than that it attempted – by association – to cash in on its name and hoped to garner some form of commercial success in so doing. Following on from this, the relative domestic (and international) financial success of *Zombi 2* (1979) encouraged producers that it might be a subgenre that would reap good commercial returns. As such, a new *filone* was initiated and numerous imitators entered the market. Thus the likes of *Paura nella città dei morti viventi/City of the Living Dead* (Lucio Fulci, 1980), *L'Aldilà/The Beyond* (Lucio Fulci, 1981), *Inferno dei morti viventi/Zombie Creeping Flesh* (Bruno Mattei, 1981), *Incubo sulla città contaminata/Nightmare City* (Umberto Lenzi, 1981), *Zombie Flesh Eaters 2, 3* and *4* and *Zombi Holocaust/Zombie Holocaust* (Marino Girolami, 1980) were quickly put into production and released in order to benefit by association. Lucio Fulci, in particular, proved particularly adept at pushing out low-grade, quick-turnaround horror that nonetheless later gained a strong cult following. In part this was due to his mastery of the low-budget formula: Fulci mastered tight shooting schedules, maintained a loyal and well-trained crew, and made films that were designed primarily for the export market.[6]

The aim was always to copy genres that were currently popular – genres that 'sold' – and exploit this popularity by making cheap, low-end rip-offs. Here, keeping abreast of developments within the most popular *filone* was crucial, as the whole enterprise of exploitation filmmaking was based on the ability to successfully 'piggy-back' on the popularity of currently successful trends. To be effective, therefore, exploitation filmmakers had to work quickly (and on low budgets) in order that their products tap into currently popular genres. Often featuring excessive violence and gore, there was little or no pretence at artistic merit. Rather they attempted to ape plots of existing films very closely and employ similar-sounding titles to films currently doing well at the box office (of which Fulci's *Zombi 2* is a prime example); while others had fantastical titles that bore little relation to the content of the films themselves. The sheer volume of these productions meant that Italian horror tended to feature prominently in grindhouse programmes, which further acted to lower its already poor critical reputation.

Understanding Italian horror

The academic study of Italian horror cinema was, until comparatively recently, limited to a relatively small number of interventions, with most of the attention it received coming from a number of fan and popular presses (see, for example, Palmerini and Mistretta, 1996; Thrower, 1999; Gallant, 2001; Jones, 2004; Paul, 2004; Harper, 2005; Slater, 2006; Lucas, 2007; Fenton, 2011; Hughes, 2011; Howarth, 2015). These have played an important and substantive role in tracing the production histories of Italian horror in general and the work of specific directors in particular.[7] While it would be inaccurate to say that Italian horror cinema has been devoid of academic study (it certainly has not), it has lacked the kind of *sustained* dialogue that helps to transform understandings of any given field. In effect, those working on Italian horror cinema have, until the recent past, only been able to provide rather isolated interventions that, while highly valuable, have not been part of a broader discursive community.

Historically book-length academic studies of Italian cinema have tended to eschew much popular genre cinema and instead concentrated on a limited number of canonical film movements, cycles and genres. In the period since the publication of Dyer and Vincendeau's ground-breaking *Popular European Cinema* (1992) much has changed – but that change has been slow to take effect. The work of a number of scholars, Dimitris Eleftheriotis, Christopher Frayling and Christopher Wagstaff primary among them, has demonstrated the rich and varied nature of genre cinema in Italy and its importance within the Italian film industry as a whole. But Italian horror cinema has only recently developed any sense of momentum behind its study. As it is, overviews of Italian film have typically tended to ignore the popular or engage with it only briefly.

This is now beginning to change and a number of recent publications have engaged with popular cinema in a way that suggests there is a welcome recognition of its place within Italian film history and, importantly, film culture. That is the case with Peter Bondanella's *A History of Italian Cinema* (2009), which in contrast to his much earlier *Italian Cinema: From Neorealism to Present* (1983) features a significant and sustained engagement with popular forms of Italian cinema, horror among them.[8] In this way, as Bondanella rightly recognised, a new history of Italian cinema could be 'rethought, reorganised and completely rewritten' (2009: x).

However, there has been a welcome growth in studies that have engaged with the idea of popular forms of cinema as an important aspect of Italian film studies (see Koven, 2006; Bayman,2011; Manzoli, 2012; Bayman and Rigoletto, 2013; Bondanella, 2014), as well as new explorations of various specific aspects of genre cinema (see, for instance, Fisher, 2011). At the same time there has also been an increasing engagement with texts that focus specifically on Italian horror cinema, which in building upon earlier interventions has allowed for the development of a dialogue surrounding its key forms, themes and histories (see, for example, Baschiera and Di Chiara, 2011; Bini, 2011; Hunter, 2014; Venturini, 2014; Mendik, 2015).

This volume seeks to make a contribution to the growing body of literature on Italian horror cinema and in so doing further unpick understandings of its often rich and complex history. The chapters offered here are not intended to cover every aspect of Italian horror cinema, but rather to offer new approaches as well as reassessments of existing ideas about the films and creative personnel involved. As such this is not intended to be the 'final' word on Italian horror cinema but rather part of an ongoing dialogue.

To this end, in Chapter 1 Russ Hunter challenges some of the previous assumptions about the roots of Italian horror cinema, arguing that a number of films exist that we might now identify as early examples of 'Italian' horror. In this way he argues that an examination of the silent era in Italian cinema will reveal a much longer engagement with some of the tropes and conventions of horror in Italy than has previously been understood.

In Chapter 2 Francesco Di Chiara investigates the 1960s 'golden age' of Italian horror cinema, characterised by a variety of foreign influences. The chapter highlights the production system of Italian popular cinema in a period that saw the growth of Italian horror and the production dynamics that eventually allowed for a proliferation of *filoni*. Looking in particular at the transnational nature of the Italian horror production of the period, Di Chiara stresses the importance of the brand value of the genre in relation to US distribution.

Stefano Baschiera engages in Chapter 3 with the 1980s, a period still understudied in relation to Italian horror production despite it marking the international canonisation of the genre. The analysis focuses in particular on the cinema of imitation and spin-off in order to look at the crucial role played by foreign markets, distribution advances and international influences in shaping the low-budget production of the period. The chapter ends with a reflection on the role played by the TV networks in the crisis affecting the genre at the end of the decade.

In Chapter 4, however, Johnny Walker notes that Italian horror has simultaneously been reinterrogated and reignited in recent years. Firstly he identifies that a strand of 'Italianate' horror has developed, which has attempted for a variety of reasons to evoke some of Italian horror's key tropes and stylistic practices. But he also highlights the ways in which technological changes have led to the development of a number of contemporary low-budget horror films emanating from Italy. In so doing he offers a challenge to the idea that Italian horror production has ceased to exist in any meaningful sense.

Peter Hutchings traces, in Chapter 5, Mario Bava's journey from critical obscurity to his current elevated position within discourses around Italian horror cinema. He argues that, to a certain extent, this change in his status has been driven by the development during the 1990s of what might be termed 'cult' discourses that have fixated on hitherto marginal areas of film culture. But Hutchings observes that there is a tension at play here between cultish forms of engagement with Bava, auteurist approaches and the dynamics of the Italian film industry within which the director operated.

Chapters 6 and 7 examine the work of Dario Argento, arguably the most well-known and highly regarded Italian horror director and – importantly – the one Italian horror director who has worked (almost) exclusively in the horror genre and been critically lauded (at least for the early part of his career). Marcia Landy in an eclectic contribution draws upon the work of Gramsci, Artaud and Deleuze among others to outline what she terms the 'Argento Syndrome' as a means to explore the filmic impact of creating and viewing violence. For Landy, Argento is cinematically self-conscious in his use of film to explore the very nature of filmmaking and violence itself. Indeed, as she notes, in Argento's work 'art is as dangerous as life'. Karl Schoonover's chapter, instead, analyses Argento's early works in order to reveal how the 'waste' that populates his films suggests an ecological imaginary of the director. Through a series of thought-provoking tenets inviting reflection on the role played by waste, leftovers and refuse in Argento's films and the relationship between the human and non-human worlds, Schoonover suggests 'their potential to register a historically specific account of the sociopolitical nature of materiality'.

In Chapter 8 Adam Lowenstein engages with the relationship between *giallo* and slasher films, revealing both the international dimension and influence of Italian horror production. Looking at Mario Bava's *Reazione a catena/ Ecologia del delitto /Bay of Blood* (1971) and Sean S. Cunningham's *Friday the 13th* (1980), the analysis reveals the roles played by the natural landscape in both films. Lowenstein invites us to look at the cross-pollination between the two sub-genres, considering how they enable a 'subtractive spectatorship' viewing the body count typical of these films as 'counting-down', revealing a desire for a depopulated and empty landscape.

Leon Hunt analyses one of the most interesting and understudied aspects of *giallo* cinema in Chapter 9 by looking at the proliferation in the 1960s of *fumetti neri* (or 'black comics'). In fact, Italian comics aimed at an adult readership, such as Angela and Luciana Giussani's *Diabolik* and Max Bunker and Magnus's *Kriminal*, present a series of common features and a shared imaginary with *giallo* productions such as Mario Bava's *Sei donne per l'assassino*.

Through an attentive textual analysis and an overview of the cultural context that signalled the emergence of the *fumetti neri*, Hunt suggests it is imperative to take into account their international roots if we are to situate them properly within the cinema of the period.

Austin Fisher examines the 'rural *gialli*' in Chapter 10 in order to locate them within the broader context of Italian cultural history to see to what extent they can be viewed as 'documents of the historical and political concerns of 1970s'. Through an analysis of films such as *Non si sevizia un paperino/Don't Torture a Duckling* (Lucio Fulci, 1972), *I corpi presentano trace di violenza carnale/ Torso* (Sergio Martino, 1973), *La casa dalle finestre che ridono/The House of the Laughing Windows* (Pupi Avati, 1976) and *Solamente nero/Bloodstained Shadow* (Antonio Bido, 1978) he engages with the question of heritage, national culture and the political memory of Italy in the 1970s in order to demonstrate the various modes of address these films negotiated.

As Craig Hatch observes in Chapter 11, there is an intimate relationship between successful horror films and the nature of their soundtracks. In the case of Italian horror soundtracks Hatch argues they endured and flourished beyond the confines of film itself, proving popular as stand-alone music. In breaking down the sectional nature of their construction and examining what he terms their 'pop music' approach to film composition, Hatch explores the broad popularity and legacy of Italian horror soundtracks, but impor- tantly also notes this self-same composition 'played a vital role in shaping the experience of the films themselves'.

Mark Bernard takes a highly innovative approach in Chapter 12 by examin- ing the use, function and impact of scenes of animal slaughter in the cannibal *filone*. In taking the work of director Ruggero Deodato and his relationship with the use of real animal death on film as a case study, Bernard uses a food studies framework to see how such work can be profitably examined. In so doing he argues that, whether they intended to or not, Italian horror directors of cannibal films expose 'the often hidden brutality behind food procurement and preparation'.

In the final chapter in this volume, Paolo Noto focuses upon the reception of Italian horror cinema in Italy's film journals and magazines during the decade that marked the height of the country's horror production, the 1970s. Noto argues that horror was met with a curious mixture of indifference and disdain, something he sees as symptomatic of a broader treatment of Italian genre cinema by the country's critical establishment.

NOTE ON USE OF FILM TITLES

Italian horror films are marked by a plethora of release titles, a phenomenon not uncommon with exploitation-style cinema in particular. In order to avoid confusion, the Italian-language release titles are used, with the most common international release title being listed where appropriate.

NOTES

1. Moreover, Argento can be considered as the first horror specialist. Other directors, such as Mario Bava, Ruggero Deodato and Sergio Martino, made popular cinema and horror was one of the many genres they were involved with.
2. All the information gathered about the co-production of *Sei donne per l'assassino* comes from: *Archivio centrale dello stato, ministero del turismo e dello spettacolo, direzione generale per il cinema, fascicoli e copioni*, folder No. 4407.
3. The company's modest initial starting capital (900,000 lira) offers a clear indication of the size of this production company.
4. In the production agreements for *Sei donne per l'assassino* the company is listed as Monachia Film Produktion (Munich) but in the final prints of the film appears as Top Film.
5. DVD extra, 'Interview with Luigi Cozzi', *Contamination*, Starz Home Entertainment (2004).
6. Italian exploitation filmmakers operated on a model similar to that perfected by Roger Corman and American International Pictures.
7. Most notable here – and standing apart from anything written on Italian horror cinema to date – is Tim Lucas's *Mario Bava, All The Colors of the Dark*. The book runs to over 1,110 pages and is a highly detailed engagement with the works of its subject.
8. Prior to this point, references to Italian horror cinema in particular tended to be much more isolated and limited (see, for instance, Wood, 2005; Celli and Cottino-Jones, 2007).

BIBLIOGRAPHY

Baschiera, S. and Di Chiara, F. (2011), 'Once Upon a Time in Italy: Transnational features of genre production 1960s–1970s', *Film International*, Vol. 8, Issue 6, pp. 30–9.

Baschiera, S. (2011), 'Vom Krimi zum *Giallo*: Mario Bavas *Sei donne per l'assassino/ blutige seide*', in F. Bono and Roschlau, J. (eds) *Tenöre, Touristen, Gastarbeiter. Deutsch-italienishe Filmbeziehungen*, Munich: Cinegraph–Richard Boorberg Verlag, pp. 169–79.

Bayman, L. (2011), *Directory of World Cinema: Italy*, Bristol: Intellect.

Bayman, L. and Rigoletto, S. (2013), *Popular Italian Cinema*, Basingstoke: Palgrave.

Bergfelder, T. (2005), *International Adventures. German Popular Cinema and European Co-Productions in the 1960s*, New York and Oxford: Berghahn.

Bini, A. (2011), 'Horror Cinema: The Emancipation of Women and Urban Anxiety', in Brizio-Skov, F. (ed.), *Popular Italian Cinema: Culture and Politics in a Postwar Society*, New York: I. B. Tauris.

Bondanella, P. (1983), *Italian Cinema: From Neorealism to the present*, New York: Ungar.

Bondanella, P. (2009), *A History of Italian Cinema*, London: Continuum.

Bondanella, P. (ed.) (2014), *The Italian Cinema Book*, London: British Film Institute.

Brunetta, G. (2009), The *History of Italian Cinema*, Princeton, NJ: Princeton University Press.

Celli, C. and Cottino-Jones, M. (2007), *A New Guide to Italian Cinema*, New York: Palgrave.

Curti, R. (2015), *Italian Gothic Horror Films, 1957–1969*, Jefferson, NC: McFarland.

Della Casa, S. (2001), 'L'horror', in De Vincenti, G. (ed.), *Storia del cinema italiano Vol. X: 1960–1964*, Venice and Rome: Marsilio/Edizioni di Bianco e Nero, pp. 319–30.

Dyer, R. and Vincendeau, G. (eds) (1992), *Popular European Cinema*, London: Routledge. Eleftheriotis, D. (2001), *Popular Cinemas of Europe: Texts, Contexts and Frameworks*, London: Continuum.

Fenton, H. (ed) (2011), *Cannibal Holocaust: And the Savage Cinema of Ruggero Deodato*, Godalming: FAB Press.

Fisher, A. (2011), *Radical Frontiers in the Spaghetti Western: Politics, Violence and Popular Italian Cinema*, London: I. B. Tauris.

Frayling, C. (1981), *Spaghetti Westerns: Cowboys and Europeans from Karl May to Sergio Leone*, London: Routledge, pp. 70–1.

Gallant, C. (2001), *The Art of Darkness: The Cinema of Dario Argento*, Godalming: FAB Press.

Harper, J. (2005), *Italian Horror*, Baltimore: Luminary Press.

Howarth, T. (2015), *Splintered Visions: Lucio Fulci and His Films*, Parkville, MD: Midnight Marquee Press, Inc.

Hughes, H. (2011), *Cinema Italiano: The Complete Guide From Classics To Cult*, London: I. B. Tauris.

Hunt, L. (2000), 'A Sadistic Night at the Opera: Notes on the Italian Horror Film', in Gelder, K. (ed.), *The Horror Reader*, London: Routledge, p. 326.

Hunter, R. (2014), 'Nightmare cities: Italian Zombie Cinema and Environmental Discourses', in Hunt, L., Lockyer, S. and Williamson, M. (eds), *Screening the Undead: Vampires and Zombies in Film and Television*, London: I. B. Tauris.

Jones, A. (2004), *Profondo Argento*, Godalming: FAB Press.

Koven, M. J. (2006), *La Dolce Morte: Vernacular Cinema and the Italian Giallo Film*, Oxford: Scarecrow Press.

Lucas, T. (2007), *Mario Bava: All the Colors of the Dark*, Cincinnati, OH: Video Watchdog.

Mendik, X. (2015), *Bodies of Desire and Bodies in Distress: The Golden Age of Italian Cult Cinema 1970–1985*, Newcastle: Cambridge Scholars Press.

Palmerini, L. M. and Mistretta, G. (1996), *Spaghetti Nightmares: Italian fantasy-horrors as seen through the eyes of their protagonists*, Key West, FL: Fantasma Books.

Pitassio, F. (2005), 'L'orribile segreto dell'horror italiano', in Manzoli, G. and Pescatore, G. (eds), *L'arte del risparmio: stile e tecnologia. Il cinema a basso costo in Italia negli anni Sessanta*, Rome: Carocci, pp. 31–41.

Paul, L. (2004), *Italian Horror Film Directors*, Jefferson, NC: McFarland.

Pulleine, T., *The Guardian*, 5 December 2003.

Slater, J. (ed.) (2006), *Eaten Alive! Italian Cannibal and Zombie Movies*, London: Plexus.

Tentori, A. and Cozzi, L. (2001), *Italian Horror Movies: A Critical Catalogue Of Nearly 200 Chillers*, Rome: Mondo Ignoto.

Thrower, S. (1999), *Beyond Terror: The Films of Lucio Fulci*, Godalming: FAB Press.

Venturini, S. (2014), *Horror italiano*, Rome: Donzelli.

Wagstaff, C. (1992), 'A Forkful of Westerns: Industry, audiences and the Italian Western', in Dyer, R. and Vincendeau, G. (eds), *Popular European Cinema*, London: Routledge, pp. 245–61.

Wagstaff, C. (1995), 'Italy in the Post-War International Cinema Market', in Duggan, C. and Wagstaff, C. (eds), *Italy in the Cold War: Politics, Culture and Society 1948–58*, Oxford and Washington, DC: Berg, pp. 89–116.

Wood, M. (2005), *Italian Cinema*, Oxford: Berg.

1. *PREFERISCO L'INFERNO*: EARLY ITALIAN HORROR CINEMA

Russ Hunter

The precise generic beginnings of horror cinema have the odd status of being both simultaneously clear and opaque. The general trend in studies of horror cinema has been to date the genre's beginnings around the release of the series of Universal's 'monster movies' beginning with *Frankenstein* (James Whale, 1931) and *Dracula* (Tod Browning, 1931). The desire to search for the antecedents, roots and origins of any genre leads film scholars to identify certain texts as key turning points that effectively lay the ground for what follows. While this view of genre can be overly deterministic, it is nonetheless true that some texts rather than others are given the status of key reference points based upon their perceived historical importance. Cinematically horror was a term that first gained currency during the mid-1930s, at a point after the release of Whale and Browning's films, in the USA and like much generic categorisation its first usage is necessarily hard to locate with any precision. As Alison Peirse has noted, although horror was not recognised as a distinctive genre by critics before the early to mid-1930s, a number of films were identified as sharing similar enough tropes to require a particular collective label. She states that:

> at varying points from 1931–1933 the word 'horror' changes from referring to the effect it has on the audience to attaching to a 'type' of film. This transition occurs at different times depending on the country in which the word is used, and whether in a newspaper, trade journal, magazine, etc. (2013: 8)

In terms of concretising our sense of genre history this presents a problem in that no one is quite sure exactly *when* this change takes place. All we know is that this is a term that gains some form of critical and industrial currency during this period. Conceptually this leaves us with the issue of whether or not we can then apply this category to films that pre-date the identification and vocalisation of this generic framework. Any process of 'imposing' generic categorisations on cinema that pre-dates the creation of these self-same terms is, of course, problematic in lots of ways. As Geraghty and Jancovich note, such a move can 'do violence to our sense of history' (2008: 2), given that we are removing a film from the context in which it was originally produced, distributed and exhibited in ways that mean we tend to ignore the complexities of the genre's history and distinctiveness.

All of which means care needs to be taken in the ways we discuss the development of the horror genre. But it can also lead to a kind of paralysis in discussing those films that 'look' like horror films to the contemporary observer but that originate before the 'horror film' took shape as a generic category. This does not mean, though, that it is impossible now to choose to apply the term horror to these films if we can find good reasons to do so, only that we are sensitive to the ways in which the term is mobilised. It is possible to both recognise a film's original generic context *and* reassess its current generic positioning. Indeed, as Altman has argued, 'genres are not inert categories shared by all (although at some moments they appear to be), but discursive categories made by real speakers for particular purposes in specific situations' (1999: 101). It is important here to remember that when *Dracula* was released on Valentine's Day in 1931 it was marketed as a kind of romantic thriller. The initial press book for the film, for instance, makes no mention of the film as horror and nor does it seek to position it as such. This is perhaps unsurprising given the lack of the industrial framework and generic category of 'the horror film' at the time. It does, however, point to ways in which genres are flexible concepts and understandings of them can change, altering our classification and perceptions of earlier works. This is important, however, as our understanding of the historical development of the horror genre is predicated upon the notion that it *starts* with both *Dracula* and *Frankenstein*. This is a reconfiguring of the same kind of industrial and critical logic that is used to date the genre's beginnings. In effect, if we argue that the genre comes into existence because the term is used *after* these two films were released, it seems counterintuitive to say we cannot go yet further back and see horror as emanating from films prior to this period. Hutchings, talking in relation to the DVD re-release of the Universal Monster Legacy Collection, of which *Dracula* and *Frankenstein* were a part, has noted the ways in which the reissue formed 'part of a broader discursive refiguring of the horror genre, one that involves a retrospective designation of films as "horror" that were not originally thought of in that way' (2008:

223). Genre histories are therefore not monoliths but alter as we discover (or rediscover) new films that match contemporary understandings of the genre.

Ernest Mathijs (2006) has argued that film receptions can often ossify into a 'final moment' whereby ideas coalesce around certain textual understandings and therefore remain, more or less, static. In effect, we come to a generally agreed upon idea of what a particular text 'means' and what its key character-istics are. Although writing specifically with regard to film receptions, it is pos-sible to extend Mathijs' conception to film genres in as much as their histories are often characterised by stability in relation to our general understandings of key historical moments. In particular, what is considered canonical in any given genre, while being added to over time, retains a core set of films that are effectively then seen as key reference points in its development. The develop-ment and early history of genres, too, often have broadly agreed upon starting points that relate to a film, or more commonly a set of films, that are viewed as urtexts from which the genre develops and (eventually) flourishes. In this case a rigid adherence to long-held generic histories does, however, concretise horror history as a linear and slightly mechanistic continuum. In effect, *Dracula* and *Frankenstein* have become such texts, and explorations of the antecedents, boundaries and influences of the genre have been limited. That is not to say that others have not explored areas of film history that could be seen as horror films, such as large parts of German Expressionism for instance, but rather that there has been a caution in explicitly linking them to the horror genre.

In this respect early Italian cinema has received relatively little critical atten-tion with regard to its development of the horror genre (for an exception, see Venturini, 2014). This chapter explores several Italian films from the silent era that pre-date this period of the genre's historical development. In so doing it identifies a number of productions that, while neither designed nor marketed as horror films, nonetheless evidence some of the qualities associated with the horror genre. I do not wish to necessarily 'reclaim' these films as horrors but rather to stress their congruence with later traditions within the genre and in so doing suggest it as a potentially fruitful area for further research. In essence the presence of such films, with their presentation of a variety of supernatural elements and stress on a battle between good and evil (often with reference to earthly manifestations of Satan and quasi-religious allusions), can be seen as an early, formative engagement with tropes that would become key to the development of 'the horror film' being formulated as a vocalised, generic term. What I want to suggest here is that further work is required, via the examina-tion of films from the pre-Universal Monster Movies period – which effectively means the pre-sound period – in order to trace those films that contribute to the *idea* that there may a thing called 'the horror film'. If, as Peirse (2013) suggests, a distinct category is recognised in the early 1930s, then an explora-tion of the kinds of films that contributed to its recognition is crucial. In this sense the aim of this chapter is to highlight a number of films that might have informed the move towards such a position.

In attempting to locate early examples of 'horror-like' films in Italy I aim to stress here that a renegotiation of what we might call the fuzzy boundaries of horror genre history should be attempted. Building a picture of how early cinema contributed to the development of the horror genre, particularly as it was articulated in the post-Universal Monster movies period, is a complex and ultimately frustrating exercise. A major epistemological problem here is the amount of Italian silent cinema that is now lost to us, which has been placed as high as 75 per cent (see, for instance, Bondanella, 2014: 7), in effect meaning that it is hard to ascertain the kind, extent and longevity of Italy's engagement with the cinematic macabre.

It is possible to try to 'reconstruct' lost films from remaining evidence – from posters, remaining stills, reviews, memoirs and a range of promotional materials – but this can never be a complete process. Ultimately we end up providing a 'best guess' for exactly what generic markers a film *appears* to have. As noted above, this can be deceptive for a variety of reasons. Frequently titles can be misleading and suggest a horror or horror-inflected film when, in reality, the film itself has no connection to the genre whatsoever. In this respect it is tempting to look at the titles of many silent Italian films and connect them to the broad sweep of horror cinema's origins. Indeed, remaining evidence for a number of films suggests they might have important contributions to make in debates around the development of the horror genre. Thus, little-known films such as *La fidanzata della morte*/'The Fiancé of the Dead' (Mario Voller-Buzzi, 1916), *L'angoscia di Satana*/'The Anguish of Satan' (Giuseppe di Luguoro, 1918), *L'autobus della morte*/'The Bus of Death' (Ugo de Simone, 1919), to name but a few, are ripe for reassessment.[1] But we also need to be careful here, too. The Roberto Roberti (a pseudonym for Vincenzo Leone, father of Sergio Leone) directed *La vampira Indiana* (1913), for instance, translates as 'The Indian Vampire'. Though the film is lost and little is known about it, Frayling (2005: 15) identifies it as 'the first Italian Western of note' and its title is therefore the generic equivalent of the linguistic 'false friend'. The lost status of many of these films is an impeding factor in developing a fuller picture of the period in question.

That noted, pinpointing the first Italian horror film, or even very broadly when Italian producers began to make horror films in any numbers, is a difficult task. Riccardo Freda's *I Vampiri* (1957) is frequently viewed as the first 'real' Italian horror film and seen to be a kind of filmic pathfinder for what was to follow. In part this is because it coincided with a boom in horror production in Britain led by Hammer – a boom whose success was in part responsible for demonstrating the commercial potential of horror cinema to Italian producers. But the film stands out because of the apparent void of horror production in

Italy prior to that point. What is notable here is that in the years preceding its release in 1957, Italian producers appear to have had little or no interest in developing horror films. To some extent, as I will outline below, there were significant periods where it was more or less impossible for them to do so, such as during the Fascist period (1922–43). But it is also true that the 1930s, 1940s and much of the 1950s saw only very sporadic horror production in Europe in general. In many ways the Italian case was no exception. Recently, however, there has been some recognition of the possible development of horror cinema prior to this point (Paul, 2005; Moliterno, 2008; Bondanella, 2009; Venturini, 2014). In particular, the existence of an Italian version of *Frankenstein* released in 1921 has led to a curiosity over the precise beginning of Italy's production of horror cinema.

A Frankenstein's monster of lost cinema

Interest in the historical manifestation of Italian horror prior to *I Vampiri* has grown considerably in recent years. In part this is because historically there has been little or no significant engagement with it, but also relates to a growing interest in the study of Italian genre cinema in general. In a post from 16 August 2011 on *sempre in penombra*, an Italian website dedicated to researching silent cinema, it was claimed that for Frankenstein adaptations 'no one . . . seems to remember the Italian version from the silent period'.[2] That film, *Il mostro di Frankenstein* (Eugenio Testa, 1921), was the third cinematic adaptation of Mary Shelley's gothic novel *Frankenstein: Or, the Modern Prometheus* (1818) in the silent era, and was produced by Albertini films, a company fronted by the actor Luciano Albertini but owned by Ernst Hugo Correll (later the production manager at UFA). The raised awareness of the film as potentially Italy's earliest manifestation of horror imagery onscreen means that it bears some detailed consideration here. The lack of a print means any attempt to identify generic horror markers is problematic but, as I will argue, it is possible to reconstruct the film in part by using a range of secondary sources. In so doing it is possible to more clearly evaluate *Il mostro di Frankenstein*'s likely place in the development of the Italian horror film.

The film is emblematic of the problems of tracing the bit-by-bit development of genres and the variety of filmic representations that inform them. Given its 'lost' status, little evidence remains about the film's text and as such it has developed the status of something of an enigma. For popular audiences this is certainly true as the film is 'lost' and as such no known copies survive. Because of this there have been no retrospective screenings, no video release, no DVD release and no access to the film via online streaming services. In effect, the film has remained obscure and has been of interest only to collectors and film historians, whose attempts to locate a print have consistently been stymied.

As far back as 1973 film collector, publisher and horror aficionado Forrest J. Ackerman noted that an Italian version of the film existed as well as stating that he had a photograph of The Monster (Ackerman in *Glut*, 1973). But this was rather an isolated interest in the film that drew little academic attention. Academic interest in the film has appeared only comparatively recently with a number of commentators either identifying it as potentially Italy's earliest example of horror cinema (see, for example, Paul, 2005; Bondanella, 2009) or as one of Italy's few examples of horror in the silent period (Moliterno, 2008: 159).

Undoubtedly the subject matter of the original novel has been crucial in suggesting that *Il mostro di Frankenstein* was *likely* to be a horror film. The success and, as noted above, key generic position of James Whale's *Frankenstein* has impacted upon how any adaptation of Mary Shelley's novel is viewed. The intimate association that *Frankenstein* now has with the genre has influenced our view of adaptations by association, providing us with 'horror' as a frame of reference for such works. Thus, *earlier* adaptations can, in this way, often very easily become caught up in the current status of *Frankenstein* and effectively be assumed to be horrors as a result. The danger in relation to *Il mostro di Frankenstein* is falling into 'educated guesswork' based upon assumptions derived from the source material. In reality very few textual details of the film are known and, given that the film is lost, historians have necessarily relied upon secondary sources in order to piece together fragmentary evidence in order to reconstruct details of the film. Indeed, despite the absence of a print for the film it is possible to glean some information about it that helps to make the picture a little clearer. While a number of posters remain in existence, a number of other sources are particularly helpful in suggesting generic markers, most notably the one remaining photograph, a Belgian flyer and the one extant review.

To begin with, it is certainly clear from the posters that remain to us that the film was not marketed as a horror. Cinema posters from the period (of which only a few remain), such as the 1922 Milanese Cinema Vittoria and Cinema Aurora, for example, respectively announce the film as a 'sensational adventure work rich with impressive situations' and an 'extraordinary film of sensational adventures'. While nothing equating to a horror-inclined film is alluded to, the generic framework being evoked is clearly very broadly that of the adventure film. This is no surprise on several counts. Firstly, it was a popular contemporary genre and one that encompassed within it a broad array of subject matters. But equally as important here is the film's star, Luciano Albertini, who was a former circus acrobat-turned-film-star famous for his onscreen acts of physical derring-do (and who was often compared by the British and American press to Douglas Fairbanks). Albertini's career success was predicated upon films that allowed him to show off his acrobatic skills, often via a variety of (seemingly) perilous scenarios, typified by films like the

Figure 1.1　The one remaining photograph of The Monster from *Il mostro di Frankenstein.*

German-produced *Der Abgrund des Todes/Cage of Death* (Luciano Albertini, Albert-Francis Bertoni and Max Obal, 1923). His was a career that had been built upon his reputation as an acrobat and to a lesser extent a muscleman. In this sense Albertini Films' decision to adapt Mary Shelley's novel and to cast Albertini in the lead role of Baron Frankenstein seems slightly quizzical in as much as there is little in *Frankenstein: Or, the Modern Prometheus* (nor indeed later adaptations) to suggest that the character had to perform any physically demanding acts.

The sole still photograph, review and flyer when analysed together are highly instructive here. While conclusions drawn from single images should be treated with caution, a number of things can potentially be gleaned from these sources. The photograph itself (see Fig. 1.1) shows The Monster (Umberto Guarracino) throttling a female victim in front of a washing line inside a slightly dishevelled room with glassless windows.[3] As such, it is clearly intended to suggest to potential viewers a 'snapshot' of what to expect from the film itself. Guarracino's Monster clearly differs from Charles Ogle's earlier heavily made-up and physically grotesque characterisation in *Frankenstein* (J. Searle Dawley, 1910), as well as lacking the heavy latex and bulky make-up of Boris Karloff's later portrayal.[4] The image also seems to suggest that this was a much more athletic and physically dynamic Monster than previous portrayals, given The Monster's clearly very humanoid form and Guarracino's evident muscularity. On its own this suggests that The Monster was unencumbered by heavy make-up and prosthetics and thus free to move much more fluidly than either Charles Ogle or Boris Karloff's performances.

But why is this important? If we combine this with the contemporary review from the cinema weekly *Kines* and evidence from the flyer then the picture becomes clearer. The review alludes to The Monster having an 'extensive knowledge of Greco-Roman fighting', which complements Hirschmann's claim that 'the storyline reputedly included a confrontation between Frankenstein and his Monster' (2012: 42). The Belgian flyer shows a hand-drawn image of The Monster (apparently in a cave) with a figure pursuing him close behind. If we combine all of this it seems likely that the confrontation (which on this basis it seems likely took place) was between Baron Frankenstein and The Monster. That is to say, between the highly athletic and muscular Luciano Albertini and the burly Umberto Guarracino. This then suggests a good reason why Albertini films chose to adapt this particular project with Albertini as the lead – it clearly offered him the opportunity to use his physical talents and use them against a literally 'monstrous' opponent. In effect it was another way to show that Albertini, a huge star in Italy and Germany in particular in his day, was the ultimate muscleman athlete.

Two things are evident from this. Firstly, that the film was clearly conceived as a star vehicle for Albertini and as such its promotion as an adventure film makes sense. But this was also an attempt to adapt an iconic gothic novel. J. Searle Dawley's 1910 adaptation had prior to this created a grotesque monster via the use of heavy prosthetics and had featured a vivid scene of The Monster being created via stop-motion photography with a skeleton slowly taking shape and appearing to grow flesh. While relatively tame now, this was a darkly impressive and horrifying special effect at the time. The text of Mary Shelley's novel, with its focus on the creation of life from dead-matter, was such that it was likely in a cinematic incarnation to contain scenes that would, to some degree, horrify. Albertini Films' adaptation can be viewed as an attempt to show off their star's physical skills and play into his star persona but *also* to do so via the adaptation of a novel that was likely to be much more macabre as a result. The image of the monster that we have – to say nothing of the fact that he is listed as The Monster – suggests a film in line with modern horror sensibilities. Thus, the film can be both partly an adventure film and also partly a horror.

Il mostro di Frankenstein was released less than a year prior to the Fascist takeover of power in 1922, after which the grounds for the production of heavily horror-inclined films were much less fertile. Stephen Gundle (2013: 32) has noted that there were no horror films in Italy during the Fascist period, and while there is still general agreement that during this era 'it would have been impossible to produce a horror film' (Bini, 2011: 54), there were in any case impediments to such a move even prior to this period. So, although for a variety of reasons Fascism may indeed have stymied any attempt to develop horror cinema in Italy right up until its fall in 1943, prior to Mussolini's takeover of government, decree laws of 1914 and 1919 placed restrictions upon what could be exhibited in public cinemas. The sustained social and moral influence of the Catholic Church, as well as its role in smaller towns as a *de facto* film distributor and exhibitor, meant that the impact of its desire for cinema that avoided 'horrific images' (de Ville, 2010: 62) was significant. These earlier decree laws placed a number of strictures upon what could be shown, and the general dictum of avoiding anything that was 'offensive to public morality and decency' (Bonsaver, 2014: 66) meant that imagery that was in any way 'horrific' was unlikely to be exhibited.

I prefer hell! Italian horror cinema before *Il mostro di Frankenstein*

It is possible to go as far back as 1911 to see, at the very least, the roots of Italy's cinematic engagement with horror imagery. The silent era saw several attempted adaptations of Dante Alighieri's epic fourteenth-century verse *La Commedia/Divine Comedy*, an iconic piece of literature of three parts (*L'Inferno*, *Il purgatorio* and *Il paradiso*). Most notable for our purposes here was *L'Inferno* (Francesco Bertolini, Adolfo Padovan and Giuseppe de Liguoro, 1911), which adapted the first part of *La Commedia*. Clearly *L'Inferno* was not designed to be a horror film and it would be absurd to suggest that. As Welle has argued, such was the prestige associated with adapting Dante, especially in such an ambitious fashion and on such a large scale, that the film played a centrifugal role in Italy in 'cinema's movement from marginality towards cultural respectability', having a significant impact upon 'the cultural prestige for the cinema among the country's traditional literary/cultural elite' (2004: 21). But, that noted, what the film does in adapting a source material whose focus is the suffering of those consigned to hell for their sins on earth, is to graphically show that suffering and torment. Its significance in terms of the Italian horror film – and indeed horror cinema more broadly – is in its contribution to the development of horror imagery in cinema as a whole. In adapting Dante's original source material for cinema, Bertolini, Padovan and de Liguoro undoubtedly contributed to the notion of cinema – and particularly Italian cinema – as an art form, but they also necessarily added to the idea of how it could explore darker, more macabre themes and ideas. In effect it made a significant contribution to what we might term the library of horror imagery that developed during this period.

The film drew not only from the art of Gustave Doré but also earlier cinematic representations of demons, the devil and the supernatural in general (which were, for instance, featured regularly in the earlier work of the likes of Georges Méliès). As Dante, accompanied by the poet Virgil as his guide, descends to various circles of hell, intertitles describing the fate of various sinners in life are quickly followed by what amount to small vignettes showing the horrors that await. One of the more infamous pieces

Figure 1.2   The fate of 'The sowers of discord and the promoters of dissension'.

of imagery from the film comes when Dante is taken to the area of hell reserved for '[t]he sowers of discord and the promoters of dissention' (see Fig. 1.2), who the intertitles tell us were 'maimed by Demons'. As a series of (apparently) maimed figures pass under their view, Virgil points towards a man who with his right hand thrusts his decapitated head towards Dante. Immediately following this we cut to a tightly framed close-up that lingers on the headless man in an attempt to further underline the grotesque nature of the scene that has just unfolded. Towards the end of the film Dante is introduced to 'The arch traitor, Lucifer' who is happily chewing on something. The intertitles reveal to us that he has 'three mouths' and 'holds the bodies of Brutus and Cassius' there. The scene features a closely cropped shot of Lucifer's mouth as he seems to joyfully eat them, an image that echoes the nightmarish chomping moon-faced creature of Méliès' *La lune à un mètre/ The Astronomer's Dream* (1898).

The film is interesting in relation to later developments in Italian horror for other reasons too. In an interesting pre-echo of the kinds of exploitation filmmaking that Italian horror producers would later become infamous for during the 1970s and 1980s, the film itself was subject to a copycat version that was in circulation at the same time. *L'Inferno/Dante's Inferno* (Giuseppe Berardi and Arturo Busnengo, 1911), produced by the Italian Helios Film, was allegedly rushed into production when it became clear that Milano Films were planning a lavish adaptation of Dante's work. It seems likely that the film was designed to take advantage of the publicity generated by Milano Films for their much larger and prestigious production. Helios was a comparatively small production company and as such its resources were necessarily limited. The net result of their activity was a lawsuit from the US distributors of the Milano Films version.

Adaptations of classic literary works such as *La Commedia* and *Frankenstein: Or, the Modern Prometheus* was common during this period and as we have seen their translation to screen often resulted in dark and horror-inclined films. Gino Moiliterno (2008) notes that among Italy's earlier horror films was not only *Il mostro di Frankenstein* but also the slightly earlier *Malombra* (Carmine Gallone, 1917). Even films with clear supernatural elements, such as *Malombra*, that might today mark them out as horror films, were conceived, produced and marketed in very different terms. In fact, *Malombra* is an interesting case in point here. An adaptation of Antonio Fogazzaro's famous gothic novel of the same name, it follows the story of Marina di Malombra (Lyda Borelli), who prior to her upcoming wedding lives in her uncle's castle. While there she reads letters from a mysterious ancestor called Cecilia, whom she discovers was driven to death by Marina's uncle. The film ends with Marina committing suicide after having murdered her uncle in revenge.

Malombra was rather straightforwardly described by *Motion Picutre News* in July 1917 as being 'based on the Italian novel', with its main selling point being the participation of Lyda Borelli, an actress they saw as having done 'remarkable work in a number of recent productions' (anonymous, 1917a). What was being sold with *Malombra* was the promise of an adaptation of an iconic Italian novel and the star presence of one of Italy's most famous divas. In the US the film was, interestingly, released as *From the Great Beyond* by Ben Blumenthal of Export and Import, with *The Moving Picture World* viewing the film as not only 'founded on the novel' but also 'built on psychic lines'. The latter, it is clear, was the cause of some confusion and they note that 'the subject of metempsychosis stumped would-be titlers completely' (anonymous, 1917b). The 'psychic lines' reference is of particular interest as one of the most iconic images of the film is a double exposure that shows a ghostly Cecilia appearing next to Marina as she reads her relative's letters.

In attempting to locate the roots (or perhaps more correctly the antecedents) of the horror film the most common strategy is to alight upon a relatively well-known film, like *L'Inferno* or *Malombra*, such as I have done here so far. Higher-profile films like *L'Inferno* tend to be much more easily accessible as – frequently – prints survive or a number of marketing and filmic materials are available for us to study. Survival of prints, in particular, means that on a very basic level it is also possible to study the film itself and examine the extent it contains elements we might view as horror-like. What this does, however, is to suggest that the antecedents of what later became 'horror' as a genre are limited to only a few films, implying that it is a limited range of films that contribute to what we understand when discussing cinematic horror. Yet the key to understanding the extent of horror-based plots, themes and images in cinema (or at least the intention to 'affect' audiences) is also to examine films that are of a lower profile but appear in much greater numbers. Given the vast amount of films produced in the silent period there are also numerous other films that hint at a much earlier engagement with the generic markers of the horror film. To take some examples, Eleuterio Rodolfi's *Preferisco L'inferno!* (1916) (literally 'I prefer hell!') and *Il cadavere di marmo* (Ugo de Simone, 1915) are the kind of films that can get easily forgotten. It is clear over the period covered here that a number of films engage with tropes that would later become staple parts of the horror film genre, most notably the appearance of the supernatural, the influence of 'dark' or satanic forces and doubts about unrestrained scientific progress and enlightenment rationality as embodied by the mad scientist or crazed inventor. With *Il cadavere di marmo*, literally 'the marble man', it is possible to see an engagement with themes and character types that would become staples of the horror genre in the period after Universal's first tranche of Monster Movies. Ugo de Simone's film from 1915 tells the tale of Alberto, a man who has lost his fortune and wants to kill himself. Just as he is trying to commit suicide by shooting himself, an old man offers him an alternative, saying he will give him a fortune to become the guinea pig for his scientific experiments'. As a result of his Faustian pact, Alberto becomes rich again and falls in love, but the old man turns out to be a mad scientist who injects him with a dangerous solution to see whether he can turn him into marble. By the end of the film Alberto is driven to despair, ultimately suffocating his tormentor.

Conclusion

What is clear, however, is that prior to the mid-1930s there were consistent – if largely disconnected – representations of the supernatural and the cinematic macabre that parallel modern conceptions of the horror genre. These do not represent a coherent tradition or genre but rather were common ways in which to explore ideas of good and evil onscreen. Given the embedded nature of Christianity in Europe's socio-political history and, in particular, the Catholic church's stress upon the ever-present dangers of Satan, it is unsurprising that filmmakers took advantage of the new medium of film to use familiar imagery for new ends. These were images that were both familiar to people and had the potential to have a particular kind of resonance. Given this, it is clear that 'Christianity's Manichean system of absolute good versus absolute evil dovetails neatly into the usual narrative pattern of much classical and contemporary Western horror' (Benshoff, 2014: 209). In this way it is also possible to see how, from the very beginning, cinema allowed a space for filmmakers to explore darker ideas and concepts using the moving image (as opposed to the painting or even the sermon). This is not the same as saying that early proponents of such cinema had a religious or moralistic motive (although some undoubtedly did) but rather that it offered new and exciting ways to utilise familiar forms of imagery.

It is important to stress that what has been presented here is a retrospective reading of some of the influences and developments that, bit by bit, can be seen as establishing cinema as a medium through which to explore the macabre. The films outlined here were not designed to be horror films and neither were they marketed as such. What is becoming increasingly evident, however, is that the long-established boundaries and fuzziness via which we understand the beginnings of the horror genre need to be challenged and reassessed. In presenting further avenues for investigation it is hoped that this chapter will form a small part of that process. The language available to us in the films explored here is, in itself, affected by this and means that there is a tendency to 'talk around' these films and not address their closeness to and connections with later works in the genre. Yet many genres, most notably film noir, have been identified only in retrospect and were originally discussed using other generic markers and other terminology. There is no reason why horror should be any different in this sense. What is key here, however, is that we recognise the bit-by-bit contribution that silent-era cinema made to the development of what would eventually be industrially vocalised as a specific genre.

In many ways, what the films explored here evidence are the ways in which early Italian cinema explored issues and images that were designed to, in some way, provoke a reaction of shock, horror or terror. Europe's long Christian heritage in general and Italy's strong Catholic association in particular meant that cinema became a natural space in which to explore and transform familiar religious tropes via a (relatively) new medium. Central then to the fact that horror imagery developed in Italy was a number of driving factors. The long cultural and sociological inheritance in art and literature of Italy's Catholicism played its part in shaping how ideas around the horrific played out onscreen. This translated into a series of short and longer-form films that explored both ideas around the dangers presented by 'sinning' but also transformed into a much broader exploration of the supernatural in general and representations of 'the monstrous'. This, when combined with the early drive to justify cinema's cultural credibility via the adaptation of well-regarded and well-known literature, led to the creation of a number of films whose place in the horror firmament is only now beginning to be recognised.

NOTES

1. There is no evidence that these films ever received international distribution, so literal English translations of their titles are provided.
2. www.sempreinpenombra.com/2011/08/16/il-frankenstein-italiano-del-1920/
3. The clarity of the image and the way in which it is posed suggest that the photograph was a promotional shot rather than a still.
4. Photographs from the earlier *Life Without Soul*, also a lost film, suggest that Guarracino's Monster shared its much more humanoid and less physically altered shape.

BIBLIOGRAPHY

Altman, R. (1999), *Film/Genre*, London: BFI.
Anonymous (1917a), 'Shepard and Van Loan to handle Bernstein Films', *Motion Picture News*, 21 July 1917, p. 403.
Anonymous (1917b), 'Export and Import Gets More Films', *The Moving Picture World*, 28 July 1917, p. 661.
Benshoff, H. M. (2014), 'Horror Before "The Horror Film"', in Benshoff, H. M. (ed.), *A Companion To The Horror Film*, Oxford: Wiley Blackwell, pp. 207–24.
Bini, A. (2011), 'Horror Cinema: The emancipation of women and urban anxiety', in Brizio-Skov, F. (ed.), *Popular Italian Cinema: Culture and Politics in a Postwar Society*, New York: I. B. Tauris, pp. 53–82.
Bondanella, P. (2009), *A History of Italian Cinema*, London: Continuum.
Bondanella, P. (2014), 'Introduction', in Bondanella, P. (ed.), *The Italian Cinema Book*, London: British Film Institute.
Bonsaver, G. (2014), 'Censorship from the Fascist Period to the Present', in P. Bondanella (ed.), *The Italian Cinema Book*, London: British Film Institute.
Geraghty, L. and Jancovich, M. (2008), 'Introduction: Generic canons', in Geraghty, L. and Jancovich, M. (eds), *The Shifting Definitions of Genre: Essays on Labeling Films, Television Shows and Media*, London: McFarland, pp. 1–14.
Giannini, G. (1921), *Kines*, 10 September 1921.
Glut, D. F. (1973), *The Frankenstein Legend: A Tribute to Mary Shelley and Boris Karloff*, Metuchen, NJ: Scarecrow Press.
Gundle, S. (2013), *Mussolini's Dream Factory: Film Stardom in Fascist Italy*, Oxford: Berghahn.
Hirschmann, K. (2012), *Frankenstein*, San Diego: Reference Point Press.
Hutchings, P. (2008), 'Monster legacies: Memory, Technology and Horror History', in Geraghty, L. and Jancovich, M. (eds), *The Shifting Definitions of Genre: Essays on Labeling Films, Television Shows and Media*, London: McFarland, pp. 216–28.
Mann, M. (2011), 'Gothic horror', in Bayman, L., *Dictionary of World Cinema: Italy*, Bristol: Intellect, pp. 154–6.
Mathijs, E. (2006), '*The Lord of the Rings* and Family: A View on Text and Reception', in Mathijs, E. and Pomerance, M. (eds), *From Hobbits to Hollywood: Essays on Peter Jackson's* The Lord of the Rings, New York: Editions Rodopi, pp. 41–64.
Moliterno, G. (2008), *Historical Dictionary of Italian Cinema*, Plymouth, MA: Scarecrow Press.
Paul, L. (2005), *Italian Horror Film Directors*, London: McFarland.
Peirse, A. (2013), *After Dracula: The 1930s Horror Film*, London: I. B. Tauris.
Schreck, N. (2001), *The Satanic Screen: An illustrated Guide To The Devil In Cinema*, London: Creation Books.

Venturini, S. (2014), *Horror italiano*, Rome: Donzelli.
Welle, J. P. (2004), 'Early cinema, *Dante's Inferno* of 1911, and the Origins of Italian Film Culture', in Iannuci, A. (ed.), *Dante, Cinema & Television*, London: University of Toronto Press.

2. DOMESTIC FILMS MADE FOR EXPORT: MODES OF PRODUCTION OF THE 1960s ITALIAN HORROR FILM

Francesco Di Chiara

Along with the Italian Western, but with an arguably more lasting effect, Italian horror cinema of the 1960s has contributed significantly to the branding of European genre cinema for an international audience. As with Italian cinema a decade earlier,[1] the success of Italian horror film was due at the same time to its compatibility with other, foreign genre products – they could fit in a double bill with an American International Pictures release, for instance – and their perceived 'otherness' in respect of the Hollywood standards. In fact, because of their graphic violence, eroticism and visual flair, these films soon gained a cult following outside of Italy, and especially throughout the 1970s with the increasing international success of Italian *giallo* and with the emergence of horror cult directors like Dario Argento and Lucio Fulci.

However, when viewed from the perspective of Italian film history, the very existence of an Italian horror genre seems to be inexplicable. As many historians have pointed out in the past, this genre seems to have flourished in a country completely devoid of a tradition of domestic gothic or mystery literature.[2] Moreover, the supposedly non-industrial quality of these films, which apparently relied only on the craftsmanship of talented directors like Mario Bava, Riccardo Freda and Antonio Margheriti, contrasts with the idea of an industrial strategy aimed at conquering foreign markets, especially because no Italian company at the time was capable of controlling the international distribution of its products. Finally, Italian horror films were often regarded as completely unrelated to other products of the Italian cultural industry.

While not completely untrue, over the last decade these remarks have been substantially challenged by new works focusing on the complex relationship that 1960s Italian horror entertains with Italian national culture,[3] and on an in-depth analysis of post-Second World War Italian genre cinema. In fact, 1960s Italian horror was indeed a minor genre, which generated modest revenues on the domestic market, and that was highly dependent on an international market model. However, from an industrial standpoint, these films appear to be a product of the new situation that the Italian film industry had been facing since the late 1950s, which somehow helped the acquisition of a brand value in the international circuits on the part of both art and popular Italian cinema. In fact, the horror genre allowed the Italian film industry to experiment with new modes of production and to develop production trends aimed at the international, rather than the domestic, market. By focusing on the 'rough start' of Italian horror film production in its first five years, this chapter aims at taking into account the characteristics of the 1960s Italian horror film from an industrial standpoint, and to assess its relationship with other branches of Italian popular culture of the time.

THE RULES OF THE GAME: THE POST-WAR ITALIAN FILM INDUSTRY AND THE ITALIAN FILM AID SYSTEM

Before analysing the modes of production and the financing of the 1960s Italian horror film, it will first be necessary to take into account the inner working of the post-Second World War Italian film industry, and its complex relationship with the Italian government. In fact, as was the case with most of the European film industries in the post-Second World War era, both Italian art and genre cinema were heavily dependent on the state aid system, especially as the last years of the Second World War had effectively been a 'full stop' for most of the Italian film industry. For instance, the main film studios in Rome, Cinecittà, had been converted to a refugee camp,[4] and most of the filming equipment present in the capital had been confiscated and taken to Venice (which, since 1943, had served as a film production hub for the Republic of Salò). Furthermore, the protectionist measures that had been conceived by the fascist regime throughout the 1930s in order to relaunch domestic production, had been abolished shortly after the war, leaving Italian producers to face extremely aggressive competition from Hollywood.

It was the then-emerging Italian art cinema, related to the new neorealist aesthetics, which to some degree set in motion the Italian film industry. In fact, the release of *Roma città aperta/Rome, Open City* (Roberto Rossellini, 1945) was not only warmly received by the Italian audience – unlike the following neorealist pictures, which mostly struggled at the box office – but also marked the beginning of unprecedented attention towards Italian film on the part of foreign markets. Firstly, Roberto Rossellini was awarded the Golden Palm as Best Director at the first edition of the Cannes Film Festival in 1946. Secondly, and most importantly, *Roma città aperta* was distributed on the US market in 1946, as it had been partly financed by a US Army officer who had acquired the rights for North American distribution. The reception on the American market was exceptionally good for a foreign production, and thus the US release of *Roma città aperta* initiated a relatively continuous interest by American distributors towards the Italian art film[5] and also favoured the export of other, less ambitious, products like genre films. Moreover, *Roma città aperta* also marked the beginning of occasional forms of co-operation between the Italian and the American film industries, as was the case with Rossellini's following *Paisà/Paisan* (1946), which was an Italian-American co-production.

However, aside from the international exploits of the art-film sector, throughout the latter half of the 1940s the whole of the Italian film industry was still suffering from a lack of state support, at a time when most European countries were developing protectionist measures or incentives for domestic production.[6] An answer to the demand for state aid from the film industry came only after the 1948 elections, which saw the rise of the conservative Catholic party Christian Democracy. In 1949, Giulio Andreotti, who had been appointed Under-Secretary for Cinematography, issued an Act that substantially reprised the pre-war legislation of the fascist regime, the *Legge Alfieri* of 1938. In fact, Andreotti reinstituted past protectionist measures, such as taxes on the dubbing of foreign films, partly for the purpose of limiting the circulation of non-domestic products.[7] Moreover, soft loans for film financing (conceived in order to overcome the low availability of private financing) and above all a tax-relief programme were both restored. Therefore, since the early 1950s every domestic production was eligible to receive a government tax refund of 10 per cent of its total gross, plus another 8 per cent reserved for works considered of particular artistic value (which was usually granted regardless of the actual quality of the film). Furthermore, the Italian government also blocked the export of revenues generated in Italy by the Italian agencies of Hollywood film distributors, thus forcing American distributors to invest that money in the Italian film industry or in other national activities.[8] The main difference between the Andreotti laws and the previous fascist legislation consisted of the fact that every company could have access to that aid, while the *Legge Alfieri* had set a minimum limit of a capital of 500,000 lira, in order to benefit only the bigger, more reliable companies.

In fact, the main consequence of the Andreotti law was both a rise in overall film production and a proliferation of small companies, which were often created in order to produce just one film and then disappeared. Another corollary of this situation was the fact that these smaller companies usually depended on bigger film distributors, who pre-acquired the distribution rights of their films, thus assuming a great part of the risk involved in film production.[9] In the case of low- to mid-budget films the Italian production system was close to what Janet Staiger (1985: 571–9) has described as a 'package-unit system of production', where the distributor acted as the main financier of a project managed by a smaller production company. Reportedly, these smaller companies frequently went under-budget in order to ensure a profit from the financing received from the distributor. This was possible because of the tendency of reutilising production props and stock shots from one production to another, as well as to the recurring presence of a group of extremely efficient professionals typified by directors such as Mario Bava and Antonio Margheriti or cinematographer Ubaldo Terzano. Therefore, the fragmentation of the Italian film industry, along with the availability of soft loans, the tax refunds and the financing on the part of the distributors, all coalesced in favouring a continuous experimentation on the part of Italian genre cinema, and conversely a certain instability of the system of genres.

The 'Filoni' and the transnational life of the Italian genre film

In examining the genre system of classical Hollywood, Rick Altman (1999) distinguishes between 'cycles' and 'genres': the former are groups of films that are all made by a same studio (or by a single producer-unit working within a larger studio) mostly using personnel under contract. When they cease to be exclusive to a single studio, cycles evolve into genres: they become widespread, broader, long-lasting categories that are shared by many production companies at the same time. Moreover, genres are recognised as such by audiences, film critics and film historians. As many Italian scholars have noted,[10] Altman's model does not perfectly fit the Italian situation. In fact, with the notable exception of wider, 'macro-genres' such as comedy or melodrama, no cycle seems to have been able to evolve into a shared, stable film genre. Traditionally, Italian film critics of the time preferred to use the term *filoni* (literally 'veins'), as most Italian film genres since the 1950s tended to spawn from foreign models and were intensively exploited (just like ore veins) by several film companies at the same time. Not exclusive to a single company (only a few Italian studios at the time kept actors or directors under contract), most of the post-war Italian film genres span an average time of about seven to ten years, and hardly fit with Altman's definition of either cycles or film genres.

However, rather than small-time operations aimed at quickly cashing in through the imitation of an already existing successful film and failing to evolve into more stable categories, I maintain that Italian post-war film genres should be regarded as productive experiments involving themes, icons and stylistic traits coming from different universes, such as foreign models, distinctively national traits, high art and Italian popular culture. These experiments were made possible by a notable amount of genre mixing and by the presence of a restricted group of professionals (for instance, directors like Freda, Bava or Margheriti, as well as screenwriters like Ennio De Concini) working within several genres at the same time. Most importantly, the outputs of these experiments were tested not only on the domestic audience but, since the late 1950s, also on European and North American audiences.

The transnational dimension of Italian genre cinema arguably started with the explosive success of *Le fatiche di Ercole/Hercules* (Pietro Francisci, 1958), which not only marked the success of the peplum, a then-minor genre that suddenly became one of the most successful production trends in late 1950s and early 1960s Italy, but also opened the doors for a wide distribution in the US. In fact, Galatea, the Italian company which had the exclusivity for the international market for Francisci's film, managed to sell the film to the American distributor Joseph E. Levine's Embassy Picture Corporation, which dubbed the film and promoted it through a wide marketing campaign involving the use of TV advertising. In North America, *Le fatiche di Ercole* was a huge success, and set the standards for the US distribution patterns of Italian genre cinema: the single films were pre-acquired by distribution companies often operating in marginal sectors, such as the drive-in circuit, and their rights were generally sold at a flat rate. In fact, Italian production companies had no control whatsoever on the overseas distribution of their films, because they did not have any distribution agencies located abroad, and therefore their penetration of the US market always remained limited. In this respect, Italian producers were often content providers for the US distributors who pre-acquired the distribution rights of their films, and consequently these films were often made at least in part according to the requests of foreign distributors.

Another element to take into account in relation to the transnational nature of Italian genre cinema is the rise of the trend of European co-productions. In fact, Italian film genres highly benefited from the trend of European film co-productions that started in 1949 with the bi-lateral agreements between Italy and France (soon followed by similar treaties with the German Federal Republic, Spain and the United Kingdom). This formula allowed companies located in different countries to pool resources and production experience in order to make bigger, more competitive films, which were able to attract a European audience typically keen on consuming American films. Most interestingly, co-productions allowed each partner involved in such agreements to benefit from the state aid offered by their respective country of origin. The most interesting aspect of these ventures is perhaps their relationship with issues of nationality, identity and branding. In fact, as Tim Bergfelder (2000) has pointed out, throughout the 1950s and 1960s European film co-productions had managed to acquire a stable brand value by underplaying their national identity, and instead producing cosmopolitan films that were able to appeal to both American and European audiences.[11] Nonetheless, despite their ostensibly cosmopolitan nature, European genre co-productions soon reached a high degree of recognisability among an international audience, allowing European genre cinema to be perceived as a brand.

THE FIRST WAVE OF THE ITALIAN HORROR FILMS

Several factors contributed to lowering the risk of genre film production in 1960s Italy: the presence of state aid in the form of soft loans and tax reliefs; the role of film distributors as film financiers; the increasing number of film co-production agreements; and finally the presence of American distributors willing to pay in advance for Italian genre films. In particular, the relationship between Italian producers and US distributors helps to explain the very existence of the Italian horror film, a genre that struggled to find its place at the Italian box office. In fact, the roughly thirty Italian horror films produced from 1957 to 1966 (the first 'wave' of Italian horror film production) rarely broke the 200 million lira threshold on the domestic market, which was the break-even point for the average Italian genre film.

Italian horror film production began in the second half of the 1950s, but only reached any momentum in the early 1960s. In fact, early Italian horror films such as *I vampiri* (Riccardo Freda, 1958) or *Caltiki, il mostro immortale/Caltiki, the Immortal Monster* (Riccardo Freda, 1959) can be regarded as isolated episodes defined mainly by genre mixing and by the tendency to replicate some features from the films produced by British company Hammer film. In fact, *Caltiki, il mostro immortale* blends horror and science fiction in a fashion that is quite similar to *The Quatermass Experiment* (Val Guest, 1955). Interestingly, *I vampiri* pre-dates, by a few weeks, *The Curse of Frankenstein* (Terence Fisher, 1957), Hammer's first proper venture in the horror genre, but retains the structure of sci-fi investigation of *The Quatermass Experiment*. Moreover, *I vampiri* draws on a multiplicity of models, such as the Italian melodrama (particularly for its opposition of 'good' and 'evil' female characters), Italian film noirs of the 1950s, and European horror films of the past, such as Dreyer's *Vampyr* (1932), which is referenced through the character of Duchess Marguerite Du Grand.

From a production standpoint, both *I vampiri* and *Caltiki, il mostro immortale* can be regarded as isolated experiments, still far from presenting the defining characteristics of the 1960s Italian horror film. In fact, the bulk of Italian film production started after the huge box office success of Hammer's *Dracula* (Terence Fisher, 1958) in the first-run circuit of Rome in 1959: from 1960 to 1966, about thirty Italian horror films were made, until this kind of production suddenly dropped. It has to be pointed out that not all of the five Italian horror films released in 1960 can be considered as relatively cheap imitations of Hammer's *Dracula*; on the contrary, they form a variegated scenario, representative of the mixed trends of early Italian horror film. The first here, *L'amante del vampiro/The Vampire and the Ballerina* (Renato Polselli, 1960), was indeed conceived as a cheap stand-in for Hammer productions, and compensated its lower production values with a more explicit representation of body horror and sex.[12] *L'ultima preda del vampiro/The Playgirls and the Vampire* (Piero Regnoli, 1960) followed in the same vein, while *Seddok l'erede di Satana/Atom Age Vampire* (Anton Giulio Majano, 1960) reprised the mixture of sci-fi elements and horror introduced by *Caltiki, il mostro immortale*. However, the two most influential Italian horror films released in 1960 were arguably the full directorial debut of cinematographer Mario Bava, *La maschera del demonio/Black Sunday*, and *Il mulino delle donne di pietra/The Mill of the Stone Women* (Giorgio Ferroni). In fact, it was from the release of these two films that Italian horror started to be conceived as a genre primarily meant for export to the US, thanks to the international network set up by mid-range production and distribution house Galatea in the late 1950s. Moreover, both *La maschera del demonio* and *Il mulino delle donne di pietra* were ambitious projects, aimed at starting a quality line of horror productions.

Co-produced by Galatea along with Jolly Film, *La maschera del demonio* was far from being a rushed-out low-budget production. Conceived by cinematographer and Galatea long-time collaborator Mario Bava, *La maschera del demonio* had a budget amounting to about 145 million lira, which represented a sort of mid-point between the cost of the average sword-and-sandal film (about 300 million lira) and small-time genre quickies conceived for the peripheral markets, which easily settled around a 70 million lira budget.[13] It is worth noting that almost no part of this money was spent directly by Galatea and Jolly: in fact, Galatea stipulated a 60 million lira pre-sale contract with Italian distributor Unidis, while 8 million lira came from the Banca nazionale del lavoro, where the soft loans to Italian producers had been housed by the Italian government.[14] *Black Sunday* partly reprised the model of Freda's *I vampiri*, but at the same time it was influenced by the more direct representation of sex and violence that characterised Hammer's take on *Dracula*. The modes of production of Bava's film were consistent with the ones already experimented with by Galatea within other film genres. For instance, *La maschera del demonio* imported a foreign (albeit at the time mostly unheard-of) star, the British actress Barbara Steele, following a trend that was launched by the importing of American bodybuilders since the success of *Le fatiche di Ercole*. Moreover, Galatea rented film equipment and facilities from a bigger company, Titanus, as was customary among mid-range and even high-range companies of the time that could not bear the costs related to owning their own studios and equipment.

Galatea aimed at producing a highly successful, medium-budget film that could please at the same time the Italian audience – which had flocked to see *Dracula* – and foreign distributors by following the trend set by Hammer productions, and at the same time differentiating *La maschera del demonio* from that model. From the pre-credit sequence, where the witch Asa (Barbara Steele) is tortured with the mask of Satan and then burnt at the stake, *La maschera del demonio* exceeds the representation of body horror and sexuality already present in the model offered by Hammer productions. In fact, this sequence not only was the first to feature the sadistic violence towards female characters which would become a trademark of Italian horror and *giallo* films, but Bava's direction famously made this scene more intense, equating sadistic and viewing pleasure by using sophisticated camera movements and POV shots. It was this blending of eroticism, graphic violence and refined camerawork that helped to define the identity of Italian horror for an international audience. However, this approach was a double-edged sword, as the film was banned from distribution in the UK until 1968.

It is also worth noting that *La maschera del demonio* was loosely adapted from a short tale by Nikolaj Gogol, and thus helped in identifying Italian horror with literary sources that were often different from the ones chosen by gothic horror productions made by British and American competitors like Hammer or American International Pictures. Most interestingly, as American distributors apparently considered the grounding of a horror film in a literary tradition as customary, the literary sources of Italian horror films were often completely made up. For instance, *Il mulino delle donne di pietra* was supposedly adapted from 'Flemish Tales' written by a non-existent Pieter Van Weigen, while *I tre volti della paura/Black Sabbath* (Mario Bava, 1963) came from totally fake sources or from works of authors who did not correspond to the ones announced in the credits.[15]

If *La maschera del demonio* is one of the most famous examples of early Italian gothic horror, the lesser-known *Il mulino delle donne di pietra* is equally representative of the experimental attitude that defined some of these early Italian horror productions. Produced by small Italian company Wanguard Film, along with the slightly bigger Explorer Film 58 and Faro Film, *Il mulino delle donne di pietra* was also co-produced with the equally small French company Comptoire D'Expansion Cinématographique (CEC), which covered 30 per cent of the film's budget. Despite the small scale of the companies involved, the film was rather ambitious: it featured a mostly international cast, including German star Wolfgang Preiss – who in the same year starred in Fritz Lang's last film *Die 1000 Augen des Dr Mabuse /The 1,000 Eyes of Dr Mabuse* (1960) – as well as emerging French star Pierre Brice. Importantly, the film was shot in Eastmancolor using the French widescreen format Dyaliscope. It has to be stressed that, although gothic Italian horror is commonly associated with the flamboyant colour photography of Mario Bava, the majority of the films were actually shot in black and white. This happened not only because colour was more expensive and had been introduced only relatively recently (in 1952) in Italian cinema, but also because of the models of choice of early Italian horror.[16] In fact, as though these films were born to follow the path set by the recent success of Hammer's products, Italian horror drew from a variety of models representing a tradition of horror cinema.

According to 1960s Italian filmmakers, classic horror cinema was still best represented by black-and-white European or Hollywood films from the 1930s, such as the aforementioned *Vampyr* (directly referenced in *I vampiri, L'ultima preda del vampiro* and *Il mulino delle donne di pietra*) or *Dr Jekyll and Mr Hyde* (Rouben Mamoulian, 1932, also referenced in *Atom Age Vampire*).[17] In the case of *Il mulino delle donne di pietra*, the choice of Eastmancolor seems to follow a similar logic, as this film is also inspired by classic horror films, albeit of a very colourful kind: *Mystery of the Wax Museum* (Michael Curtiz, 1933) and *House of Wax* (André De Toth, 1953). In fact, the film blends the theme of the vampire, which was already present in Freda's *I vampiri* – here an evil scientist kidnaps young girls and uses their blood to cure his ill daughter – with the theme of the evil artist present in these two classic Warner Bros. productions, as corpses of dead girls are disguised as morbid wax sculptures. Both *Mystery of the Wax Museum* and *House of Wax* are notable for their visual spectacular values: the former was, along with *Terror X* (Michael Curtiz, 1932), one of the first examples of two-colour Technicolor in the 1930s, while *House of Wax* was conceived as the first 3D entry of Warner Bros. Therefore, *Il mulino delle donne di pietra* can be considered as a film experimenting with another approach in respect to *La maschera del demonio*. Here the visual pleasure is created not just by the relationship between eroticism, graphic images of decay – which are nonetheless present in the last reel of the film – and sophisticated camerawork. In fact, this film also relies on several hallucinating sequences that are also enhanced by the colour photography and by the production values displayed in the film, which are far superior to those of *La maschera del demonio* and of the other Italian horror films released the same year.

It is worth noting that, other than using colour photography and a widescreen format, *Il mulino delle donne di pietra* also featured location shooting in the Netherlands (where the action takes place). An odd choice, probably imposed by the French co-producer (who actually paid for the expenses of the location shooting), especially considering that all the exterior shooting of the other Italian horror films happened on the backlots of the studios surrounding Rome.[18] Unsurprisingly, all of these choices impacted upon the budget of the film, which reached a total of 185 million lira, costing almost 30 per cent more than *Black Sunday*. In the end, *Mill of the Stone Women* was a very

complex financial operation, to which the three Italian co-producers contributed a sum of 60 million lira, while the rest came from the French co-producer,
the Cinecittà studios and the pre-sale to Italian distributors.[19]

DOMESTIC FILMS MADE FOR EXPORT

La maschera del demonio and *Il mulino delle donne di pietra* were two different, yet somehow complementary, experiments in starting a new production
trend of Italian horror films able to appeal to an international audience. In
their own way, both of these films tried to replicate narrative and thematic
elements already present in *I vampiri,* but mixed them with graphic violence,
eroticism and a visual flair that allowed them to compete against the products made by Hammer or American International Pictures. However, on the
domestic market this attitude did not pay off, as neither Bava's nor Ferroni's
films earned much more than the 127 million lira[20] garnered by *I vampiri* a
few years earlier. In fact, in the end *Il mulino delle donne di pietra* and *La
maschera del demonio* lost, after a five-year run in Italian cinemas, 15 million
and 25 million lira respectively.[21] Although it is difficult to ascertain exactly
how much the two films earned for the sale of the distribution rights on
foreign markets, it was clearly only through the sale to American distributors
that the two films might have been able to generate revenues. In both cases,
the sale operation was managed by Galatea, which, in addition to being the
producer of *La maschera del demonio,* was also the owner of the foreign rights
for *Il mulino delle donne di pietra.* The latter was the only Italian horror film
to enter the catalogue of Parade Pictures in 1963, three years after its debut
in Italian theatres. *La maschera del demonio* was arguably easier to sell, as
it allowed Galatea to start a continuous and profitable relationship with
American International Pictures.

At the time, Galatea's partner on the US market, Levine, was abandoning
low-budget genre films in favour of products able to reach a wider audience.
In fact, it continued to partner Galatea in more highbrow projects like Pietro
Germi's comedy *Divorzio all'italiana/Divorce Italian Style* (1961) and the
Second World War epic *Italiani brava gente/Attack and Retreat* (Giuseppe De
Santis, 1964). Therefore, for its horror production Galatea turned to monster-
movie specialists James Nicholson and Samuel Z. Arkoff, who at the time
were producing Roger Corman's first venture into gothic horror, *The Fall of
the House of Usher* (1960). By picking up *La maschera del demonio* for distribution in the US, Nicholson and Arkoff's company, American International
Pictures, started a long relationship with Italian horror, providing Italian
producers with an important commercial outlet for their genre productions.
In fact, despite being a black-and-white film, *La maschera del demonio* was
used by American International Pictures as the main attraction in double-bill

programmes,[22] and drove interest towards Italian horror films. Moreover, in 1961 Barbara Steele starred in Roger Corman's second Poe adaptation, *The Pit and the Pendulum*.

Thus, Italian horror proved to be disappointing on the domestic market but, like the sword-and-sandal before, it clearly had some potential interest for foreign distributors. Therefore, after the unsatisfactory domestic performance of these 1960 prototypes, subsequent Italian horror productions experimented with yet another approach. Firstly, production dropped between 1961 and 1962, with only three titles released compared to five in 1960 alone. Secondly, one of the two Italian horror films released in 1962, *L'orribile segreto del Dr Hichcock/The Horrible Dr Hichcock* (Riccardo Freda), set a new standard with its style and modes of production. Directed and produced by the makers of the first Italian horror, *I vampiri*, *L'orribile segreto del Dr Hichcock* reprised the most successful elements of both *La maschera del demonio* – for instance, a strong and perverse eroticism, and graphic violence – and *Il mulino delle donne di pietra* – with its frequent hallucinatory sequences combined with an anti-naturalistic colour photography. However, *L'orribile segreto del Dr Hichcock* mixed these same elements with a narrative structure referencing 1940s woman's films,[23] in particular *Rebecca* (Alfred Hitchcock, 1940), with several citations from other films directed by Alfred Hitchcock. As far as production values are concerned, this film followed the path set by the horror films directed by Roger Corman. For instance, instead of the more complex narrative and the frequent exterior scenes of *Il mulino delle donne di pietra*, *L'orribile segreto del Dr Hichcock* focused on a few characters moving in a closed environment, entirely reconstructed in the studio, and whose perverse feelings were enhanced by the use of colour. Furthermore, in comparison to *La maschera del demonio*, the complex camerawork seems to have been replaced by the more cost-effective movements of zoom lenses and by film editing. Not surprisingly, *L'orribile segreto del Dr Hichcock*'s final budget amounted to only 96 million lira,[24] which was about 50 million lira less than *Black Sunday*, despite the ever-increasing inflation of early 1960s Italy.[25] Therefore, even despite the disappointing result at the domestic box office (142 million lira over a five-year run), *L'orribile segreto del Dr Hichcock* was still able to recoup its budget and to generate an (albeit modest) revenue.

The sale to foreign markets was still a crucial element for making Italian horror a profitable genre. *L'orribile segreto del Dr Hichcock* was dubbed into French and sold to French distributor Cosmopolis in September 1962 (three months after its debut in Italian theatres), to UK distributor Compton-Cameo Films in 1963, and finally to Sigma III Corporation for US distribution. It was only after the release of *L'orribile segreto del Dr Hichcock* that Italian horror production rose again to an average of five to six films from 1963 to 1965, before dropping to only two titles in 1966 and then entering a hiatus until the end of the decade. Most companies limited their output to only one or two horror films and, not surprisingly, the only Italian company to maintain a relatively steady relationship with this genre was Galatea, because of its continuing relationship with American International Pictures. Before entirely leaving film production in 1965, they produced two more films directed by Bava: the first example of the *giallo*, *La ragazza che sapeva troppo/The Girl Who Knew Too Much* (Mario Bava, 1962), and *I tre volti della paura/Black Sabbath* (Mario Bava, 1963) starring Boris Karloff.

CONCLUSIONS

In the 1960s Italian horror remained a minor genre in Italian production, but nonetheless gave life to a respectable thirty titles in a span of less than ten years, before the horror *filone* was put on hold by the Italian Western and *giallo*, which had much broader audience appeal. The conditions for the existence of this genre reside in the risk reduction represented by state aid policies, but above all in the interest demonstrated by foreign distributors and co-producers. Nonetheless, despite the practice of hiding the names of their directors and actors behind English-sounding monikers (like Robert Hampton for Riccardo Freda), these films maintained a strict relationship with other elements of the Italian popular culture of the time. In fact, many of these films have a relationship with sensational crime comics like *Diabolik* (published since 1962), or with the Italian horror pulp books that were sold at news-stands, like the book collections *I libri di Dracula* and *KKK I classici dell'orrore*, which both appeared shortly after the release of Hammer's *Dracula* in 1959. It has to be pointed out that these books often offered source material to Italian horror films, as was the case with *La vergine di Norimberga/The Virgin of Nuremberg* (Antonio Margheriti, 1963), which was adapted from a novel released in the aforementioned *KKK* series. Most interestingly, the start of Italian horror film production coincided with the launch of magazines devoted to a form of horror known as *fumetti* (photo-novels). One of the most successful media of 1950s Italy, the photo-novel was usually aimed at a female audience and contained melodramatic stories. However, the early 1960s saw the rise of horror photo-novel series such as *Malìa, il fotoromanzo del terrore*, full of sensationalist eroticism and graphic violence. These photo-novels also presented original stories, but mostly adapted horror films by adding balloons to stage shots and/or film stills: therefore, there is a photo-novel adaptation for most of the Italian films produced in the 1960s, most predominantly those that had enjoyed less success in film theatres. Finally, Italian distributors (or even Italian agencies of the Hollywood majors) were conscious of the existing relationship between the horror film and other branches of the Italian cultural industry, and exploited it in the advertisement of their films. For instance, part of the graphic material conceived by Warner Bros. Italy for promoting *La maschera del demonio*, which the company had distributed in Italian theatres, explicitly replicated the layout of the covers of the extremely successful book collection *I gialli Mondadori*, which had introduced crime novels to an Italian audience in the 1920s.

Before the Western and alongside sword-and-sandal cinema, Italian horror created a brand for Italian genre films in front of an international audience, as demonstrated both by the relationship between AIP and Galatea, and by the fact that almost all Italian horror films produced in the first half of the 1960s were picked up by US distributors. Moreover, Italian horror proved to be an extremely modern genre, capable of entering into a complex relationship of cross-promotion with other products of the Italian cultural industry.

NOTES

1. See Hawkins (2002).
2. See Venturini (2014: 5–9).
3. In particular, Simone Venturini (2014) has pointed out how an 'horrific' sensibility not necessarily related to a proper horror genre had flourished in Italian cinema as early as the 1910s, while Alberto Pezzotta (2014) has investigated the complex relationship between the Italian horror eroticisation of violence and the new sensibility typical of the years of the 'economic boom' (1957–63).
4. See Steimatsky (2008). Moreover, other fully equipped studios like those owned by major film company Titanus had also been confiscated by the US Army to be used as barracks. However, several other minor studios were still operational, as pointed out by Farassino (1988).
5. For the role played by *Roma città aperta* in initiating the birth of an American 'art cinema' distribution circuit, see Balio (2010: 40–61). Hawkins (2004) has also pointed out how the positive reception of the film was due not only to its artistic quality, but mostly to the more direct representation of sex and violence as compared to the strict rules of the Motion Picture Association of America (MPPDA).
6. See Nowell-Smith (1998).
7. These taxes also helped the production of national films: in fact, Italian companies gained a 'dubbing voucher' (which meant they were exempted from paying taxes on dubbing) for every domestic film they produced. Moreover, these companies could also sell their government vouchers to distribution companies, thus gaining income.
8. For the Andreotti laws and the MPPDA–ANICA agreements, see Corsi (2001) and Quaglietti (1980).
9. See Della Casa (2001: 39) and Venturini (2001: 38).
10. See Pescatore (2003), Eugeni (2004) and Noto (2011). However, I maintain that Altman's model works well in the case of broader categories such as comedy or melodrama, and above all in the case of large-scale production companies such as Titanus. See Di Chiara (2013).
11. On horror film co-productions, also see Baschiera and Di Chiara (2010).
12. See Pezzotta (2014).
13. The financial data come from the film's folder preserved in the Italian Central Archives of the State in Rome: Archivio Centrale dello Stato, Ministero del Turismo e dello Spettacolo, Direzione Generale Cinema, Copioni e fascicoli, CF3302.

14. See Archivio Centrale dello Stato, Ministero del Turismo e dello Spettacolo, Direzione Generale Cinema, Copioni e fascicoli, CF3302.
15. See Pezzotta (2014: 39).
16. For an analysis of the colour technologies employed by Italian horror, see Pitassio (2005).
17. Another point of reference for the Italian horror films released in 1960 could be *Les yeux sans visage/Eyes Without a Face* (George Franju), a French and Italian co-production released the same year. For early Italian horror cinema's preference for black-and-white photography, see also Masi (1982).
18. For instance, the exterior shooting of *Il mulino delle donne di pietra* amounts to 18 million lira, while Galatea spent only 5 million lira for the exteriors of *La maschera del demonio*.
19. See Archivio Centrale dello Stato, Ministero del Turismo e dello Spettacolo, Direzione Generale Cinema, Copioni e fascicoli, CF3241. The Italian co-producers apparently did not apply for the governmental soft loan.
20. All information about box office revenues of Italian films of the 1960s is taken from Rondolino and Levi (1967). These data refer to the total gross earned after the approximately five-year run of Italian films through the different circuits (first-, second- and third-run cinemas).
21. The total gross of *La maschera del demonio*, which cost 144 million lira to make, was 130 million lira after a five-year run. *Il mulino delle donne di pietra* only made 160 million lira in the same time frame.
22. For the activities of American International Pictures as a distributor of Italian horror films, see McGee (1984: 137–8).
23. For an analysis of the 'female gothic film', see Elsaesser (1992).
24. See Archivio Centrale dello Stato, Ministero del Turismo e dello Spettacolo, Direzione Generale Cinema, Copioni e fascicoli, CF3923.
25. The average inflation rate in Italy increased from 2.05 per cent in 1961 to 4.69 per cent in 1962. See: www.inflation.eu/inflation-rates/italy/historic-inflation/cpi-inflation-italy-1962.aspx [last accessed on 31 May 2015].

BIBLIOGRAPHY

Balio, T. (2010), *The Foreign Film Renaissance on American Screens 1946–1973*, Madison: Wisconsin University Press.
Baschiera, S. and Di Chiara, F. (2010), 'Once Upon a Time in Italy: Transnational Features of Genre Production 1960s–1970s', *Film International*, 8:6, pp. 30–9.
Bergfelder, T. (2000), 'The Nation Vanishes. European Co-Production and Popular Genre Formula in the 1950s and 1960s', in Mette, H. and MacKenzie, S. (eds), *Cinema and Nation*, London and New York: Routledge, pp. 139–51.
Corsi, B. (2001), *Con qualche dollaro in meno. Storia economica del cinema italiano*, Rome: Editori Riuniti.
Della Casa, S. (2001), 'I generi di profondità', in De Vincenti, G. (ed.), *Storia del cinema italiano 1960–1964*, Vol. X, Venice and Rome: Marsilio-Edizioni di Bianco & Nero, pp. 294–331.
Di Chiara, F. (2013), *Generi e industria cinematografica in Italia: il caso Titanus (1949–1964)*, Turin: Lindau.
Elsaesser, T. (1992), 'Mirror, Muse, Medusa: Experiment Perilous', in Païni, D. and Vernet, M.(eds), *Le portrait peint au cinema/The Painted Portrait in Film*, special issue of *Iris*, 14/15, pp. 147–59.
Eugeni, R. (2004), 'Sviluppo, trasformazione e rielaborazione dei generi', in Bernardi,

S. (ed.), *Storia del cinema italiano 1954–1959*, Vol. IX, Venice and Rome: Marsilio-Edizioni di Bianco & Nero, pp. 77–97.

Farassino, A. (1988), 'Il costo dei panni sporchi. Note sul "modo di produzione" neorealista', in Zagarrio, V. (ed.), *Dietro lo schermo. Ragionamenti sui modi di produzione cinematografici in Italia*, Venice: Marsilio, pp. 135–43.

Hawkins, J. (2002), 'Sleaze Mania, Euro-Trash and High Art: The Place of European Art Films in American Low Culture', in Jancovich, M. (ed.), *Horror, the Film Reader*, London and New York: Routledge, pp. 125–34.

Masi, S. (1982), *La luce nel cinema. Introduzione alla storia della fotografia nel film*, L'Aquila: Cooperativa cinematografica 'La lanterna magica'.

McGee, M. T. (1984), *Fast and Furious. The Story of American International Pictures*, Jefferson, NC: McFarland.

Noto, P. (2011), *Dal bozzetto ai generi. Il cinema italiano dei primi anni Cinquanta*, Turin: Kaplan.

Nowell-Smith, G. (1998), 'Introduction', in Nowell-Smith, G. and Ricci, S. (eds), *Hollywood and Europe: economics, culture, national identity. 1945–95*, London: BFI, pp. 1–17.

Pescatore, G. (2003), 'I generi come forme seriali', in Antonini, A. (ed.), *Il film e i suoi multipli*, Udine: Forum, pp. 53–6.

Pezzotta, A. (2014), 'Il boom? È gotico (e anche un po' sadico)', *Bianco & Nero*, 579, pp. 34–48.

Pitassio, F. (2005), 'L'orribile segreto dell'horror italiano', in Manzoli, G. and Pescatore, G. (eds), *L'arte del risparmio: stile e tecnologia*, Rome: Carocci, pp. 31–41.

Quaglietti, L. (1980), *Storia economico-politica del cinema italiano 1945–1980*, Rome: Editori Riuniti.

Rondolino, G. and Levi, O. (1967), *Catalogo Bolaffi del cinema italiano: tutti i film italiani del dopoguerra*, Turin: Bolaffi.

Staiger, J. (1988), 'The Hollywood Mode of Production 1930–60', in Bordwell, D., Staiger, J. and Thompson, K. (eds), *The Classical Hollywood Cinema. Film Style & Mode of Production to 1960*, London and New York: Routledge, pp. 311–37.

Steimatsky, N. (2009), 'The Cinecittà Refugee Camp (1944–1950)', *October*, 128, pp. 23–50.

Venturini, S. (2001), *Galatea S.p.A. (1952–1965): storia di una casa di produzione cinematografica*, Rome: AIRSC.

Venturini, S. (2014), *Horror italiano*, Rome: Donzelli.

3. THE 1980s ITALIAN HORROR CINEMA OF IMITATION: THE GOOD, THE UGLY AND THE SEQUEL

Stefano Baschiera

ITALIAN HORROR AND THE 1980S CRISIS

In the first half of the 1980s, Italian horror cinema thrived amid a significant moment of crisis and structural changes in the national film industry and infrastructure. During the decade, the crisis of Italian cinema, which began in the 1970s, worsened significantly and affected all sectors of the industry.[1] Specifically, the exhibition sector continued to struggle and witnessed an apparently irreversible resizing of the number of cinema theatres in the country and a massive decline in the number of the increasingly expensive tickets sold (Corsi, 2001: 116–23).[2] The second- and third-run theatres – in particular, the provincial ones – which constituted the backbone of Italian cinema-going faced the crisis of the sector first, soon followed by more prestigious urban exhibition centres.

The national film industry was adapting to and attempting to rationalise the uncontrolled emergence of private television networks. In fact, they were not only the main competitors of theatrical exhibition but, as I shall discuss later, they became the key players in national film production. The first consequence was a consistent withdrawal to the national signalled by the gradual departure from the international stage that Italian cinema was accustomed to, as well as the more limited ability to attract foreign investments and to participate in ambitious European co-productions (Corsi, 2001: 139–41).

While art cinema struggled with the challenges of a generational renewal and a generalised lack of ambition of producers, a creative crisis also hit the last haven of Italian cinema: its genre production. The inevitable move of popular cinema from third-run theatres to the small screen began to impact the quantity and quality of the films produced.

Arguably, the crisis did not impact horror cinema. In truth, the production of horror films quantitatively thrived during the late 1970s and early 1980s. As Paolo Russo points out, between 1977 and 1985 seventy-five films belonging to the horror genre were produced, with seventeen films made in the years 1977 to 1980, 'for an average percentage close to the six per cent (of the entire production) a figure which is undoubtedly relevant in particular if compared with the numbers of the previous decades' (Russo, 2005: 441). During the 1980s, two films by Dario Argento (*Inferno*, 1980 and *Tenebre/Tenebrae*, 1982) were among the few titles not belonging to the comedy genre that managed to enter the top ten of the national box office.[3]

Overall, the crisis of the exhibition sector did not affect horror production because, with a few exceptions, since the 1950s the national market was hardly the first source of revenue for Italian horror films. A consequence of the reliance on foreign markets can be seen in the transnational dimension of the production based on co-production agreements, employment of international casts, use of English pen-names, foreign settings and locations, and the involvement of American distributors for the financing of the films.[4] As discussed later, these (and other) features that characterised the mode of production of Italian horror cinema became increasingly prominent in the 1980s.

Moreover, during the decade, with the development of VHS distribution, Italian horror cinema developed a new form of fandom and reached a cult status, particularly in the US, UK, Germany and Japan. In the same period it encountered a problematic canonisation (see Church, 2014) because, on the one hand, fans and critics promoted a new understanding of the genre through an authorship approach focused on directors such as Mario Bava, Dario Argento and Lucio Fulci; on the other hand, Italian horror became synonymous with extreme cinema and with visually graphic excesses, as can be grasped by the recurring presence of those films in the UK video nasties lists (see Egan, 2007).

THE NEGLECTED DECADE: SCHOLARLY APPROACHES TO 1980S
ITALIAN HORROR

Despite its international relevance, little scholarly attention has been dedicated to the production of the genre in the 1980s. In fact, the main publications dedicated to the genre end their analysis at the end of the 1970s. This is the case, for instance, for recently published works on Italian horror (Pitassio, 2005; Curti, 2009; Di Chiara, 2009; Venturini, 2014) and on the general production of Italian popular cinema (Manzoli, 2012).

Overall it can be argued that the reason for this recurring time frame when dealing with Italian popular cinema is related to the changes in the film production landscape. I am thinking of the crisis of the exhibition sector, the loss of key producers such as Dino De Laurentiis and Aurelio Grimaldi, and the unregulated emergence of private networks and their involvement in film financing. These changes, which initially began in the mid-1970s, affected genre production in the following decade and left a general feeling that the 'golden age' was inevitably past and unrepeatable.

In the 1980s, the Italian horror landscape was even more fragmented and diverse than before. In many respects the decade offered some of the most iconic films associated with Italian horror as a whole, such as *E tu vivrai nel terrore! L'aldilà/The Beyond* (Lucio Fulci, 1981), *Cannibal Holocaust* (Ruggero Deodato, 1980), *Lo squartatore di New York/The New York Ripper* (Lucio Fulci, 1982), *Dèmoni/Demons* (Lamberto Bava, 1985) and *La chiesa/The Church* (Michele Soavi, 1989). Equally, the decade witnessed a seemingly disorderly proliferation of highly derivative, very low-budget films which further advanced the concept of 'cinema of imitation',[5] based on (unofficial) sequels and/or remakes quickly able to exploit the popularity of a particular title and sub-genre. Even if we consider only the years 1980 and 1981, it is possible to list films such as *Alien Terror/Alien 2* (Ciro Ippolito, 1980), *La casa sperduta nel parco/House on the Edge of the Park* (Ruggero Deodato, 1980), Luigi Cozzi's *Contamination – Alien arriva sulla Terra/Contamination* (1980) and Bruno Mattei's *Virus – l'inferno dei morti viventi/Hell of the Living Dead* (1980) as examples of this trend.

Generally speaking, in the 1980s film production does not seem to add any successful new features to the strengths (and weaknesses) of the industrial system put in place in the previous decades, and it continued to be characterised by several short-lived and small-sized production companies. In the same way, from a textual perspective there are no significant innovations in plots, styles and themes. Instead, the Italian horror of the 1980s takes to extremes both the fragmentation of the production and recurring motifs such as the reliance on the representation of sex and gory violence. Therefore, I would argue that the struggle to offer a holistic vision of the genre during the 1980s is the first reason why the decade has been regularly left out from scholarly works. In fact, production during this period does not offer sufficient originality, either in terms of style or industrial approach, to be considered as an 'age' on its own.

The second reason can be found in the new understandings of Italian horror cinema. As previously mentioned, with the international recognition and canonisation of the genre, and the sub-cultural capital it generated, an authorship approach began to emerge. This originated with the fanzines and was then employed in marketing strategies as well as in scholarly and critical works. Therefore, the condition of the genre during the 1980s has been primarily approached through the study of the oeuvre of specific directors, with Argento being the clear frontrunner given the number of book-length studies dedicated to him. The 1980s are thus mainly understood through the (limited) filmic production of the period by canonised 'horror auteurs' (mainly understood as Mario Bava, Dario Argento, Lucio Fulci) whose careers began in a previous decade.

Another way in which the 1980s Italian horror has been analysed by scholars is through its most iconic sub-genres: cannibal and zombie films. Looking, for example, at the former, which started at the end of the 1970s, there is no doubt that it became seen as most representative of the genre across the two decades, attracting academic attention because of its initial originality, its development from the 'schockumentaries' tradition, and a 'textual consistency' that was difficult to find in other horror series.

To sum up, 1980s Italian horror cinema was investigated through an authorial lens or through its most recognisable (and consistent) sub-genres. Instead, I would like to examine the 1980s as the period where some of the key features of horror production in Italy are most evident. In order to do that, we must embrace the flourishing of highly derivative productions as an opportunity to investigate one of the most interesting characteristics of Italian low-budget popular cinema and the horror genre in particular: the imitation film.

THE IMITATION GAME IN ITALIAN POPULAR CINEMA

In order to look at the role played by the imitation film in Italian horror cinema of the 1980s, it is necessary to understand how the concepts of imitation and intertextuality work within Italian popular cinema. First, we need to step back and consider the 1970s, the period when the emergence of private TV broadcasters and the crisis of the film industry promoted changes that would cross over into the following decade. During the second half of the 1970s, imitation and intertextual exchange with popular culture contributed both to the growth of traditional genres (adventure, fantasy and sci-fi cinema) and the large pool of films which borrowed from other media, such as the music industry, TV shows and comic books (Manzoli and Menarini, 2005: 398). These exchanges with popular culture led to fragmentation in sub-genres and *filoni*, which enabled the generation of series of films with repetitive narrative structures and plot developments.

One of the thematic features common to the generic proliferation of those years was the strong presence of sex and violence (Manzoli and Menarini, 2005: 398). While eroticism featured in the comedies of the time, an increased representation of violence became the dominant characteristic of genres such as the adventure film, the Western, *poliziottesco* and, of course, horror. With the exception of comedy and *poliziottesco*, the imitation films, highly derivative of American productions, continued to hide their national traits. In fact, as Manzoli and Menarini (2005) argue, without the association with a strong director's name, genre production in Italy constantly had to pretend to be American in order to attract an audience.

It is difficult to find a Hollywood success of those years that was not imitated or parodied in Italy. *Conan the Barbarian* (John Milius, 1982), for instance, generated Italian fantasy films such as *Ator l'invincibile/Ator, the Fighting Eagle* (Joe D'Amato, 1982), *Ator 2 – l'invincibile Orion/The Blade Master* (Joe D'Amato, 1984), *Gunan il guerriero/Gunan, King of the Barbarians* (Franco Prosperi, 1982), *Thor il conquistatore/Thor the Conqueror* (Tonino Ricci, 1983) and *The Barbarians* (Ruggero Deodato, 1987). A film such as *The Karate Kid* (John G. Avildsen, 1984) was followed by *Il ragazzo dal kimono d'oro/Karate Warrior* (Fabrizio De Angelis, 1987) and its long series of sequels (six in total).

The same happened with the Italian 'post-apocalyptic' cinema that owed much to the success of *Mad Max* (George Miller, 1979), *The Warriors* (Walter Hill, 1979) and *Escape From New York* (John Carpenter, 1981). As Manzoli and Menarini (2005) maintain, works such as Enzo G. Castellari's series of films *1990: I guerrieri del Bronx/1990: The Bronx Warriors* (1982), *I nuovi barbari/Warriors of the Wasteland* (1983) and *Fuga dal Bronx/Escape from the Bronx* (1983) are good examples of the ability of the Italian production to ride the wave of American genre success. The most interesting case of cinema of imitation, however, can be seen with Spielberg's *Jaws* (1975), which quickly generated a long series of imitations such as Enzo G. Castellari's *L'ultimo squalo/Great White/The Last Shark* (1980), Sergio Martino's *Il fiume del grande caimano/The Great Alligator* (1979), *Shark: Rosso nell'oceano/Devil Fish* (Lamberto Bava, 1984), *Killer Crocodile* (Fabrizio De Angelis, 1989) and many more.[6]

These films are exemplars not only for their ability to hide their national belonging but, as with other imitation films, they cope with their budgetary limitations in respect to the original through a strong accent on exoticism and graphic violence. Moreover, they show the ability of a producer/director like Ovidio G. Assonitis, who was at the forefront of the production of imitation films, to build a film around a prominent international cast. This is the case not only of *Tentacoli/Tentacles* (1977), which features Henry Fonda, John Huston and Shelley Winters, but also of *Piranha 2/Piranha Part Two: The Spawning* (1981), which featured a directorial contribution from James Cameron.

It can be argued that at the start of the 1980s, Italian horror cinema re-emerged after a period of crisis mainly because of the new popularity of the genre as a whole on the international market, thanks to the works of directors such as Tobe Hopper, Wes Craven, John Carpenter and in particular George A. Romero. These filmmakers presented Italian horror production with the opportunity to capitalise on its ability to quickly develop imitation sub-genres based on successful films. However, once again, it was the international market that offered the most significant slice of the potential revenue.

ITALIAN HORROR AND THE 1980S INTERNATIONAL MARKET

In line with what happened to genres such as the spy story, the adventure, the mythological, story and the Western, the emergence of horror cinema in Italy in the 1950s can be ascribed to an attempt by Italian producers of low-budget films to exploit the relatively new popularity of the genre on the domestic second- and third-run distribution circuit. In particular, towards the end of the 1950s films by British Hammer and by American International Pictures generated a certain amount of interest in the genre which prompted new production (Della Casa, 2001: 319).

However, the production of films such as *La maschera del demonio/The Mask of Satan* (Mario Bava, 1960) and *Danza macabra/Castle of Blood* (Antonio Margheriti, 1963) was a long way from meeting the national box office success of *Dracula* (Terence Fisher, 1958), despite their fake international origin and their 'new' depiction of sex and violence (see Di Chiara, 2009 and Pezzotta, 2013). Indeed, during the 1960s the sum of the box office returns of horror, *giallo* and sci-fi was equal to one-twentieth of that of adventure films alone (Pitassio, 2005: 36).[7]

Therefore, from its beginning the genre relied on the international market, and in particular on American distribution, in order to generate income. *La maschera del demonio* is a clear example of a film that, thanks to a partnership between its production company Galatea and American International Pictures (AIP), managed to gain its main source of revenue from the drive-in circuit. Italian horror producers began to rely on (or to aspire to) the advances for the distribution in foreign markets to help the financing of their films, in addition to the mechanism of the secured minimum, which was the financial backbone of independent productions.

The secured minimum, in fact, was mainly used by 'independent producers who relied on national or regional distributors to take their films, receiving from them initially a secured minimum of the proceeds of distribution on account' (Ventavoli, 2003: 218). Therefore, the secured minimum 'was paid by the independent regional agents to the producers directly or through a "central" distributor. In essence it was a sum that was supposed to match the probable minimum return of the film in their particular area' (Ventavoli, 2003: 218).

The importance of foreign markets for the development of Italian horror cinema and the mechanism of the secured minimum demonstrate, once again, the key role played by distribution. Recent scholarly works have stressed the need to look at distribution in order to understand film genre.[8] For instance, Lobato and Ryan argue that thinking about genre 'through distribution provides a different way of addressing some of the typical concerns of genre studies, such as patterns of generic evolution, aesthetic histories of individual genres/sub-genres, and debates around categorization and canonization' (Lobato and Ryan, 2011: 190). In particular, their research stresses the role of distribution as the gatekeeper for their ability to withhold or circulate texts and to indirectly regulate the degrees of access to them.

Pitassio perfectly explains the key role distribution played in Italian horror cinema when he claims that:

> The founding characteristics of popular cinema do not stem from the formative objective of the production system but, more specifically, from its distributional apparatus. This allows a widespread flow of products and clichés, tangible objects and subdued technologies. The 'secured minimum', in this sense, provides a distributor with an extraordinary contractual power over any operational choices, thus facilitating the metamorphosis of the genre into a more flexible trend. This also determines an order of priorities, privileging the effect over its predisposition, the result over its building. In other words, it dictates a spectacular attraction over the textual organisation that validates it, including a technological attraction towards experimenting with original tools. (Pitassio, 2005: 36)[9]

I would argue that this is a key characteristic of Italian popular cinema in general and of horror cinema in particular. The crucial role played by the distribution apparatus can be seen as part of a production system characterised by fragmentation in small companies and dictated by the financial need to rely on practices of imitation and the recycling of American models.

A clear example of this has been offered by Kevin Heffernan's analysis of the distribution of Mario Bava's ambitious 'art-horror' *La casa dell'esorcismo/ Lisa e il diavolo/Lisa and the Devil* (1972), his largest-budget film (see Heffernan 2007: 144–63). The film, produced by Alfredo Leone, was meant as the follow-up to the box-office success *Gli orrori del castello di Norimberga/ Baron Blood* (Mario Bava, 1971), which was distributed by AIP. Both Allied Artists and AIP were interested in the distribution rights and ready to offer upfront a significant amount of money (approximately a quarter of the production budget) to secure them. However, after its premiere at the 1972 Cannes film festival, *La casa dell'esorcismo* was without a distributor because, for AIP, it was too 'arty, obscure and campy' (Heffernan, 2007: 156). After a year without American distribution, Leone asked Bava and the actress Elke Sommer to reshoot a new sub-plot involving a demonic possession. The new cut, called *The House of Exorcism*, was then screened in 1974 to potential distributors looking to exploit the international success of *The Exorcist* (William Friedkin, 1973). The fascinating story of the distribution of this film does not end here and it is more complicated than this brief summary. However, it is important to note, once again, the role that imitation and falsification played in the production of popular genres and the fundamental importance of international markets.

Since the introduction of the 'Industry Code of Self-Regulation' (CARA) in 1968 by the Motion Picture Association, which allowed the representation of graphic violence in its rating categories, R-rated horror films 'have explicitly visualised graphic violence and taboo subject matter to a degree unprecedented in the commercial American cinema' (Gregory A. Waller, 2000: 148). The production of films that challenged censorship boundaries undoubtedly reached its peak during the 'gore/slasher' period of the 1980s thanks to films like *Friday the 13th* (Sean S. Cunningham, 1980) and *Slumber Party Massacre* (Amy Holden Jones, 1982).

This slasher production ran in sequels, cycles, sub-genres and repetitive formulae (Waller: 262) and created a new demand for horror films made quickly, independently and with low budgets. In fact, the majors did not get involved in the production of cheaply made genre films, but instead preferred to act as distributors (as happened, for instance, with Paramount and *Friday the 13th*), compromising in some ways the development of the genre but creating a more fierce competition among independent producers.

From the end of the 1970s, Italian imitations needed quickly to adapt to the fast-paced emergence of sub-genres (rape revenge, post-apocalyptic, etc.) that characterised the American productions of the time. The low budgets and graphic violence of the slasher films, for instance, presented a new opportunity as well as a challenge for Italian production companies such as Fulvia Films and Dania Films to quickly develop their diverse catalogues.

LOW-BUDGET IMITATIONS IN THE 1980S

The production of Italian horror films in the 1980s shows the features (and the limits) of the overall production of low-budget popular cinema. In this regard, Pescatore and Manzoli have addressed a new theoretical approach to the question of low budgets in Italian popular cinema in a series of contributions (Manzoli and Pescatore, 2004, 2005).[10] Looking at the genre cinema of the 1960s, they engage with these low-budget productions by distinguishing three levels.

The first comprises the development of the local technologies that are a 'low cost alternative in respect to the foreign technological innovations, in relation in particular to the American film industry' (Manzoli and Pescatore, 2004:

100). The second level refers to aesthetics, understood as 'a label of recognisable phenomena: auteurs, styles, conventions, linguistic modes, intertextual or intermedial contributions' (ibid.). The system looks at the practices of falsifying these phenomena by 'the plagiarism of linguistic forms [. . .], the recycling of external aesthetics borrowed from other media [. . .] or internal aesthetics (parodies of high-brow cinema)' (ibid.). The third level is a mediation and negotiation between the other two levels. Italian genre cinema is understood as being in continuous negotiation between technical and aesthetic competences.

Looking at these levels, Manzoli and Pescatore argue that they correspond to the main shortcomings of Italian popular cinema, namely 'the lack of a laboratory, understood as a place for the technological development for the production; the lack of strong authorial, productive and stylistic labels able to attract a popular audience; the lack of an internal dynamics within the national genres able to stimulate further "genrefication" processes' (Manzoli and Pescatore, 2004: 101).

However, within these limitations, popular cinema was still able to innovate, as is evident from the production of horror cinema. Cannibal films, for instance, with their reliance on a documentary aesthetic and outdoor shooting in exotic locations, present a constant level of negotiation between recycling the documentary aesthetic (typical of the *mondo* movies) and elements taken from several sub-genres of the period (from zombie to soft-core). They continue with the practice of plagiarising forms belonging to other genres, such as the adventure film. Overall, one could argue that the 'found footage' plot device used in *Cannibal Holocaust* (Ruggero Deodato, 1980) is one of the most effective and original manifestations of the negotiation between technical availability (the use of a 16 mm camera) and aesthetic features.

Although Manzoli and Pescatore do not engage with the question of distribution, this aspect plays a crucial role in the three conceptualised levels. The same negotiation occurring at the third level is due to a production system which relies strongly on a secured minimum and advances. Plagiarism, faking and recycling are by-products of this system and it can be argued that Italian horror cinema, with its reliance on foreign distribution, existed as long as it managed to sustain this negotiation between cheap technology and recognisable/imitative aesthetics.

This is evident not only by looking at the long series of 'zombie' films, with titles evoking to different degrees those of Romero – such as Fulci's *Paura nella città dei morti viventi/The City of the Living Dead* (1980) and Mario Girolami's *Zombie Holocaust* (1980) – but also the borrowing of sub-genre tropes and iconography in films such as Fulci's *L'aldilà* or Lamberto Bava's *Dèmoni*.

In particular, there is one feature belonging to the 'level of aesthetic' and involving the mode of imitation that I would like to draw attention to: the use of international locations and settings. Early Italian horror films re-created in studios their gothic settings whereas *giallo* productions were characterised by the figure of the traveller and the representation of European capitals and 'exotic' locations, revealing in this way a showcase of touristic attractions and a hedonistic international 'jet-set' (see Baschiera and Di Chiara, 2009). Cannibal films and shockumentaries, instead, take the idea of 'exoticism' to a completely different level, with films shot in Malaysia, Sri Lanka, Thailand, etc. Shooting in New York was an exceptional occurrence for a film like Fulci's *Zombi 2*; on several occasions the American landscape was 're-created' in Italy in films such as *Autostop rosso sangue/Hitch Hike* (Pasquale Festa Campanile, 1977). In contrast, the 1980s were characterised by Italian horror productions set and shot in the US. I am thinking of films such as *L'aldilà*, *La casa sperduta nel parco*, *Miami Golem* (Alberto De Martino, 1985) and *Uccelli assassini/ Zombie 5: Killing Birds* (Claudio Lattanzi and Joe D'Amato, 1987). After *The Texas Chain Saw Massacre*, *Halloween* and *The Last House on the Left*, horror tales moved to different spaces in America, from the countryside to (sub)urban areas; Italian productions followed suit, also thanks to new partnerships and collaborations with American companies and distributors.

Consequently, the period witnessed an increased mobility of crew, with fewer films actually shot in Italian studios and locations, and Italian directors being directly employed by American productions. This was the case, for instance, for the controversial Romano *Nightmare/Nightmare in a Damaged Brain* (Romano Scavolini, 1981). Produced by the independent company Goldmine Productions, which made only this film, and widely distributed by 21st Century Film Corporation, it was shot in Florida and New York with an American cast.

VHS AND A NEW UNDERSTANDING OF ITALIAN HORROR CINEMA

As previously mentioned, the 1980s saw an increased availability of Italian horror cinema thanks to the quick adoption of VHS players (see McDonald, 2007). In fact, the rapid development of new ancillary markets in the US during the 1980s with the emergence of rental stores marked a further growth of the niche demand for extreme content.

In his thorough study of the home video distribution of 'splat' cinema, Mark Bernard reminds us how the distribution of films on video did not have to abide by the MPAA ratings. Therefore, films on VHS 'were routinely released as "Unrated", a label that was able to escape the pornographic stigma of the X rating' (Bernard, 2014: 75). In this way, video distribution represented an easier alternative for those 'unrated' films that would have struggled to get a theatrical run. Most importantly, Bernard argues that '[a]side from more lenient regulatory policies, home video was a viable avenue for the release of "Unrated" films for several other reasons. With home video, greater responsibility is shifted to the consumer and away from the producer, distributor or retailer' (Bernard, 2014: 75).

This, of course, is just one of the reasons why the VHS distribution circuit was a promising venue for the producers of low-budget horror films. We have also to consider how the Hollywood majors did not show an immediate interest in home video and were at least sceptical towards this new format of home entertainment, which was promoted for its 'timeshifting' and was seen as a risk for the owners of copyrighted material (see Frederick Wasser, 2008: 121; Janet Wasko, 2003: 126). The renting of tapes, which emerged in 1978, was also not an immediately viable business model for the studios as it was 'covered by First Save Doctrine, a provision of the Copyright Act of 1976 that allows the legitimate buyer of copyrighted work to dispose of the copy as he or she wishes' (Wasko, 2003: 127). The growing demand for new films to fill VHS catalogues, in particular for rental outlets, seemed to favour unrated, low-budget production. On the one hand, this was because of the opportunity to rely on graphic covers for the videotape cases displayed in the 'adult only' area of the store (see Guins, 2005); on the other hand, this was due to the demands of the market for new catalogues. As Wasser argues:

> independent producers and mini-major studios such as Orion, Vestry, De Laurentiis, Carolco (allied with LIVE), and Cannon did not have big libraries and therefore expanded their production through the mid-1980s in anticipation that the global market would pay for more new movies. In contrast the Hollywood majors did not substantially increase the number of productions (they already had libraries of popular titles) but instead increased the money spent on making and marketing their films. (Wasser, 2008: 124–5)

There was another incentive for independent producers to make new films that could also appeal to the videotape market: the high price-tag of unrated VHS. In truth, these were generally 'marked up to defray financial risks for producers and distributors' (Bernard, 2014: 82).[11] As a result, the films attracted mainly 'fans', promoting a series of collection practices that would result in an important factor in the understanding of the sub-cultural capital of the genre (ibid.).

The unrated VHS proved once more the role of distribution 'in the understanding of the propagation of exploitation cinema' (Church, 2015: 11), with the availability of different cuts of the same film and the choice of evocative covers and ever-changing titles (see Guins, 2005: 19–21; Egan, 2007: 59).

Overall, during the 1980s, cable TV and VHS offered a new international market to Italian horror that received a new scrutiny, exposure and, as already mentioned, canonisation. Even the fact that the American majors, instead of engaging directly with the production of the films, preferred to distribute inde-pendent productions created possible new visibility for Italian horror cinema, which was also becoming an 'extreme' label for a niche fandom community.

THE CRISIS TOWARDS THE 1990S: TV KILLED THE HORROR STARS

The first signs of the crisis of Italian horror production occurred towards the end of the decade, in a period when the genre seemed to meet a wider audience in the national market. In fact, even after 1985 it was possible to find Italian horror productions among the 'top 50' films at the box office, for instance *Dèmoni, Dèmoni 2 . . . l'incubo ritorna/Demons 2* (Lamberto Bava, 1982), *La chiesa/The Church* (Michele Soavi, 1989) and of course the constantly present Argento with *Opera* (1987).

The popularity of American horror films – *The Evil Dead* (Sam Raimi, 1983), *Poltergeist* (Tobe Hopper, 1982), *The Thing* (John Carpenter, 1982), *Friday the 13th*, Wes Craven's *A Nightmare on Elm Street* (1984), for instance – contributed to the creation of a general interest for the genre, pushing it to the mainstream. This can also be proven by looking at the astonishing popular-ity of an Italian horror comic book like *Dylan Dog* (1986–).[12]

Despite the possibility of Italian horror meeting, arguably for the first time, the interests of the domestic market, by the late 1980s and early 1990s the production of horror cinema dropped significantly. Koven lists in his overview of the 'spaghetti nightmare' some of the causes of the crisis: the competition in the home video market with low-budget American films (which did not need the extra cost of English dubbing), the difficult generational change (which implies an authorship approach to the genre), and, finally, the fact that 'by early 1980s spaghetti nightmare films had gone just about far as they could' (Koven, 2014: 209).

However, a number of other production-related issues slowly brought the genre to an end. First of all, by the close of the 1980s American horror seemed to be locked in a tiresome cycle of repetitive plots and endless sequels. While the emergence of the slasher contributed to burst the Italian production of horror films, the international crisis of the genre was almost an end to it. Considering the low-cost productions emanating from Italy, we can under-stand how negotiation of the technological and aesthetic levels was not able any longer to produce innovation. On the one hand, in fact, the technologi-cal gap was increasingly wide because of the developments in special effects made in Hollywood for blockbuster productions. On the other hand, from an aesthetic perspective, there was a shortage of new horror sub-genres which deserved to be 'falsified' and recycled.

Nonetheless, while these were 'external' causes for the crisis of Italian horror cinema, the main reason can be found in the changes taking place in the national film production, with TV networks emerging as the main financiers of national cinema. Starting from the decision by the Constitutional Court in 1976 that the Italian public broadcaster (RAI) did not have a monopoly at the regional level, a long period of unregulated development of private TV networks in Italy completely changed the production landscape.[13]

The end of the 1970s witnessed the birth of hundreds of regional TV stations, which based their activities on the often unregulated selling of advertising space and on the broadcasting of free films, usually American imports. Their offering strongly jeopardised the existence of second- and third-run cinemas and accentuated the crisis of theatrical releases, creating a disparity between the financial capabilities of cinema and TV networks (Corsi, 2012: 43). As a consequence, the crisis of cinema-going led to a reduction in funds going back to the production, compromising the system of the secured minimum. As Ventavoli argues:

> since the Eighties the important role played by releasing films at the cinema and relative connection with the S.M. [Secured Minimum] Italy has been gradually replaced by television sales. The old segment of the proceeds (Italian market – foreign market – government subsidies) no longer covers the whole of the costs but only a tiny or at least a very minor part, while the advance sale or the television coproduction has to cover the greater part. Thus the entire old system has been shattered and the popularity rating that was once based on the number of actual tickets sold is measured today in terms of audience and related advertising potential. (Ventavoli, 2003: 221)

In the period between 1984 and 1990 a duopoly was created with two multimedia empires, RAI and Silvio Berlusconi's Fininvest, which were able to control the entire cycle of a film from its production to its TV run. In 1984 Fininvest formed Reteitalia, its film-producing branch, which applied the same 'TV approach' to cinema, making films that could first of all generate revenue during the TV run (Corsi, 2012: 44).

As Barbara Corsi points out, 'from 1984 to 1995, the year when the label is substituted with that of Mediaset and then Medusa, Reteitalia produced 155 films, more than any other Italian production company in the history of Italian cinema' (Corsi, 2012: 44).

However, these films were clearly aimed at a generic public in order to exploit the final TV broadcasting destination. Corsi (2012) defines this as 'nice cinema' in the sense that it is a cinema that aims to be average and to avoid controversy and complications. The dominant role played by TV broadcasters in financing films significantly limited the flexibility and variety of small productions in the country, compromising low-cost genre production by bending it to the needs of TV broadcasting. It is noteworthy that horror was among the genres initially produced by Reteitalia. I am thinking in particular of the production of eight feature films for TV broadcast, all directed by Lamberto Bava, which were grouped in two series. The first series, *Brivido giallo* (1987/1988), comprises four films: *Una notte al cimitero/Graveyard Disturbance*, *Per sempre/Until Death*, *La casa dell'orco/The Ogre* and *A cena col vampiro/ Dinner with a Vampire*. The second series, called *Alta tensione* (1988–9), featured: *Il gioko/School of Fear*, *Testimone oculare/Eyewitness*, *L'uomo che non voleva morire/The Man who didn't want to Die* and *Il maestro del terrore/The Prince of Terror*.

It is clear from this list the way in which TV broadcasters tried to replace the production of popular cinema, attracting its personnel. Eight feature films in the span of two years can be viewed as an impressive feat and commitment to the possible life of the genre. Several of these films found a distributor and were released on the American market under evocative titles, in an attempt to perpetuate the 'imitating, plagiarising, recycling' characteristics of Italian popular cinema. However, these films did not have any particular filmic source of 'sequel' ambition. The technical limitations dictated by the medium were evident, starting with the 1:33 format. Moreover, if the spectacle of the gore was the main attraction and recognisable feature of the Italian productions, here the films had to meet the requirements of TV's generic audience. Not only was the violence tamed, but films such as *Una notte al cimitero* and *A cena col vampiro* tried to appeal to the TV spectatorship by adding comedy elements and self-reflexivity to the storyline. Moreover, the series titles *Brivido giallo* and *Alta tensione* evoke the Italian passion for mystery TV more than the horror genre.

Reteitalia did not stop there, though. It was also involved in the production of Lamberto Bava's *La maschera del demonio* (1989). As a co-production involving five countries, this remake can be seen as one of the last attempts to keep alive the horror genre and, again, was mainly designed for TV distribution. Despite this project and what can clearly be seen as an attempt to attract the VHS audience of the original film, it was not widely distributed.

As Olney points out, 'by the end of the 1980s, Euro horror was no longer shown on network television in the United States, and the grindhouses and drive-ins that once were the reliable venues for its exhibition had been mostly driven out of business by the explosive growth of multiplex theatre chains' (Olney, 2013: 218). New Italian productions could only live on the channels of the national broadcasters where, however, they had to face the fierce competition of American films.

This ideally closed a circle. As the original *La maschera del demonio* managed to generate an international understanding of Italian horror cinema, thanks to AIP distribution and those features that made the genre recognisable and profitable, its remake created for the small screen did not meet an international audience. Italian horror cinema at the dawn of the 1990s was mainly represented by the works of a few recognisable directors: Argento in primis, who still had a monetisable name. However, the system of production of popular genres based on distribution demands was completely upset, leaving horror cinema at the margins of the national industry.

NOTES

1. For a critical overview on 1980s Italian cinema, see Miccichè (1998) and Zagarrio (1998), among others.
2. On the crisis of Italian cinema-going, see Corsi (2001: 116–23) as well as Jaykar and Waterman (2008).
3. Box-office data from *Il giornale dello spettacolo*. For an analysis of the Italian 1980s box office, see Fiorentini (2011).
4. On the role played by international markets on the production of Italian popular cinema, see Wagstaff (1995).
5. With regard to 'cinema of imitation', I am referring to all the attempts made by Italian cinema to make cheaper 'knock-offs' of foreign (often American) genre films. Italian producers often 'disguised' these works as American films by hiding the Italian nationality of the actors and filmmakers involved.
6. For an analysis of the Italian *Jaws*-imitation films, see Denis Lotti (2015).
7. On the role played by international collaboration in the development of Italian horror cinema, see Di Chiara's chapter in this book.
8. For an overview of the scholarly works on distribution, see Perren (2013).
9. This and other translations from Italian are made by the author.
10. All the translations from Italian in this text are by the author.
11. See Tim Lucas's 1986 overview of the available versions of Argento's films in the American home video market.
12. The comic book is published by Sergio Bonelli Editore, which since the 1940s has focused its production on the development of genres (Western, sci-fi, etc.). Interestingly, *Dylan Dog* shares some features with horror film production, from foreign locations (it is set in London) to imitating American films.
13. For a comprehensive overview of this topic, see Schlesinger (1990); Monteleone (2005); Barra and Scaglioni (2013); D'Aiola (2013).

BIBLIOGRAPHY

Barra, L. and Scaglioni, M. (2013), 'Berlusconi's Television, Before and After: the 1980s, Innovation and Conservation', *Comunicazioni Sociali*, No. 1, pp. 78–89.

Baschiera, S. and Di Chiara, F. (2010), 'A Postcard from the Grindhouse: Exotic Landscapes and Italian Holidays in Lucio Fulci's *Zombie* and Sergio Martino's *Torso*', in Weiner, R. and Cline, J. (eds), *Cinema Inferno: Celluloid Explosions from the Cultural Margins*, Lanham, MD, Toronto and Plymouth, MA: Scarecrow Press, pp. 101–23.

Bernard, M. (2014), *Selling the Splat Pack: The DVD Revolution and the American Horror Film*, Edinburgh: Edinburgh University Press.

Church, D. (2014), 'One on Top of the Other: Lucio Fulci, Transnational Film

Industries, and the Retrospective Construction of the Italian Horror Canon', *Quarterly Review of Film and Video*, Vol. 32, No. 1, pp. 1–20.

Church, D. (2015), *Grindhouse nostalgia. Memory, home video and exploitation film fandom*, Edinburgh: Edinburgh University Press.

Corsi, B. (2001), *Con qualche dollaro in meno*, Rome: Editori Riuniti.

Curti, R. (2015), *Italian Gothic Horror Films, 1957–1969*, Jefferson, NC: McFarland.

D'Aiola, A. (2013), 'Piccolo grande schermo. Quando la televisione fa il cinema', in Grasso, A. (ed.), *Storie e culture della televisione italiana*, Milan: Mondadori, pp. 269–82.

Della Casa, S. (2001), 'L'horror', in De Vincenti, G. (ed.), *Storia del cinema italiano Vol. X: 1960–1964*, Venice and Rome: Marsilio/Edizioni di Bianco & Nero, pp. 319–30.

Di Chiara, F. (2009), *I tre volti della paura – Il cinema horror italiano (1957–1965)*, Ferrara: UnifePress.

Egan, K. (2007), *Trash or Treasure? Censorship and the Changing Meanings of the Video Nasties*, Manchester: Manchester University Press.

Fiorentini, C. (2011), *La sottigliezza del tempo libero. Analisi dei consumi cinematografici nell'Italia anni '80*. Unpublished Tesi di Laurea, University of Bologna.

Guins, R. (2005), 'Blood and Black Gloves on Shiny Discs: New Media, Old Tastes, and the Remediation of Italian Horror Films in the United States', in Schneider, S. J. and Williams, T. (eds), *Horror International*, Detroit: Wayne State University Press, pp. 15–32.

Heffernan, K. (2007), 'Art House or House of Exorcism? The Changing Distribution and Reception Contexts of Mario Bava's *Lisa and the Devil*', in Sconce, J. (ed.), *Sleaze Artists. Cinema at the Margins of Taste, Style and Politics*, Durham, NC and London: Duke University Press. pp. 144–66.

Jaykar, K. P. and Waterman, D. (2008), 'The rise and fall of the Italian Market', in McDonald, P. and Wasko, J. (eds), *The Contemporary Hollywood Film Industry*, Oxford: Wiley-Blackwell.

Koven, M. J. (2006), *La Dolce Morte: Vernacular Cinema and the Italian Giallo Film*, Oxford: Scarecrow Press.

Koven, M. J. (2014), 'The *Giallo* and the Spaghetti Nightmare', in Bondanella, P. (ed.), *The Italian Cinema Book*, London: BFI, pp. 203–10.

Lobato, R. and Ryan, M. D. (2011), 'Rethinking Genre Studies Through Distribution Analysis: Issues in International Horror Movie Circuits', *New Review of Film and Television Studies*, Vol. 9, No. 2 (June), pp. 188–203.

Lotti, D. (2015), 'Mare Monstrum: Il riverbero di Jaws nei sequel illegittimi: mockbuster, imitazioni, ripoff (e documentari) di produzione italiana (1976–1995)', in *Cinergie*, No. 7, March, available at www.cinergie.it/?p=5443 [accessed April 2015].

Lucas, T. (1986), 'The Butchering of Argento', *Fangoria*, Vol. 7, No. 66, August, pp. 14–17.

Manzoli, G. and Pescatore, G. (2004), *L'arte del risparmio: stili e tecnologia*, Bianco & Nero, No. 549, pp. 97–101.

Manzoli, G. and Pescatore, G. (eds) (2005), *L'arte del risparmio: stile e tecnologia. Il cinema a basso costo in Italia negli anni Sessanta*, Rome: Carocci.

Manzoli, G. and Menarini, R. (2005), 'Cinema italiano di imitazione. Generi e sottogeneri', in Zagarrio, V. (ed.), *Storia del cinema italiano Vol. XIII 1977–1985*, Venice and Rome: Marsilio/Edizioni di Bianco & Nero, pp. 398–415.

Manzoli, G. (2012), *Da Ercole a Fantozzi. Cinema popolare e società italiana dal boom economico alla neotelevisione (1958–1976)*, Rome: Carocci.

McDonald, P. (2007), *Video and DVD Industries*, London: BFI Palgrave.

Miccichè, L. (1998), 'Il lungo decennio grigio', in Miccichè, L. (ed.), *Gli schermi opachi, il cinema italiano degli anni '80*, Venice: Marsilio Editori, pp. 3–16.

Monteleone, F. (2005), 'Il cinema come genere televisivo', in Zagarrio, V. (ed.), *Storia del cinema italiano Vol. XIII 1977–1985*, Venice and Rome: Marsilio/Edizioni di Bianco & Nero, pp. 56–66.

Needham, G. (2002), 'Playing with genre: an introduction to the Italian *giallo*', *Kinoeye*, Vol. 2, Issue 11. www.kinoeye.org/02/11/needham11.php [accessed April 2013].

Olney, I. (2013), *Eurohorror*, Bloomington and Indianapolis: Indiana University Press.

Perren, A. (2013), 'Rethinking Distribution for the Future of Media Industry Studies', *Cinema Journal*, Vol. 52, No. 3 (2013), pp. 165–71.

Pezzotta, A. (2013), *Mario Bava*, Milan: Il castoro.

Piselli, S. and Morrocchi, R. (1996), *Bizarre Sinema! – Horror All'Italiana 1957–1979*, Berkeley: Gingko Press.

Pitassio, F. (2005), 'L'orribile segreto dell'horror italiano', in Manzoli, G. and Pescatore, G. (eds), *L'arte del risparmio: stile e tecnologia. Il cinema a basso costo in Italia negli anni Sessanta*, Rome: Carocci, pp. 31–41.

Russo, P. (2005), 'Mettere in scena l'angoscia. Dario Argento e l'horror', in Zagarrio, V. (ed.), *Storia del cinema italiano – Vol. XIII 1977–1985*, Venice and Rome: Marsilio/Edizioni di Bianco & Nero, pp. 433–43.

Schlesinger, P. (1990), 'The Berlusconi Phenomenon', in Baranski, Z. G. and Lumley, R. (eds), *Culture and Conflict in Postwar Italy*, New York: St Martin's Press, pp. 272–85.

Ventavoli, L. (2003), 'Secured Minimum: Some Clarifications', in Della Casa, S. (ed.), *Captains Courageous, Italian producers 1945–1975*, Milan: Electa, pp. 218–22.

Venturini, S. (2014), *Horror italiano*, Rome: Donzelli.

Wagstaff, C. (1995), 'Italy in the Post-War International Cinema Market', in Duggan, C. and Wagstaff, C. (eds), *Italy in the Cold War: Politics, Culture and Society 1948–58*, Oxford and Washington, DC: Berg, pp. 89–116.

Waller, G. A. (2000), 'Introduction to American Horrors', in Gelder, K. (ed.), *The Horror Reader*, London and New York: Routledge, pp. 256–64.

Wasko, J. (2003), *How Hollywood Works*, London: Sage.

Wasser, F. (2008), 'Ancillary Markets – Video and DVD: Hollywood Retools', in McDonald, P. and Wasko, J. (eds), *The Contemporary Hollywood Film Industry*, Oxford: Wiley-Blackwell, pp. 124–5.

Zagarrio, V. (1998), 'Polveri e arcipelaghi, Movimenti, incontri, attraversamenti del decennio', in Miccichè, L. (ed.), *Schermi opachi. Il cinema italiano degli anni Ottanta*, Venice: Marsilio Editori, pp. 34–5.

4. KNOWING THE UNKNOWN BEYOND: 'ITALIANATE' AND 'ITALIAN' HORROR CINEMA IN THE TWENTY-FIRST CENTURY

Johnny Walker

Since the year 2000, European horror cinema has undergone a major revival. After the 1990s, which saw very few European horror films made, the first fifteen years of the twenty-first century witnessed a groundswell in production from France, Germany, the Netherlands, Spain, Serbia and the UK. Italy was also part of this 'new wave', though its horror films typically did not reach as wide an audience, nor experience the critical recognition, of its continental neighbours. Italian horror during this period also faced a great irony. Whereas several filmmakers from America and Europe pastiched the Italian horror boom of the 1960s, 1970s and 1980s with films that were widely distributed and commercially well received, Italian directors shooting horror films either in Italy or elsewhere typically lacked access to 'formal' distribution (Lobato, 2012) and therefore their films were not as widely seen.

It is the purpose of this chapter to explore what 'Italian horror' has meant in the twenty-first century as a historically grounded and transnational concept on the one hand, and a contemporaneous mode of production on the other. The chapter begins by considering those films that, while lacking the involvement of Italian resources and investors, set out explicitly to recall some of the most influential moments of Italian horror cinema's history. It will consider, specifically, how such films – what I will be collectively referring to as 'Italianate' horror – can be considered as both 'art' and 'exploitation'. The chapter will then proceed to consider the shape of Italian horror production since 2000, and how it managed to stay buoyant in a marketplace crowded with high-profile international production.

ITALIANATE HORROR

The term 'Italianate' is often used to refer to 'Italian-style' architecture dating back to the 1840s, which was popular in both America and England and drew inspiration from 'Tuscan late-Medieval farmhouses' (Hopkins, Jr, 2009: 102). The use of the term can also be found in various books dealing with early nineteenth-century English fashion (Brand, 2011: ix), and late nineteenth- to early twentieth-century works of art (Jaffe, 1992). However, in spite of its implied lack of currency in the twenty-first century, the presence of what C. P. Brand in 1957 dubbed 'Italo-mania' (2011: ix) has been widely felt across international film production in recent years: firstly, across the field of horror and exploitation cinema; and secondly, in the realm of art cinema.

From the former camp, one might single out the work of Quentin Tarantino, whose fannish myriad of Italian hat-tips include a 'revisioning' of Enzo G. Castellari's 1975 exploitation film *Quel maledetto treno blindato/Inglorious Bastards* (as *Inglorious Basterds* in 2009) and a 2013 'sequel' to Sergio Corbucci's violent Spaghetti Western from 1966, *Django* (*Django Unchained*). The films of Tarantino's protégé, Eli Roth, can also be understood as possessing notable Italianate streaks. The ultra-violent *Hostel II* (2007), for instance, is laced with corporeal set pieces that recall the scenes of 'violence and bodily mutilation' that have come to signify the horror films of Lucio Fulci (Grant, 2000: 68). *Hostel II* also features cameos by the Italian genre star Edwige Feneche (who featured in a string of Italian sex comedies and *gialli* in the 1970s) and Italian horror director Ruggero Deodato. Similarly, Roth's *The Green Inferno* (2014) lifts its title and central themes directly from Deodato's *Cannibal Holocaust* (1980).[1] A host of direct-to-video/DVD cheapies, from the retroactive 'cannibal' film *Welcome to the Jungle* (Jonathan Hensleigh, 2007), to the gory British-gangster-film-meets-*poliziottesco A Day of Violence* (Dan Ward, 2009), and the *giallo*-like *Kolobos* (David Todd Ocvirk and Daniel Liatowitsch, 1999) and *Fantom Kiler* [sic.] series (Roman Nowicki, 1998–2008),[2] can also be thought of as being Italianate in both style and spirit. These kinds of 'retrosploitation' (Church, 2015) films point towards the enduring appeal of Italian horror's 'golden age' with filmmakers beyond Italy and their global audiences, by nostalgically relishing some of the more iconic films' exploitative elements. Such films have emerged at a time when indigenous Italian horror production – which is similarly indebted to a past era of exploitation cinema (discussed below) – lacks visibility in most markets.

Perhaps one of the most intriguing developments amid the flurry of non-Italian production, however, is a cycle of *art* films that share the intertextual revelry of the aforementioned Italianate movies, but have managed to gain a certain amount of critical credibility that most of the other horror pastiches have not.[3] The first art film in question is the French/Belgian production

Amer (Hélène Cattet and Bruno Forzani, 2009), which, through three chapters, traces the sexual awakening of Ana (Cassandra Forêt/Charlotte Eugène Guibeaud/Marie Bos) from young girl, to teenager, to woman. The second film in this cycle is the British production *Berberian Sound Studio* (Peter Strickland, 2011), in which Gilderoy (Toby Jones), a British sound-designer, applies the visceral sound effects to a supernatural Italian horror film. The third film, which is also the second by *Amer*'s directorial team, is the France/Belgium/Luxembourg production *L'étrange couleur des larmes de ton corps/The Strange Colour of Your Body's Tears* (Hélène Cattet and Bruno Forzani, 2013), which tells of a man's (Klaus Tange) mental breakdown following the disappearance of his wife. These films are arguably more comparable with the films of the 'new European extremism' (Kendall and Horeck, 2011) than they are with the work of Tarantino, Roth and others, as they foreground a variety of tropes one would tend to associate with the avant-garde. Indeed, they have been collectively heralded in mainstream critical discourse for their stylistic innovation and pretentions to art house sensibilities, and have thus been granted a centrality to mainstream press discourse that contemporary Italian horror production, by comparison, has not. Yet, for all that these films carry an aura of high culture, in that they celebrate more overtly the *auteurist* legacies of Dario Argento and Mario Bava rather than their *cult* legacies outside of Italy, the films are still imbued with a sense of self-reflexive appreciation of Italian horror's more unsavoury associations.

Amer, *Berberian Sound Studio* and *L'étrange couleur des larmes de ton corps* conflate the commercial prospects of exploitation cinema with the intellectualistic arena of the art film and thus contribute to a long tradition in Italian horror in spite of their non-Italian production origins. Leon Hunt, in his essay about Dario Argento's *Opera* (1987), acknowledges classic Italian horror's pretentions to 'art'. Via David Bordwell's work on the art film, Hunt argues that much of Dario Argento's work from the 1970s and 1980s can be thought of as 'art films' because they comprise 'patterned violations of the classical norm', display preferences for 'an unusual angle, a stressed bit of cutting, a prohibited camera movement' and the deliberate 'failure to motivate cinematic space and time by cause-effect logic' (Bordwell quoted in Hunt, 2009: 328). Furthermore, Peter Hutchings has recognised how Argento specifically is revered as a 'great film artist' by British fans who seek to valorise his work above lesser examples of ironically appreciated paracinema (Hutchings, 2003: 135), while Andy Willis has argued that the films of Argento, Mario Bava, Lucio Fulci and Ruggero Deodato adopt a position 'somewhere between' art and the less-credible area of exploitation, through juxtaposing realism and other art film tropes against gory prosthetic effects (Willis, 2006: 110).

Characteristic of much exploitation cinema, *Amer*, *Berberian Sound Studio* and *L'étrange couleur des larmes de ton corps* are commercial properties out to capitalise on the (cult) reputation of the most decorated and widely seen works of key Italian directors, through film form, specific textual allusions, their soundtracks and thematic congruencies. *Amer*'s title sequence, for instance, sees the screen divided into three panels that recall specifically the 'split-screen' party sequence in Fulci's *Una lucertola con la pelle di donna/ Lizard in a Woman's Skin* (1971). The emphasis placed throughout the film on close-ups of people's eyes, and the general theme of 'looking' at scenes of terror, chimes with the issues of 'visibility, spectatorship, and horror' that have been said to be at the core of films like *Opera* (Hunt, 2009: 333). The blue, red and green light filters that are used all through the film echo the psychedelic cinemascapes of Bava's *Reazione a catena/A Bay of Blood* (1971) and Argento's kaleidoscopic *Suspiria* (1977), while its score comprises a mix of harsh synthesised melodies and smooth jazz – compositions that are, in fact, lifted directly from Italian *gialli* of the 1970s.[4]

Berberian Sound Studio makes repeated nods to Italian horror, too. The film that Gilderoy works on has a characteristically elaborate title, *The Equestrian Vortex*. Having 'Equestrian' in the title directly alludes to Argento's revered 'animal trilogy', *L'uccello dalle piume di cristallo/The Bird with the Crystal Plumage* (1970), *Il gatto a nove code/The Cat o' Nine Tales* (1971) and *4 mosche di velluto grigio/Four Flies on Grey Velvet* (1971), as well as to the flurry of similarly titled films that sought to capitalise on Argento's success, such as *La tarantola dal ventre nero/Black Belly of the Tarantula* (Paolo Cavara, 1971), *L'iguana dalla lingua di fuoco/The Iguana with the Tongue of Fire* (Riccardo Freda, 1971) and *Non si sevizia un paperino/Don't Torture a Duckling* (Lucio Fulci, 1972). Meanwhile, the word 'Vortex' corresponds with the audacious, surrealist, and otherworldly sensibilities of supernatural films such as Argento's *Suspiria* and Fulci's *L'aldilà/The Beyond* (1981), the latter of which actually sees the protagonists pass through a 'vortex' into the wastelands of Hell.

In *Berberian Sound Studio* we learn that *The Equestrian Vortex* tells of the awakening of an evil witch à la *Suspiria* and *Inferno* (Dario Argento, 1980), and features the kinds of grisly attacks on young women for which Argento and his contemporaries have become so infamous (see Clover, 1992: 42; Knee, 1996). Not insignificantly, the film-within-the-film's director, Giancarlo Santini (Antonio Macino), views film violence (namely, a scene involving a woman being sexually violated with a hot poker) as being intrinsic to his artistic vision and responsibilities as a filmmaker. As he states with gusto: 'It is my duty to show!' *Berberian Sound Studio* is also littered with other intertextual nods to canonical Italian genre cinema: the person who changes the film reels in the post-production suite is identified only by their black leather gloves – much like the killers in numerous *gialli*; and the title sequence of *The Equestrian Vortex* (which, incidentally, is all that we see of the film) is a moody animation in black, red and white which swirls in and out of focus, à la the opening credits of *Un pugno di dollari/A Fistful of Dollars* (Sergio Leone, 1964).

Finally, *L'étrange couleur des larmes de ton corps* also makes repeated nods to classic Italian horror. Its title, as with *The Equestrian Vortex*, is decidedly opaque, attesting perhaps to an awkward English translation or, more likely, to the similarly abstract titles of other *gialli* such as Giuseppe Benati's *L'assassino ha riservato nove poltrone/The Killer Reserved Nine Seats* (1974) and Pupi Avati's *La casa dalle finestre che ridono/The House with Laughing Windows* (1976). The film abandons narrative, preferring long impressionist scenes instead, and replicates the blue, green and red light filters from *Amer* throughout. Moreover, the scene in which a woman has her nipple flicked and scraped by the killer's knife is a direct nod to a similar scene in Fulci's notorious *Lo squartatore di New York/The New York Ripper* (1982) where a woman's nipple is sliced off with a razor blade. As with *Amer*, the soundtrack of *L'étrange couleur des larmes de ton corps* is lifted from controversial Italian exploitation films, as in the credit sequence that utilises the theme from Giulio Berutti's 'nunsploitation' movie *Suor Omicidi/Killer Nun* (1979).

For all their exploitation qualities, the films pertain to 'art' in a number of ways. Unlike most exploitation films, *Amer* and *Berberian Sound Studio* are widely celebrated works, while the more divisive *L'étrange couleur des larmes de ton corps* has still managed to command mainstream champions. These films have also been cited individually in the mainstream press for their intellectual pretentions, as well as for circumventing the standard aural, visual and narrative conventions of the commercial mainstream. For example, in his review of *Amer*, Philip French comments on how the film's 'soundtrack . . . is ominously exaggerated', how the 'close-ups are extreme', how 'colours change melodramatically to fit the shifting moods' and that, come its conclusion (or lack thereof), it is left up to the audience to make any real sense of it. 'This is art-house horror,' French concludes, 'a pure cinema for connoisseurs, a return to late-19th-century decadence' (French, 2011). Similarly, Wendy Ide of the *Times* praised *Berberian Sound Studio* as 'an impressively eccentric and genuinely original piece of cinema' (Ide, 2013: 24), while *The Strange Colour of Your Body's Tears*, though not as well received as either *Amer* or *Berberian Sound Studio*, was nevertheless dubbed 'a ludicrous head trip of a movie . . . full of spirals and fractals, mystery and menace' (Brookes, 2014), as well as '[h]igh-art horror' and 'architectural art nouveau' (Muir, 2014). What is immediately apparent from these reviews is how the films are framed not as 'exploitation films' or as 'rip-offs', but rather as self-aware, well-schooled and, consequently, innovative (or, in the case of *L'étrange couleur des larmes de ton corps*, perhaps a bit too indulgent).

They are not simply horror, but *art house horror*, a designation that implies their superiority over run-of-the-mill genre fare. According to French (2011), *Amer* is 'a pure cinema', an expression which infers a cinema that is untarnished by the generic falsities of the commercial mainstream. French also prefers to use the term 'connoisseurs' to describe *Amer*'s audience – an elite group he seems to include himself in – rather than terms such as 'geeks', 'nerds' or 'fans', which have traditionally carried negative connotations (Duffett, 2013: 37–8). Importantly here – and unlike the term 'fans' – the word 'connoisseurs' points towards knowledge or intellect, not 'obsession'. Moreover, the film is presented to French's readership as 'decadent' rather than off-puttingly *excessive*, an adjective often used to invoke cult 'paracinema' and its audience's taste practices (Sconce, 1995). Ide similarly celebrates incongruity in her review of *Berberian Sound Studio*. While one could argue that a generic trait of Italian horror is its lack of coherence and abandoning of narrative, Ide finds this 'eccentric' and 'original' rather than reductive or simply generic. In other words, these films pertain to art cinema because of their sublime imagery, and the supposed challenges they present their audience through narrative.

For all their art-house associations, the context from which these films have emerged is the same context as those populist Italianate films discussed earlier. Recent High Definition Blu-Ray versions of *Inferno*, *L'aldilà* and *Cannibal Holocaust* continue to afford films that were at one time deemed controversial, immoral and ephemeral a new cultural status. Digital remastering has permitted them cultural reassessment and new-found recognition of their once unacknowledged artistry (see, for example, Guins, 2005: 27). In the UK, these kinds of releases, from art-house companies such as Arrow Films (through its 'Arrow Video' brand), have given Italian horror films once banned in Britain,[5] such as *Zombi 2/Zombie Flesh-Eaters* (1979) and *L'aldilà*, new cultural cachet that belies their grindhouse distribution origins – which Tarantino openly invokes in his films (Church, 2015) – and their Betamax legacies – as invoked in low-fi, shot-on-video DVD movies such as *A Day of Violence*. What is particularly interesting about *Amer*, *Berberian Sound Studio* and *L'étrange couleur des larmes de ton corps*, then, is their assumed status in comparison to other kinds of horror films being produced today – not least, in Italy.

Contemporary Italian horror cinema is typically regarded as being far less innovative than critics and audiences have heralded its artful Italianate counterparts. In fact, with the exception of a mere handful of films, most recent Italian horror productions have not been theatrically released, nor have they been featured in mainstream press discourse. Having examined the value of Italian-ness in horror cinema to non-Italian horror filmmakers and critics, it is to Italy, and the apparent disinterest of audiences in native horror film production, that we must now turn.

ITALIAN HORROR

In the early 2000s, the film industry trade press optimistically reported that '[a]uteur-driven, art house films' which had 'dominated the headlines in Italy for as long as anyone can remember' were to give way to a host of 'producer-led' genre pictures (Rodier, 2003a: 20) that were 'easier for a distribution company' to place with an audience, notably thrillers (Gosetti quoted in ibid.). The 'thriller' has an interesting historical relationship with the horror film. It has often been the case that many films which may have been otherwise marketed as 'horror' have, instead, been marketed as 'thrillers' due to the negative associations that 'horror film' carries with contemporaneous mainstream audiences. Perhaps the best example of this practice is the Oscar-winning 'up-market' psychological thriller *The Silence of the Lambs* (1991), which was released at a time when most 'horror' films were made in the critically reviled 'teen slasher' mould (Hutchings, 2004: 2). Indeed, the slasher cycle, which saturated the horror theatrical market throughout the 1980s, has repeatedly been blamed by some for having killed the genre off during this period, leading to a slump in production in the 1990s (see, for example, Pirie, 2008: 213).

A recent Italian example of a horror film that was marketed as a 'thriller' is Alex Infascelli's serial killer movie, *Almost Blue* (2000). One journalist did pick up on its horror elements, heralding it as 'scary as anything seen in Italy since early Dario Argento' (Marshall, 2000); however, it was mostly reported as being a 'thriller', with the press drawing comparisons with US psychological thrillers *Seven* (David Fincher, 1995) and *Fargo* (Joel and Ethan Coen, 1996) (see ibid.). Dario Argento's output since the 2000s also falls into this category. For example, *Il cartaio/The Card Player* (2004) was marketed, and referred to in the press, as a 'thriller' (Rodier, 2003b; anonymous, 2003; Rodier, 2004b). Additionally, the film, along with Argento's previous film *Non ho sonno/Sleepless* (2000), was received much more poorly than his more violent and subversive canonical works (see Hunter, 2010: 68, 73, n. 14). The main reason for this is that while Argento had (and continues to have) a stable presence in home video markets all over the world, the horror genre remained unpopular with Italian cinema-going audiences during this period. *Screen International* conducted a survey of Italian cinema in 2005, which revealed that 'comedies' and 'romantic comedies' collectively generated an average of $11.3 in ticket sales in Italy in the 2000s; 'action films' generated an average of $3.5; and dramas and thrillers generated an average of $2.3 each (Rodier, 2005: 20). 'Horror', however, was rendered 'not applicable' (ibid.). To this end, Argento was pressured in the early 2000s 'not to show blood' in his films (Argento quoted in Rodier, 2003b), and to tone down them down for a general theatrical audience and television syndication (Cozzi, 2014). As *Screen Daily* reported upon the release of *Il cartaio*, the production company and distributor, Medusa Films, was 'more interested in today's cinema going masses than the ultra-niche market of diehard Argento fans' (Marshall, 2004); the result being that both *Non ho sonno* and *Il cartaio* performed well domestically (generating $2.6m and $3.6m in box office receipts respectively),[6] but have since been relegated to the direct-to-DVD market of cult horror fans on the strength of Argento's *past* reputation.[7]

In light of these industry pressures – and the simple fact that no other Italian horror filmmakers have been able to secure wide theatrical distribution for their films – contemporary Italian horror has mostly been made, as in the 1970s and 1980s, for international export. This has meant that, of the Italian horror films that have managed to find a way out of Italy, whether at festivals, on DVD or Video On Demand, the vast majority of films have been recorded in, or have since been dubbed into, English, and have been designed to capitalise on subgeneric strands of horror popular with cinema-going audiences worldwide. Examples of this practice include Bruno Mattei's *Snuff killer – La morte in diretta/Snuff Trap* from 2003, which lifts its plot directly from the late-1990s Nicolas Cage star vehicle, *8mm* (Joel Schumacher, 1999). Another example is Federico Zampaglione's *Shadow* (2009). Its plot, which sees a former American soldier abducted by a deformed Nazi doctor in the European wilderness, resonates with a number of popular rural horrors of recent years that place city types in hostile environments, such as the French/Romanian *Calvaire* (Fabrice Du Welz, 2004), the British *Eden Lake* (James Watkins, 2008) and the North American *The Last House on the Left* (Dennis Iliadis, 2009).

Similar to the subterranean monster that inhabits the London Underground in the widely distributed British/German horror film *Creep* (2004), the monstrous Nazi in *Shadow* is also slim, bald, and uses a medical table to perform gruelling experiments on his victims. The film's Nazi theme also parallels popular European horror such as *Frontière(s)/Frontier(s)* (Xavier Gens, 2009), in which a young girl and her friends are captured by a neo-Nazi family and subjected to a host of experiments, as well as contemporary 'Nazisploitation' movies, such as *Outpost* (Steve Barker, 2009) and *Død snø/Dead Snow* (Tommy Wirkola, 2009), which were produced primarily for consumption on home-viewing media. Dario Argento's *Giallo* (2010) also tuned in to contemporary trends. In the film, a detective (Adrian Brody) hunts for a serial killer who kidnaps and tortures attractive young female models. The theme of entrapment, and the scenes in which young female protagonists are tied up and tortured, resonate with a host of 'torture porn' movies such as *Hostel* (Eli Roth, 2005) and *Martyrs* (Pascal Laugier, 2008).[8] Moreover, while the 'cat and mouse' relationship between the detective and the killer in *Giallo* is a trope found in most *gialli*, in the context of contemporary horror production this factor also chimed nicely with the high-octane investigative element of the *Saw* franchise (various, 2004–10). Significantly, *Giallo* is a much gorier film than

Argento's other work of the period and was therefore a telling example of the state of contemporary Italian cinema at the time of its release. The gore factor which was seen to limit Argento's demographic in the early 2000s was deemed workable because of the returns being made on 'extreme' films in theatres and on DVD in the US and beyond.

But not all recent Italian horror films have emulated mainstream trends. In fact, the producers of many low-fi Italian horror productions have striven to differentiate their films completely from the mainstream, with films that are produced very cheaply, shot very quickly and lack even the remotest chance of developing an audience beyond the most peripheral of cults. This is certainly the ethos that has underwritten most of the post-2000 films directed by Bruno Mattei, a director best known in cult circles for the *Dawn of the Dead* rip-off and video nasty, *Virus/Zombie Creeping Flesh* (1981) and a string of other zombie, cannibal and action films in the 1980s. Throughout the 2000s, Mattei was the only Italian horror filmmaker from the 1970s and 1980s continuing to make exploitation films with any regularity and consistency, with shot-on-video films that were mostly made in direct homage to his own (and his contemporaries') cult output, such as the mondo film *Mondo Cannibale* (2003), the 'women in prison' film *Anime perse/The Jail: The Women's Hell* (2006) and the zombie film *L'isola dei morti viventi/Island of the Living Dead* (2007).

Adopting a similar anti-mainstream ethos is director Ivan Zuccon and his independent company, Studio Interzona, which has specialised in micro-budget gothic horror films based on the work of H. P. Lovecraft since the early 2000s. If one considers the budgets of Dario Argento's films after 2000, which ranged from $3m to $12m, or the $1.4m shooting budget for Zampaglione's *Shadow*,[9] Studio Interzona's budgets are minute in comparison. Indeed, the company's shooting budgets have ranged from only a few thousand dollars (*L'altrove/Darkness Beyond*, Ivan Zuccon, 2001) to $35k (*La casa sfuggita/The Shunned House*, Ivan Zuccon, 2003) to, for its most recent film, $150k (*Wrath of the Crows*, Ivan Zuccon, 2013) (Zuccon 2014).

The lack of capital available for horror cinema from the Italian film industry has also meant that directors have in some instances had to self-fund their movies or explore alternative modes of distribution. For instance, *Il bosco fuori/The Last House in the Woods* (2006) was entirely self-funded by its director Gabriele Albanesi,[10] while Alex Infascelli's *H2Odio/Hate 2.O* was sold through Italian news-stands with a national daily newspaper because, according to its director, 'the picture would typically struggle in the cut-throat world of local theatrical distribution' (Infascelli quoted in Rodier, 2006).[11] The lack of available financial resources has also meant that production companies and distributors specialising in micro-budget films have been under immense pressure to stress the distinctiveness of their products in a vain attempt to gain visibility in a highly crowded marketplace. Two approaches have typically been adopted.

Figure 4.1 'New Generation Italian Horror': the UK DVD box art for the release of *Unknown Beyond* and *The Shunned House*.

The first approach has been the promotion of films as the wares of emerging new talent: new auteurs who are set to add to the grand tradition of cult Italian horror. This has been apparent in the UK, where the distributor Redemption Films – responsible for distributing Argento's *Profondo rosso* on VHS for the first time in Britain in the mid-1990s – also handled the distribution of Studio Interzona's *Maelstrom – Il figlio dell'altrove/Unknown Beyond* (Ivan Zuccon, 2001) and *La casa sfuggita/The Shunned House*. Both films were marketed on DVD in uniform packaging, with each cover featuring a still from the respective film rendered in blue. Across the top of each sleeve, a red band displayed the legend, 'New Generation Italian Horror' (see Fig. 4.1). This marketing tactic was similar to the ways that the films of Argento and Fulci were being marketed in America through Anchor Bay's 'Argento Collection' and Shout Factory's 'Deodato Collection', and in the UK through Screen Entertainment's 'Fulci Collection' and 'Deodato Collection'. In spite of Zuccon's output being virtually unknown to audiences, Redemption's strategy sought to mirror the uniformity of the other companies' auteur-led series 'in order to invoke value statements that valorize the director's work as an art object' (Guins, 2005: 29). This figuratively elevated Zuccon from being an obscure director to being positioned as a leader in 'New Generation Italian Horror', stressing a blood-line to his cult forefathers as he carried Italian horror's torch into the new millennium.

The second approach to marketing new Italian horror as distinctive has been through promoting films as 'pioneering' in regards to their production and distribution methods. The most visible examples of this practice have come from the production company Necrostorm. Based in Rome and headed by Giulio De Santi, Necrostorm's self-funded films, which so far include the revenge film *Adam Chaplin* (Emanuele De Santi, 2011), the futuristic horror/sci-fi *Taeter City* (Giulio De Santi, 2012) and the POV slasher film *Hotel Inferno* (Giulio De Santi, 2013), all share a penchant for ultra-violence, political incorrectness and high body counts. In other words, Necrostorm produces films that are deliberately anti-mainstream, and strives to offend the mainstream sensibilities that are said to characterise contemporary Italian cinema.[12] According to its website, Necrostorm is 'the first company that takes care of every production steps [sic]: from design, to direct distribution', and which, 'using the latest technologies and production techniques' aims to 'create Horror, Sci-Fi and Fantasy products ... with a style forgotten by the big companies, but still loved and needed by the fans'. Necrostorm's distinctiveness thus is threefold, and relates to its company branding as an innovator.

Firstly it is positioned as a producer of *innovative films*. Its marketing is keen to emphasise there is no other company operating under the same premise, nor are there films currently in production which are comparable. This relates mostly to the company's film style, which fuses the aesthetic of 1980s horror cinema, computer games and Japanese animation. For example, the futuristic police story *Taeter City*, in which violent criminals are not sent to jail but minced into fast food and sold back to society, was advertised on Necrostorm.com as giving rise to 'A NEW SPLATTER SCI-FI SUBGENRE' and of guaranteeing the audience 'AN 80's [sic] MOVIE VIBE, INSANE TECHNOLOGY, MANGA STYLE, CRAZY ACTION, BLOOD, BLOOD AND AGAIN BLOOD' (accessed 20 May 2014). Another example is *Hotel Inferno*, a film told (and experienced) entirely from the perspective of a hit man, which was marketed through Necrostorm.com as 'the first POV splatter movie', and which, in the true spirit of Italian exploitation business strategies, preceded the release of the glossy 'POV' remake of Bill Lustig's *Maniac* (1980) by some months in 2013.

Secondly, Necrostorm boasts an *innovative approach to production*. It is its trademark gory special effects which have gained it most recognition, and which broadly account for its modest cult reputation. These effects are shown clearly in the company's first feature, *Adam Chaplin*, in which the hulking titular character (Emanuele De Santi) kills his way through his city's underworld to find, and brutally massacre, the criminal organisation that murdered his wife. While the plot may well be familiar – it has been likened to *The Crow* (Alex Proyas, 1994) and the anime classic *Hokuto no Ken/Fist of the North Star* (Toyoo Ashida, 1986)[13] – the film boasts a new artificial blood effect that was integral to its marketing and subsequent reception among genre sites as 'an ass-kicking gorefest of astounding magnitude' (Jones, 2012). The effect in question is the so-called Hyperrealistic Anime Blood Symulation or 'HABS' – a polymer designed to react under intense pressure. As Necrostorm.com explains:

> Thanks to HABS, it's possible to spread out a huge amount of blood avoiding the vaporization of Fake Blood that normally occurs using the traditional techniques. (accessed 19 May 2014)

The result is an in-camera (i.e. non-digital) fake blood effect that, according to the website, 'you can normally admire only in anime cartoons'. Indeed, the final scene in *Adam Chaplin*, which is a showdown between Adam, the corrupt police and the head of the mafia, Denny (Chiara Marfella/Christian R.), shows HABS to great effect. The scene shows: Adam repeatedly punching a police officer in the face so that the front part of their skull smashes into a bloody pulp; Adam punching police officers' heads off so that they spin in the air and splatter on the ground; Adam snapping police officers' arms and legs off and smashing their heads against a white-washed wall (see Fig. 4.2); Adam shooting Derek's (Giulio De Santi) arm off at point-blank range with a rifle (so that it breaks off and lands in a bloody mess behind him); and Adam ripping out Denny's lower ribs, so that blood pours like a waterfall from his insides.

Figure 4.2   Hyperrealistic Anime Blood Symulation (HABS) in action.

The third way that Necrostorm presents itself as an innovator is through its *relationship with its fans*. The company sees this relationship as being integral to its success. Through its online forum it '[collects] all the fans' requests and suggestions: and we try to insert/apply them to our products. We give the fans what they really want to see' (accessed 17 May 2014). On the forum the fans ask questions about the films (in the thread 'YOUR QUESTIONS'), to which the company offers speedy replies (in the thread 'OUR ANSWERS'). This positive relationship is evidently maintained through mutual self-respect and self-identification. The business rhetoric, like that quoted above, points to the company's similarities with its audience, and its drive to make films that those working for the company will enjoy as much as its consumers. Necrostorm is a company different from 'the big companies' – those organisations that have 'forgotten' the audience that truly matters (ibid.). And among the 'forgotten', it is implied, are the workers at Necrostorm itself, who have branched off from – or, rather, have rejected – the mainstream to produce films for the fans and for themselves.[14] Indeed, one can ascertain from the excited and hyperbolic language used on its various ads and products that those working at Necrostorm are fans as well. This goes for the aforementioned ad for *Taeter City*, but also for the company website which features such legends as '80's/90's ARE BACK!', and the end credits of its films which acknowledge a host of cult film directors – such as Peter Jackson and John Carpenter – as having provided Necrostorm with inspiration.[15]

This is where the paradox of Necrostorm lies. On the one hand, the company looks to the future, boasting of its innovation and progressiveness through its use of cutting-edge technology and special effects. On the other hand, it is retroactive, seeking to re-create a 'vibe' associated with a specific era of cult cinema (an era that is 'forgotten' and thus, it is suggested, no more). At a time when Italianate art horror continues to gain visibility and critical respect, Necrostorm positions itself as a producer of exploitation films that relate to the ways Italian horror was seen the first time round by an international audience: not as avant-garde masterpieces, but rather as exploitation curiosities that hark back to the video era. This would partly explain the dual DVD and VHS release of *Taeter City* that was available from the Necrostorm store for a limited time only, which effectively allowed the viewer to genuinely experience the film's '80's vibe' through 80s technology.[16] It would also explain why Necrostorm strives to produce deluxe fan packages, which, through DVD-R technology, are burned-to-order, and include signed posters as well as a variety of merchandise which relates directly to the film (such as the 'All You Can Eat' burger vouchers and 'Biker Officer' identification cards which come included with the DVD of *Taeter City*). This offers the fans what 'the bigger companies' do not: a respect for these films, their histories and their 'ultra-niche' audiences, as well as a realistic future for Italian horror production.

CONCLUSION

In a book chapter published in 2005, Andy Willis discussed the state of Italian horror cinema at that time and looked despairingly to its future:

> The lack of opportunities for [young Italian horror filmmakers] means that they will very likely be forced to participate in projects that are much more conservative [than the canonical works of revered Italian horror directors] in their conception . . . It is unfortunate that younger directors . . . are unlikely to have the chance to develop and experiment with the limits of the horror genre as they may have done in an earlier era. (Willis, 2006: 129)

In a sense, Willis was right. As this chapter has shown, if we were to judge using the criteria of mainstream 'opportunities' and international visibility, *Italianate* horror cinema has certainly made more of an impression on the film world than recent *Italian* horror cinema. Moreover, Italianate art horrors *Amer*, *Berberian Sound Studio* and *L'étrange couleur des larmes de ton corps* have mirrored a critical reassessment of the Italian horror film that contemporary Italian horror has not really been a part of. The flipside of this, as this chapter has also revealed, is that several young filmmakers have, in a sense, benefited from the 'lack' of support from the Italian film industry and mainstream press discourse, and have *not* been constrained by their low budgets as Willis anticipated. On the contrary, existing outside the mainstream has afforded filmmakers a sense of freedom that they might not otherwise have been able to experience if working within the constraints of mainstream Italian film production.

Of course, not all low-budget Italian horror films find an audience, and many never get made. A case in point is the recent project *The Book*, which promised to bring together 'Italian masters' such as Ruggero Deodato, Lamberto Bava and Sergio Martino to make a horror anthology film. However, to the disappointment of those involved in the project, the film ultimately failed to hit its budget target on the crowd-funding website, Indiegogo.[17]

But companies like Studio Interzona and Necrostorm have indeed managed to find an audience (however small), and have used their outsider status to produce innovative films of varying types in spite of their 'conservative' production contexts and lack of mainstream support. To this end, contemporary Italian horror perhaps shares an unanticipated similarity with its Italianate art horror counterpart. While Italianate art horror has been afforded credibility within the commercial mainstream and thus can lay claim to more visibility than contemporary Italian horror, *Amer*, *Berberian Sound Studio* and *L'étrange couleur des larmes de ton corps* remain interesting in critical circles for the same reason why Necrostorm and Studio Interzona's output remains popular with their niche audiences: because of their experimentation, their indulgences, but above all, their cult connoisseurship.

Notes

1. 'The Green Inferno' is the term used by the protagonists in *Cannibal Holocaust* to describe the Jungle that the cannibals inhabit. On film style in *Cannibal Holocaust*, see Jackson, 2002.
2. On the *Fantom Kiler* films, see Carter, 2013.
3. Of course, the exception to this rule is the multi-award-winning Tarantino. But, by and large, the films of directors like Eli Roth have rarely been critically acclaimed. Rather, they are mostly (when they are reviewed in the mainstream press at all) condemned. For Roth specifically, this is mostly due to his associations with the vilified 'torture porn' cycle. See Jones, 2013: 27–39 and Bernard, 2014.
4. Songs include, among others, the theme from Sergio Martino's *The Case of the Scorpion's Tail* (1971) by Bruno Nicolai and the theme from Massimo Dallamano's *What Have They Done to Your Daughters?* (1974) by Stelvio Cipriani.
5. These films, when released on video in 1980s Britain, were among a final thirty-nine titles that were banned under the Obscene Publications Act (OPA). The term historically attributed to these controversial films is 'video nasty'. For insight into the legal and journalistic history of the video nasties, see Petley, 2011; and for a discussion of the legacy of the video nasties in horror and film collector circles, see Egan, 2007.
6. On *Sleepless*, see Rodier, 2003b. On *The Card Player*, see Rodier, 2004a.
7. In the UK, Arrow Video remarketed Argento's contemporary thrillers *The Stendhal Syndrome* (1996), *Sleepless* and *The Card Player* with *Terror at the Opera* as 'The Neo-Giallo Collection', in keeping with the company's lavish releases of Argento's critically revered films. For a discussion of how Argento's decreasing popularity with critics has paralleled the critical reappraisal of his past work and the consolidation of his reputation as a cult auteur, see Hunter, 2010.
8. On 'torture porn' as a category, and its broad associations, see Jones, 2013.
9. Budgets acquired from *Internet Movie Database Professional* and *Screen Daily*.
10. Albanesi is interviewed in the 'Backstage on *The Last House in the Woods*' documentary included on the Region 1 DVD release of *The Last House in the Woods* (Ghosthouse Pictures, 2006).
11. It is worth noting that this method of distribution is a common practice in Italy, especially for locally inflected independent films, such as the Sardinian parody of *My Big Fat Greek Wedding* (Joel Zwick, 2002), *Padre, figlio e spirito sardo* (Alessandro Sanna, 2004).
12. Often, 'mainstream' Italian cinema is read in relation to the influence of contemporary Hollywood. See Ferrero-Regis, 2009: xxi.
13. See Zedword, 2013 and Kenny, 2012.
14. Linda Badley (2009: 52–3) has written about how American DTV producers strive for the same political ideal.
15. It is likely that Peter Jackson is mentioned for the films he made pre-*Lord of the Rings*, such as the low-budget exploitation films *Bad Taste* (1987) and *Braindead* (1992).
16. At the time of writing, the US distributor BrinkVision is planning a simultaneous

DVD/VOD/VHS release of the micro-budget Argentinian 'neo-*giallo*' *Sonno profondo* (Luciano Onetti, 2013).
17. See www.indiegogo.com/projects/the-book-the-italian-masters-return [accessed 20 May 2014].

BIBLIOGRAPHY

Anonymous (2003), 'ITALY Production lists – August 22 2003', *Screen International*, 20 August, www.lexisnexis.com [accessed 20 August 2014].
Badley, L. (2009), 'Bringing it all back home: Horror cinema and video culture', in Conrich, I. (ed.), *Horror Zone: The Cultural Experience of Contemporary Horror Cinema*, London: I. B. Tauris, pp. 45–63.
Bernard, M. (2014), *Selling the Splat Pack: The DVD Revolution and the American Horror Film*, Edinburgh: Edinburgh University Press.
Brand, C. P. (2011 [1957]), *Italy and the English Romantics*, New York: Cambridge University Press.
Brooks, X. (2014), 'The New Review: Critics: Film: And the rest . . .', the *Observer* review arts pages (13 April), available at: www.lexisnexis.com [accessed 30 May 2014].
Carter, O. (2013), '"Slash Production": Objectifying the serial 'kiler' in Euro-Cult Cinema fan production', in MacDonald, A. (ed.), *Murders and Acquisitions: Representations of the Serial Killer in Popular Culture*, London and New York: Bloomsbury, pp. 123–44.
Church, D. (2015), *Grindhouse Nostalgia: Memory, Home Video and Exploitation Film Fandom*, Edinburgh: Edinburgh University Press.
Clover, C. (1992), *Men, Women and Chainsaws: The Modern American Horror Film*, Princeton: Princeton University Press.
Cozzi, L. (2014), 'Industry Panel 2', *Spaghetti Cinema: Italian Horror* conference, University of Bedfordshire, 10 May.
Duffett, M. (2013), *Understanding Fandom: An Introduction to the Study of Media Fan Culture*, London and New York: Bloomsbury Academic.
Egan, K. (2007), *Trash or Treasure? – Censorship and the Changing Meanings of the Video Nasties*, Manchester: Manchester University Press.
Ferrero-Regis, T. (2009), *Recent Italian Cinema: Spaces, Contexts and Experiences*, Leicester: Troubador.
French, P. (2011), '*Amer* – review', *The Guardian* [online], 9 January, www.theguardian.com/film/2011/jan/09/amer-film-review [accessed 11 May 2014].
Grant, M. (2000), 'Fulci's Wasteland: cinema, horror and dreams of Modernism', in Mendik, X. and Harper, G. (eds), *Unruly Pleasures: the Cult Film and its Critics*, Godalming: FAB Press, pp. 63–71.
Guins, R. (2005), 'Blood and black gloves on shiny discs: New media, old tastes, and the remediation of Italian horror films in the United States', in Schneider, S. J. and Williams, T. (eds), *Horror International*, Detroit: Wayne State University Press.
Hopkins, Jr, G. D. (2009), *Creating Your Architectural Style*, Louisiana: Pelican.
Hunt, L. (2009), 'A (sadistic) night at the *Opera*', in Gelder, K. (ed.), *The Horror Reader*, London: Routledge.
Hunter, R. (2010), '"Didn't you used to be Dario Argento?": the cult reception of Dario Argento', in Hope, W. (ed.), *Italian Film Directors in the New Millennium*, Newcastle upon Tyne: Cambridge Scholars Publishing.
Hutchings, P. (2003), 'The Argento effect', in Jancovich, M., Lázaro-Reboll, A.,

Stringer, J. and Willis, A. (eds), *Defining Cult Movies: The Cultural Politics of Oppositional Taste*, Manchester: Manchester University Press, pp. 127–41.

Hutchings, P. (2004), *The Horror Film*, Harlow: Pearson Longman.

Ide, W. (2013), 'Film choice', *The Times*, 23 November, p. 24.

Jackson, N. (2002), '*Cannibal Holocaust*, Realist Horror, and Reflexivity', *Post Script*, Summer 2002, 21, p. 10.

Jaffe, I. B. (ed.) (1992), *The Italian Presence in American Art, 1860–1920*, Rome: Istituto della Enciclopedia Italiana.

Jones, G. (2012), '*Adam Chaplin* (DVD)', *Dreadcentral* [online] 27 October, www.dreadcentral.com/reviews/adam-chaplin-uk-dvd#axzz32ApgvBWo [accessed 15 May 2014].

Jones, S. (2013), *Torture Porn: Popular Horror After Saw*, Basingstoke: Palgrave Macmillan.

Kendall, T. and Horeck, T. (2010), 'Introduction', in Kendall, T. and Horeck, T. (eds), *The New Extremism in Cinema: From France to Europe*, Edinburgh: Edinburgh University Press, pp. 1–17.

Kenny, M. (2013) '*Adam Chaplin*', *Mike's Pop Culture Blog* [online], 29 December, www.mikespopculture.com/movies/13945254 [accessed 19 May 2014].

Knee, A. (1996), 'Gender, genre, Argento', in Grant, B. K. (ed.), *The Dread of Difference: Gender and the Horror Film*, Austin: University of Texas Press.

Labato, R. (2012), *Shadow Economies of Cinema: Mapping Informal Film Distribution*, London: BFI.

Marshall, L. (2000), '*Almost Blue*', *Screen Daily*, 30 November, www.screendaily.com/almost-blue/404368.article [accessed 20 May 2014].

Marshall, L. (2004), '*The Card Player (Il Cartaio)*', *Screen Daily*, 6 January, www.screendaily.com/the-card-player-il-cartaio/4016700.article [accessed 20 May 2014].

Muir, K. (2014), '*The Strange Colour of Your Body's Tears*', *The Times* [online], April 11, www.lexisnexis.com [accessed 21 August 2015].

Petley, J. (2011), *Film and Video Censorship in Modern Britain*, Edinburgh: Edinburgh University Press.

Pirie, D. (2008), *A New Heritage of Horror: The English Gothic Cinema*, London: I. B. Tauris.

Rodier, M. (2003a), 'Revenge of the genre flick', *Screen International*, 1417, p. 20.

Rodier, M. (2003b), 'Dario Argento set to shoot *The Card Player*', *Screen International*, 23 February, www.lexisnexis.com [accessed 20 August 2014].

Rodier, M. (2004a), 'Italy', *Screen International*, 20 January, www.lexisnexis.com [accessed 20 August 2014].

Rodier, M. (2004b), 'Italy', *Screen Daily*, 20 January, www.screendaily.com/italy/4016926.article [accessed 20 May 2014].

Rodier, M. (2005), 'Native wisdom: local genres that hit the spot – Italy', *Screen International*, 1524 (18 November), p. 20.

Rodier, M. (2006), 'Italian distributor pioneers straight-to-newsstand distribution', *Screen International*, 3 May, www.lexisnexis.com.

Sconce, J. (1995), '"Trashing" the academy: taste, excess and an emerging politics of cinematic style', *Screen*, 36:4, pp. 371–93.

Willis, A. (2006), 'Italian horror cinema: Between art and exploitation', in Hope, W. (ed.), *Italian Cinema: New Directions*, Oxford: Peter Lang, pp. 109–30.

Zedword (2013), '*Adam Chaplin*', *Horror In the Hammer* [online], 23 June, www.horrorinthehammer.blogspot.co.uk/2013/06/adam-chaplin-review.html [accessed 19 May 2014].

Zuccon, I. (2014), Interview with author (May).

5. BAVAESQUE:
THE MAKING OF MARIO BAVA AS
ITALIAN HORROR AUTEUR

Peter Hutchings

In 2007 the writer/critic Tim Lucas published *Mario Bava: All the Colors of the Dark*. This massive tome, glossily produced, extensively illustrated, and over 1,100 pages long, has since been described, with some justification, as 'one of the most impressive books ever to have been written about any director' (Williams, 2011: 162). The end result of over thirty years' research, *Mario Bava: All the Colors of the Dark* has served to underline, reinforce and possibly clinch once and for all Mario Bava's status as a major figure not merely in Italian horror cinema but in world horror as well. However, such status has been bestowed entirely retrospectively, for during his directorial career – which ran from 1960 through to the mid-1970s – Bava, while a respected figure in the Italian film industry, received little critical attention and was not generally known to the film-going public, either in his native Italy or elsewhere.

In *Mario Bava: All the Colors of the Dark*, Lucas ascribes this obscurity to Bava's own modesty and dislike of publicity. Notwithstanding the idiosyncrasies of personality, the national and generic contexts within which Bava operated were also not especially amenable to the promotion of the director as a key creative figure or as being in any other way of importance. Indeed, horror cinema as it existed internationally from the 1930s through to the 1970s produced few 'star' directors who generated any kind of critical following or whose names featured prominently in movie publicity. In their own distinctive ways James Whale, director of the horror classics *Frankenstein* (1931) and *Bride of Frankenstein* (1935), the self-publicising William Castle in the 1950s and 1960s, and (in as much as he was a horror director) Alfred Hitchcock were notable exceptions, but the majority of horror directors laboured unobtrusively behind the scenes. Often they were figures, like Bava, who had worked their way up through the film industry over a period of years or decades and, again like Bava, who did not restrict themselves to the horror genre but operated in a variety of other genres as well. To give a few examples, Hollywood-based directors such as Erle C. Kenton, Reginald LeBorg, Rowland V. Lee and George Waggner, British-based directors Terence Fisher, Sidney Hayers and Don Sharp, and Bava's fellow Italian directors Riccardo Freda, Antonio Margheriti and Massimo Pupillo variously made significant contributions to the horror genre during the 1930s, 1940s, 1950s and 1960s without attracting much attention, outside of a few mentions in film reviews. In all sorts of ways, Bava's career as director seems to fit into this generally self-effacing model of horror direction.

Since the 1950s, the bestowing of the status of artist or, to use the cinephile argot, of 'auteur' on a film director has often operated in terms of an elevation from obscurity to a position of critical esteem. Indeed, the controversy generated by the auteurist approaches to cinema developed in France, the United States and Great Britain during the 1950s and 1960s stemmed in large part from their privileging of directors – often Hollywood-based directors – not considered noteworthy by other critics, frequently coupled with a disregard for filmmakers in possession of already established critical reputations. While the development of Bava's reputation as an Italian horror maestro certainly has about it the requisite auteurist quality of rescue from critical oblivion, it has nevertheless been played out in a very different critical and historical context from that associated with the original auteurist enterprise. For one thing, it has taken place later, primarily from the 1980s onwards, and thus posthumously (Bava died in 1980). For another, it seems to have been based mainly on the circulation of Bava's films on video and subsequently on DVD and BluRay rather than on their initial cinematic releases.

Critically, the ways in which Bava has been presented as significant have been influenced and to a certain extent shaped by cult-, paracinematic- and trash-based approaches to cinema that have developed in the same period. While it will not do to lump together these different approaches, it is striking how cinematic formats or film cycles important to Bava's career, or at least to the way that his career has been discussed and written about since his death, are also important in various ways to these approaches. Most notable here are the Italian *giallo* and Italian gothic horror, although one might also reference in this regard the trashy appeal offered by Bava's costume dramas, his science-fiction film *Terrore nello spazio/Planet of the Vampires* (1965), and his comic-book adaptation *Diabolik/Danger: Diabolik* (1968). Additionally, Bava's work has become caught up in broader changes in the critical and commercial fortunes of Italian genre cinema of the 1960s, 1970s, and early 1980s as this cinema too has become a focus not just for cult-based critical activity but also for entrepreneurial activity involving the aforementioned repackaging of Italian genre 'classics', including Bava's films, on DVD and BluRay.

At the same time, Bava's career as a whole cannot be fully encompassed or explained by this 'cultist' turn in the evaluation of Italian popular film genres. The fact that he contributed to numerous Italian genres, not all of which have been 'cultified', makes it difficult to place him wholly within any particular conceptualisation of Italian cult cinema. Indeed, the commitment evident in Lucas's *Mario Bava: All the Colors of the Dark* to inclusivity, to the recording of absolutely every available detail about Bava's filmmaking activity, has only served to problematise the cohesiveness of Bava's work not just in terms of his cult credentials but in more old-fashioned auteurist terms as well. It follows that Bava's current cult-canonical reputation potentially obscures as much as it clarifies or enlightens. Looking back beyond the cult Bava to a Bava more obviously situated within a particular industrial context reveals a director whose career was, in certain respects at least, more typical than it was extraordinary, although at the same time it was also a career which was idiosyncratic and unpredictable. Arguably, what looking at this career in all its obscurity brings with it is a sense of some of the practicalities and contingencies of Italian popular film production from the 1950s through to the 1970s, qualities that have sometimes been lost in later approaches more focused on just the cult-friendly aspects of Bava's work.

Pioneering Bava

It is a mark of success for the cult-based reappraisal of Italian horror cinema that it now exerts influence on non-cult writings about Italian cinema. Take as an example the 2009 book *A History of Italian Cinema*, written by the eminent Italianist Peter Bondanella. Earlier histories of Italian cinema made little or nothing of Italian popular genres, especially fantasy-based ones such as horror or the peplum, but Bondanella devotes separate chapters to the peplum, the Western, the *poliziesco* and to the cult favourites Italian horror and the *giallo*. Unsurprisingly perhaps, and in accord with Bava's present reputation, he is discussed mainly in the horror and *giallo* chapters (with passing references to some of his other work in the peplum and *poliziesco* chapters). In sub-sections entitled, respectively, 'Freda and Bava: The Classic Italian Horror Film' and 'The Birth of the Giallo: Mario Bava', the director is presented as a pioneer in the development of generic formats (Bondanella, 2009: 308, 376). Bava is thus rendered significant not just because he directed the first commercially successful Italian gothic horror *La maschera del demonio/Mask of Satan* (also known as *Black Sunday* and *Revenge of the Vampire*, 1960), as well as completing the 1957 horror *I vampiri* (although this was credited to Riccardo

Freda) and several other gothic horrors, but also because he directed films now thought of as key early or formative *gialli*, namely *La ragazza che sapeva troppo/The Girl Who Knew Too Much* (1963) and *Sei donne per l'assassino/ Blood and Black Lace* (1964).

An increasingly common feature in critical writing on these gothic horrors and *giallo* films is to see them as helping to initiate a broader European tradition of exploitation-based horror – or Eurohorror, in short – that stands apart from what is often presented as a more straitlaced and moralistic Anglo-American version of horror, offering instead an experience that is more assaultive, explicit, disturbing and potentially transgressive. For example, Ian Olney characterises Eurohorror movies as 'exploring the boundary between sex and violence in ways that were rare in the more puritanical British and American horror movies being made at the time' (Olney, 2013: 7). Writing about Bava's *La maschera del demonio* in particular, Danny Shipka adopts a similar approach: 'Arriving on the scene just after Franju's *Les Yeux sans visage* (*Eyes Without a Face*, 1959) and prior to Jess Franco's *Gritos en la noche* (*The Awful Dr Orloff*, 1961), *La maschera* was one of the three seminal films that opened the door to a new brand of exploitation film' (Shipka, 2011: 37).

It is clear from this and other critical writing that just as Bava's reputation has largely been established retrospectively, so the category of Eurohorror in relation to which that reputation is strongly bound has also been formed in retrospect, long after the heyday of European horror production, and, moreover, has evolved primarily through what Raiford Guins has described as a 'remediation' of films via first video and subsequently DVD and BluRay. This has frequently served to remove the films concerned from their various original contexts of production and reception so that they can join each other in the new international category that is 'Eurohorror' (Guins, 2005; for more on this, see Hutchings, 2012). Indeed, this process of recontextualisation, which involves viewing or re-viewing films from the 1960s and the 1970s in the present, is often acknowledged in works on Eurohorror, not least Olney's and Shipka's, as an integral part of the Eurohorror experience. It is also striking how central Italian horror cinema has been in the development of this way of thinking about European genre cinema; as Shipka notes, '[i]f European exploitation films were to have a central geographic point, that center would be Italy' (Shipka, 2011: 19). In support of this, one only has to look to the British Film Institute Screen Guide *100 European Horror Films* where thirty-eight of the chosen 100 titles are Italian, and in which Bava and Dario Argento are the most cited directors, with seven entries each (Schneider, 2007).

The extent to which Bava's Italian gothic or period horrors can or should be viewed as distinct and separate from Anglo-American period horrors from the same period, including work by American producer-director Roger Corman

and the British Hammer company, is debatable. They certainly were not critically viewed in that way at the time of their initial release. Indeed, back in the
early 1960s Howard Thompson in the *New York Times* managed to mistake
La maschera del demonio (under its American release title *Black Sunday*) for
'a British-made melodrama', presumably because its two stars, Barbara Steele
and John Richardson, were British and in broad terms the film in some way
resembled British horror (*New York Times*, 8 March 1961, p. 37). At least
other critics noticed that these films were Italian in origin but they also had
no problem in assigning them a place within a pre-existing entertainment
market, with, for example, the US trade magazine *Film Bulletin* summing up
La maschera del demonio as a 'weird, engrossing horror yarn with plenty of
exploitation gimmicks. Good box office item for action, ballyhoo markets'
(*Film Bulletin*, 6 March 1961, p. 16). Writing in the mid-1960s, horror historian Carlos Clarens saw Bava's gothic horror *La frusta e il corpo/The Whip
and the Body* (1963) and his *giallo* film *Sei donne per l'assassino* as 'deriving
from the Hammer product', the latter presumably from Hammer's cycle of
psychological thrillers (Clarens, 1968: 193). More recent critical writing on
Italian gothic horror cinema and Bava's contribution to that format, including Bondanella's and Rick Worland's work on the genre, has also tended to
subsume it within an internationally based gothic horror that includes British
and American productions (Bondanella, 2009; Worland, 2015). It seems from
this that the positioning of Bava as a founding father of 'Eurohorror' is far
from universally accepted, even though the foregrounding of Bava generated
by Eurohorror discourses and practices has served to make his work more
visible within other approaches.

The Italian *giallo* thriller has proved just as important as gothic horror, if
not more so, to the formation of a cultist appreciation of Italian horror cinema
and an appreciation of Bava as a pioneering Eurohorror filmmaker. Here too,
and more problematically than was the case with gothic horror, what might
initially appear to be a solid commercial category evident in 1960s and 1970s
Italian film production turns out to be something rather more elusive, with
this having implications for the way in which we might understand Bava as a
director of *giallo* films or indeed as a Eurohorror pioneer.

It is not uncommon for critics writing about the *giallo* to acknowledge that
the English-language definition of the term differs from its original and considerably broader Italian usage. For Mikel Koven, '[t]he term giallo acts as a
metonym for the entire mystery genre' (Koven, 2006: 2). Operating from a
slightly different perspective, Lucas notes, 'over the years the words "*giallo*"
and "*thriller*" have become synonymous in popular Italian usage' (Lucas,
2007: 449). By contrast, '[a]s the term has come to be understood outside of
Italy, it denotes a particularly lurid brand of thriller that dotes more on the
details of cruel and outrageous murder than on the art of detection' (Lucas:

450). However, the status of the English-language version of the *giallo* is not always as clear as it might be. Is it, as Koven suggests, a sub-category of the Italian version of the *giallo* that, confusingly, has been given the same name, presumably by English-language critics, as the main category itself? In other words, is it a sub-generic cycle that was recognised by filmmakers and audiences while *gialli* of this type were being produced during the 1960s and 1970s? Or is it a group of films that has been put together by critics (and potentially exploitation fans as well) after that period is over as one of the products of the 'remediation' of Italian genre cinema identified by Guins?

In this respect, it is interesting to look at Bava's *La ragazza che sapeva troppo*, a murder mystery set in Rome, as the first *giallo* or proto-*giallo*. Gary Needham and Mikel Koven share Bondanella's view that the film is, in Needham's words, 'the first true Italian giallo' (Needham, 2003: 136; also see Koven, 2006: 3–4). Lucas is more cautious, pointing out that '[i]n Italy, *La Ragazza che sapeva troppo* is regarded as neither the first Italian thriller nor the first giallo' (Lucas, 2007: 449). However, he then qualifies this by connecting the film with what he sees as an increased luridness in the Italian thriller evident from the 1950s onwards, so that ultimately it 'is not quite a giallo in the sense that the term is used today: it doesn't possess all the necessary generic criteria, most conspicuously in its lack of color and graphic violence. However, it was the earliest theatrical release to acknowledge the gialli, not only as an influence on its storytelling and *mise-en-scene*, but as part of the story it tells' (Lucas, 2007: 450). In this instance, Lucas is referring particularly to the film's opening sequence, in which we are shown the heroine, an American visiting Rome, reading what appears to be a lurid crime thriller (a detail that Needham also picks up on and in the same way) of the kind in which she herself will shortly become involved.

Here, frankly, *giallo* has become a rather blurry concept. Is the novel that features in *La ragazza che sapeva troppo*'s opening sequence meant to be taken as a *giallo* in the English-language sense of the term or instead in the Italian one, albeit in the more lurid or garish mode identified by Lucas? It is certainly arguable that the English-language version of *giallo* often appears to be founded more on the 1970s psychological thriller/horror films directed by Dario Argento and his imitators than it is on anything directed by Mario Bava. For example, note the descriptions of *giallo* provided by Needham and Olney. Indeed, *La ragazza che sapeva troppo* not only seems distant from better-known later *giallo* films but could also quite readily be put in other contexts, if one so wished. Its title, which in English means 'The Girl Who Knew Too Much' (although the film is also known as *The Evil Eye*), alerts us to its self-proclaimed status as a Hitchcock-style thriller, and it could be seen as contributing towards a slew of Hitchcockian or sub-Hitchcockian psychological thrillers that were a regular part of cinema-going fare during the

1960s, including productions from Great Britain (not least, Hammer's series of psychological thrillers), the United States and Germany. Often these non-Italian films featured qualities later associated with the *giallo*, for example the tourist caught up in a criminal conspiracy while abroad in Europe in the British thriller *Taste of Fear* (Seth Holt, 1961) or the American thrillers *Midnight Lace* (David Miller, 1960) and *Charade* (Stanley Donen, 1963). Worthy of mention in this context is the British Agatha Christie mystery *Murder, She Said* (George Pollock, 1961). This commences, in a manner that anticipates the opening of *La ragazza che sapeva troppo*, on a train with the amateur detective Miss Marple reading a lurid crime novel just before becoming an eye witness to a murder committed on a passing train by a killer wearing black gloves (a sartorial detail that would come to be associated with the *giallo* but which is lacking in *La ragazza che sapeva troppo*) which she herself subsequently investigates. A series of German adaptations of Edgar Wallace stories produced from the late 1950s onwards were also decidedly *giallo*-like stylistically, and have been seen by some critics as an influence on the Italian *giallo* (although their orientation more to crime than horror means that they are rarely discussed in the context of Eurohorror: for an exception, see Hanke, 2003).

Clearly none of these non-Italian films are offering themselves as *giallo*, at least in the English-language version of the term, but the fact that they and other such non-Italian productions can be seen as possessing *giallo*-like qualities suggests that the *giallo* category as developed by English-language critics is to some degree contingent and arbitrary in its attempt to seal off Italian production from broader international patterns and cycles of production. If *La ragazza che sapeva troppo* thus acquires a certain indeterminacy insofar as its relation to what appears to be a slippery definition of what a *giallo* actually is, Bava's next thriller, *Sei donne per l'assassino* (which literally means 'Six Women for the Murderer') is a much more promising candidate for *giallo* status. To borrow Tim Lucas's terms, it features in an unrestrained way both the colour and the violence lacking in *La ragazza che sapeva troppo*. A masked killer stalks and very violently murders a series of beautiful women working as models in a fashion house, with stylistic imperatives favoured over narrative in a manner usually associated with the *giallo* format (although, if one is paying attention, there is a logical plot there as well). However, this film, like *La ragazza che sapeva troppo*, lacks some of the conventions of the English-language version of *giallo*. This means that, for example, Koven argues that one needs to combine elements from both *La ragazza che sapeva troppo* and *Sei donne per l'assassino* in order to produce the formative moment for the *giallo* film more generally (Koven, 2006: 6). *Sei donne per l'assassino*'s distance from what is generally viewed as the highpoint of *giallo* production, namely the 1970s, is also an issue, especially in the context of popular Italian cinema of the period where cycles of films were usually generated very quickly.

The six-year gap between it, which might reasonably be seen from an English-language perspective as the last *giallo* film of the 1960s, and the 1970 release of Argento's first film *L'uccello dalle piume di cristallo/The Bird with the Crystal Plumage* becomes something of a problem when trying to establish that there was a popular Italian *giallo* cycle or sub-genre in train during the 1960s.

Matters become yet more complicated, for an understanding both of the *giallo* and of Bava's position in relation to this format, when one takes into account Bava's later ostensibly *giallo* productions, all of which appear in the early 1970s and in various ways turn out to be strikingly different from each other and from *La ragazza che sapeva troppo* and *Sei donne per l'assassino*. For example, *Il rosso segna della follia/Hatchet for the Honeymoon* (1970) carries over the fashion milieu from *Sei donne per l'assassino* but is not a murder mystery (we know who the killer is from the opening sequence onwards) and also contains supernatural elements. By contrast, *Reazione a catena* (1971), which goes under several titles including *Bay of Blood* and *Twitch of the Death Nerve*, contains the violence one expects of a *giallo* and features murder mystery elements but, unusually for a *giallo*, has a rural setting. It also offers a more visceral and indeed openly exploitative experience than that conjured by Bava's other more visually and culturally sophisticated *giallo* films, and it has frequently been invoked as an influence on the decidedly downmarket American slasher *Friday the 13th* (Sean S. Cunningham, 1980). Ironically, perhaps, the Bava film that arguably most resembles the *giallo* as described by English-language critics is the murder mystery *5 bambole per la luna d'agosto/Five Dolls for an August Moon* (1970), which has generally been seen as one of the director's least impressive pieces of work.

Returning to Bava's gothic horror films from the first half of the 1960s, one finds a comparable variety of approaches. In particular, *La frusta e il corpo* and *Operazione Paura/Kill Baby ... Kill* (1966) offer considerably more psychologised horror scenarios than that found in Bava's earlier *La maschera del demonio*, with ghosts in each case explicitly identified as emerging out of psychologically disturbed characters. One might balk at Lucas's comparison of *Operazione Paura* with Stanley Kubrick's *2001: A Space Odyssey* (1968) as two films 'which represent a point of embarkation when these genres begin to venture away from traditional linear narratives towards literally new dimensions in story telling that dared penetrate into areas ambiguous, abstract, and intuitive' (Lucas, 2007: 674). However, *Operazione Paura*, which was an acknowledged influence on Fellini's 'Toby Dammit' episode in *Histoires extraordinaires/Spirits of the Dead* (Federico Fellini, Louis Malle and Roger Vadim, 1968), certainly offers hallucinogenic moments of a kind and intensity not found elsewhere in Bava's gothic work, not least the sequence in which, inexplicably, the film's protagonist chases a figure through what appears to be a series of identical rooms only to find that he is chasing himself.

The heterogeneity evident in Bava's gothic and *giallo* work is a challenge to any auteurist reading predicated on there being an overall cohesion to his films. However, it is also clear that the presentation of Bava as a pioneer in relation to retrospectively constructed conceptualisations not just of Italian horror (which for many critics incorporates the *giallo*, or at least their version of it) but also of European horror more generally has involved in effect a kind of critical and commercial packaging of his work, or at least some of that work, that began back in the 1980s and which has continued to the present day. Bava has thus come to be assigned a role within the trajectory of Italian exploitation horror and/or the critical category of Eurohorror as a father figure and a distinguished contributor to these areas, although, as has already been suggested in this chapter, this has tended to involve only a partial view of his career as a filmmaker. This way of thinking about Bava has also arguably exaggerated the extent to which his films connected with or anticipated important, if sometimes vaguely defined, formats such as *giallo*, and the extent to which those same films were perceived as being radically different from Anglo-American product at the time of their initial release.

THE INDUSTRIAL BAVA

Early on in *Mario Bava: All the Colors of the Dark*, Tim Lucas claims that 'Bava was the postwar Italian cinema – at least for a period spanning three decades (1945–75)' (2007: 24). It is certainly the case that first as a cinematographer and subsequently as a director, Bava seems to have worked in just about every major Italian popular genre of that period. As a director, he did not just make horror films or thrillers but also pepla (*Ercole al centro della terra/Hercules in the Haunted World*, 1960), Viking movies (*Gli invasori/Erik the Conqueror*, 1961; *I coltelli del vendicatore/Knives of the Avenger*, 1966), Westerns (*La strada per Fort Alamo/The Road to Fort Alamo*, 1964; *Roy Colt & Winchester Jack*, 1970), science fiction (*Terrore nello spazio*, 1965), crime comedies (*Le spie vengono del semifreddo/Dr Goldfoot and the Girl Bombs*, 1966; *Diabolik*, 1968), sex comedies (*Quante volte . . . quella note/Four Times That Night*, 1971), and gritty realist crime drama (*Cani arrabbiati/Rabid Dogs*, 1975).

Such a career path suggests a filmmaker for hire responding to whatever opportunities the market offered. Indeed, one might argue that what might seem a remarkable variability in Bava's work so far as theme and style are concerned derives in large part from the fact that he never managed to establish a secure, long-term position for himself within any stable production set-up. In this he might be compared with the British horror director Terence Fisher, who for many years formed part of what essentially was a repertory company at Hammer, or Bava's fellow Italian director Dario Argento, who throughout the first part of his career worked mainly with his father and brother as his producers and was thus able to sustain a more consistent approach to the kind of films he made. By contrast, throughout his directorial career Bava was bounced unceremoniously from independent producer to independent producer, usually operating at the lower end of the industry so far as budgets were concerned, although occasionally becoming involved in slightly more prestigious projects (notably the Dino De Laurentiis-produced *Diabolik*).

Complicating matters yet further so far as Bava's position in the Italian film industry is concerned, Lucas identifies numerous other films – under the heading 'Bava's Secret Filmography' – to which Bava made uncredited directorial contributions. The best known of these is the horror film *I vampiri*, which as noted earlier was completed by Bava in the absence of credited director Riccardo Freda and which was a clear influence on Bava's subsequent *La maschera del demonio*. However, Lucas finds quite a few others in a variety of genres and indeed claims, in contradiction to the majority of Bava filmographies, that Bava's directorial debut was not *La maschera del demonio* at all but instead a little-known science fiction film *La morte viene dallo spazio/The Day the Sky Exploded* (1958) (2007: 216). Additionally, Bava was not always wholly responsible for the direction of the films for which he was credited as director, with his son Lamberto directing sections of Bava's final film *Shock/Beyond the Door II* (1977).

Adding yet more complexity to Bava's profile is the fact that his films have often existed in more than one version. This was not uncommon for Italian genre films in the 1960s and 1970s, which were regularly altered for release outside of Italy, most notably through clumsy dubbing into English (with subtitling reserved for more prestigious art house productions) and the addition of new titles. In Bava's case, for instance, *La maschera del demonio* (literally 'The Mask of the Demon') became, variously *The Mask of Satan*, *Revenge of the Vampire* and *Black Sunday*; *I tre volti della paura* ('The three faces of fear') became *Black Sabbath*; *La ragazza che sapeva troppo* became *The Evil Eye*; *Sei donne per l'assassino* was turned into *Blood and Black Lace*; *Operazione Paura* ('Operation Fear') became *Kill Baby . . . Kill* (a rare improvement on the Italian original); and *Reazione a catena* ('Chain reaction') became, variously, *Bay of Blood*, *Bloodbath* and, most memorably if also nonsensically, *Twitch of the Death Nerve*. Bava's films were altered in other more egregious and intrusive ways, however. For the films released in the United States by American International Pictures, what were often evocative original musical scores were replaced by more traditional scores by American composer Les Baxter, among them *La maschera del demonio* and *I tre volti della paura*. The *Evil Eye* version of *La ragazza che sapeva troppo* acquired a different final sequence, shot by Bava, and softened a drugs theme evident in the Italian original. A lesbian-themed plot in *I tre volti della paura* was removed by dubbing for the *Black Sabbath* version; additionally the three stories that comprised this anthology film were reordered, and a new introduction and conclusion also provided. Perhaps most spectacular in this regard was the fate of *Lisa e il diavolo/Lisa and the Devil* (1973), now generally thought of as Bava's poetic masterpiece but which was extensively reshot as *The Exorcist* (William Friedkin, 1973) knock-off *The House of Exorcism*.

It is hard to think of any other notable horror director whose career seems so shrouded in such obscurity and yet who at the same time was so thoroughly defined through a particular industrial context. On the one hand, this extraordinary array of credits, official and unofficial, and multiple versions provides opportunities for critics to track down 'originals' (or, in the case of recent BluRay releases of *La ragazza che sapeva troppo* and *Cani arrabbiati*, to present us with alternative versions of the same film) and also to develop an authorial profile that cuts across ostensible differences between films and to some degree transcends those differences. To this end, in his analyses of Bava's films, Lucas frequently identifies what he considers 'Bavaesque' qualities to do with a felicitous piece of lighting or some thematic resonances, although even he has occasionally to admit that Bava seems more invested in some projects than others.

On the other hand, and as noted earlier in this chapter, the extraordinarily detailed description of the various turns in Bava's career offered by Lucas's book also has the potential to 'unmake' Bava as auteur, and particularly as a gothic- or *giallo*-oriented auteur. There is little here of the marginality or anti-establishment behaviour often associated with cult or Eurohorror artists (Mathijs and Sexton, 2011: 67–75); Bava might never have been an 'A' list director but Lucas convincingly establishes that he was an industry insider, whose reliability rendered him consistently employable and who was often fully engaged with the different versions of his films (even in the unhappy case of *Lisa e il diavolo*). It is interesting in this regard that Lucas, in what is at heart a thoroughly industry-facing account of Bava's career, displays little interest in Bava's credentials as a figure in cult or Eurohorror discourses (even though he regularly provides commentary tracks on DVDs and BluRays marketed in those terms) but rather promotes Bava as a great, if underappreciated, cinematic artist whose 'ability to express at once the dark side of himself and his country confirms him as an artist of more than cult-level significance' (Lucas, 2007: 21).

Indeed, there is a potential here for a more thoroughgoing unmaking of Bava as auteur precisely through focusing on a career trajectory forged within and defined by a particular set of industrial and generic contexts over which Bava himself had little or no control. This is not to deny the remarkable artistry evident in some – but by no means all – of Bava's films, although even in Lucas's magisterial study it is not always clear how consistent or 'authored' this artistry is across the full range of Bava's work. By contrast, one might profitably focus precisely on the changes of direction and awkward transitions in Bava's filmography – elements that an auteurist account might seek to explain away – as a way of illuminating particular sets of industrial circumstances.

It is worth considering the latter part of Bava's career in this respect, and especially *Reazione a catena* and *Lisa e il diavolo*. The former clearly marked a noticeable change of direction for the director in what for him were unprecedentedly explicit representations of sex, nudity and violence. Indeed, Lucas himself notes that on viewing the film, actor Christopher Lee, who had earlier worked with Bava on *La frusta e il corpo*, 'was at once appalled and again concerned for the state of his old friend's mental health' (Lucas, 2007: 539). Be that as it may, *Reazione a catena*, for all of the artistic 'Bavaesque' qualities detected there by Lucas, is also and self-evidently an attempt by Bava to reorientate himself in relation to the horror market during a period in which, both in Italy and elsewhere, horror cinema was becoming more explicit as the restraints of censorship were gradually being rolled back. In a different way, Bava's penultimate film, the crime drama *Cani arrabbiati* – which was abandoned before its completion because of problems with its funding but which eventually achieved a release long after Bava's death – marked a similar, if yet more startling, attempt at career rejuvenation, with its gritty realism a complete departure from anything previously assayed by this director.

Perhaps the most extreme instance of a tension between artistry and industry in Bava's career comes with *Lisa e il diavolo*. After the commercial success of the horror film *Gli orrori del castello di Norimberga/Baron Blood* (1972), Bava was given considerable latitude by producer Alfredo Leone for his next film, and in *Lisa e il diavolo* he came up with what Kevin Heffernan has characterised as 'nonlinear narrative, painterly compositions, wild exaggerations of Italian horror film conventions, and dizzying allusions to religion, mythology, and art history' (Heffernan, 2007: 145). This bringing together of genre elements with elements associated with art house productions has proved important in later discussions of Eurohorror, where such hybridity figures as one of the challenges that Eurohorror offers to conventional cultural hierarchies. It is a quality that is clearly evident in the early films of Dario Argento and, in a manner more comparable with *Lisa e il diavolo*, in Belgian director Harry Kumel's vaguely surreal and oneiric *Le rouge aux Lèvres/Daughters of Darkness* (1971) and *Malpertuis* (1971). However, this quality did not go down well with the original US financial backers of *Lisa e il diavolo*, which ended up after extensive reshooting, some directed by Bava himself, as *The House of Exorcism*.

No one has a kind word to say for *The House of Exorcism*, which is manifestly a crude attempt to cash in on the success of *The Exorcist*, with all the requisite vomiting and cursing that one might expect of such a project. At the same time, and for all its clumsiness, it arguably fits into Bava's 1970s career more than *Lisa e il diavolo* does, with again an emphasis on explicit shock imagery that one finds in *Reazione a catena* and *Cani arrabbiati* (although the latter, like *Lisa e il diavolo*, was not released during the 1970s). By contrast, *Lisa e il diavolo*, with its references back to an Italian gothic horror that had long since lost its box-office appeal, seems a nostalgic or backward-looking project in its original context of production. The original cut of *Lisa e il diavolo* finally appeared in 1995 and has since become a Eurohorror 'classic', with viewers warned off the *House of Exorcism* version 'as it barely retains the essential core of the original production' (Schneider, 2007: 141). However, instead of thinking of the relation between the two versions in terms of an implacable artistic/industrial divide, one might better consider that relationship sequentially. *The House of Exorcism* certainly seems to fit much better into the context of European horror production during the 1970s, and indeed was a considerable commercial success at the time, while the more obviously authored and artistic *Lisa e il diavolo* accords better with the contemporary world of Eurohorror, which, as we have seen, is in its own way as nostalgic and retrospective as the world conjured by Bava's 'masterpiece' and which moreover has supported the development of the idea of Bava as an authentic horror maestro.

The fact that Bava in effect disappears in *The House of Exorcism* – his name comes off the credits, the film generally displays little of his artistry – is hardly the only time he does this in his career. Drifting in and out of productions, sometimes credited and sometimes not, with different levels of engagement depending perhaps on his own artistic sensibilities but also on the circumstances of the productions themselves, this is the other Bava, the Bava so embedded in the film industry and in popular genres and cycles of the day that it is sometimes hard to make him out as a creative personality. Thinking about him in this way does not diminish his achievement unduly – some of his films remain extraordinary pieces of work – but it does ground the achievement in something solid, material and nuanced. All those different versions of films, all these obscure credits, start to become the point rather than functioning as obstacles to understanding and appreciation. They alert us to particular national and international production collaborations and contexts. They also encourage us to think about the role of the producer in Italian popular cinema, something that is clearly important but which to date has received little critical attention. They might also push us towards a consideration of the full range of popular Italian film cycles rather than adopting a selective focus – perhaps too selective – on just a few of these. It is to Tim Lucas's credit that for all his dedication to the idea of Bava as a great cinematic artist he has provided so much industrial and contextual information outside of that focus that can support other ways of thinking about Bava. It is an acknowledgement of the richness and complexity of Bava's career in Italian cinema that it feels as if there is yet more to be said about Mario Bava as an Italian film director.

BIBLIOGRAPHY

Bondanella, P. (2009), *A History of Italian Cinema*, London: Continuum.
Clarens, C. (1968), *Horror Movies: An Illustrated Survey*, London: Secker & Warburg.
Guins, R. (2005), 'Blood and Black Gloves on Shiny Discs: New Media, Old Tastes, and the Remediation of Italian Horror Films in the United States', in Schneider, S. J. and Williams, T. (ed.), *Horror International*, Detroit: Wayne State University Press, pp. 15–32.
Hanke, K. (2003), 'The "lost" horror film series: the Edgar Wallace krimis', in Schneider, S. J. (ed.), *Fear without Frontiers: Horror Cinema Across the Globe*, Godalming: FAB Press, pp. 111–23.
Heffernan, K. (2007), 'Art House or House of Exorcism? The Changing Distribution and Reception Contexts of Mario Bava's *Lisa and the Devil*', in Sconce, J. (ed.), *Sleaze Artists: Cinema at the Margins of Taste, Style, and Politics*, Durham, NC and London: Duke University Press, pp. 144–66.
Hutchings, P. (2012), '*Resident Evil*: The Limits of European Horror', in Allmer, P., Brick, E. and Huxley, D. (eds), *European Nightmares: Horror Cinema in Europe since 1945*, London: Wallflower, pp. 13–24.
Koven, M. J. (2006), *La Dolce Morte: vernacular cinema and the Italian giallo film*, Lanham, MD: Scarecrow Press.
Lucas, T. (2007), *Mario Bava: All the Colors of the Dark*, Cincinnati: Video Watchdog.
Mathijs, E. and Sexton, J. (2011), *Cult Cinema: an introduction*, Malden, MA: John Wiley & Sons.
Needham, G. (2003), 'Playing with genre: defining the Italian giallo', in Schneider, S. J. (ed.), *Fear without Frontiers: Horror Cinema Across the Globe*, Godalming: FAB Press, pp. 135–60.
Olney, I. (2013), *Euro horror: classic European horror cinema in contemporary American culture*, Bloomington: Indiana University Press.
Schneider, S. (ed.) (2007), *100 European Horror Films*, London: British Film Institute.
Shipka, D. (2011), *Perverse Titillation: The Exploitation Cinema of Italy, Spain and France, 1960–1980*, Jefferson, NC: McFarland.
Williams, T. (2011), 'Mario Bava; All the Colors of the Dark' (review), *Horror Studies*, 2:1, pp. 162–70.
Worland, R. (2015), 'The Gothic Revival (1957–1974)', in Benshoff, H. M. (ed.), *A Companion to the Horror Film*, Chichester: Wiley Blackwell, pp. 273–91.

6. THE ARGENTO SYNDROME: AESTHETICS OF HORROR

Marcia Landy

The Argento Syndrome is my term for discussing filmmaker Dario Argento's consistent, even obsessive, explorations on film of the nature and effects of creating and viewing violence. Argento's films are an unrelenting investigation of the cinematic uses of memory, trauma and distorted vision, and the cinematic body as threatened site of attack, mutilation and death. The films are symptomatic of a politics and aesthetics that invoke the powers of internalised and externalised forms of horror, particularly tied to the twentieth century and to the uses of media technology, including computer-generated effects. In their blurring of fact and fantasy, challenges to representation, hallucinatory quality and particular strategies to incorporate the viewer into their images, they address a world where the real and illusory have lost their clarity and where art is as dangerous as life. Argento is a filmmaker whose cinematic work is very self-conscious of the uses of horror 'as a meditation on the aesthetics of filmmaking itself' (Schneider, 2007: 60).

In the early years of its development from the 1890s to the First World War, Italian cinema was identified with comedy films, romances, *divismo* (star films) and historical spectacles. However, the effects of fascism and war from the mid-1920s to the fall of the regime in 1943 introduced conflicts over the direction of film production in the immediate post-Second World War era. These centred around what came to be identified nationally and internationally as neorealism, with its focus on the effects of the war, the hardships of everyday survival, and the emphasis on humanist solidarity in contrast to the propagandistic and Hollywood-style films identified with the cinema of the twenty years of fascism (Bertellini, 2004: 4). Neorealism offered a version of cinema averse to genre forms, but, in fact, in the cinema 'no profound cultural and/or political break occurred' (Ricci, 2008: 165–8).

In the late 1950s into the 1970s, a blend of genre and neorealism emerged in popular comedic and melodramatic forms. In the industry's pressure to produce a profitable cinema of quality and of popularity, 'historical' and mythical peplum (costume) epics emerged and achieved local and international acclaim (subsequently to be overtaken by the popularity of Spaghetti Westerns). These films, identified with low-budget forms of production, were watched by youthful and cinephilic sectors of the Italian and international populations. The films offered a contrast to an art cinema that, from the 1960s through the 1970s, also gained international attention through films by auteurs such as Roberto Rossellini, Federico Fellini, Michelangelo Antonioni, Pier Paolo Pasolini and Bernardo Bertolucci. By contrast, the films of Mario Bava, Lucio Fulci and Dario Argento, among other filmmakers, were relegated to a mode of cinematic expression associated with exploitation and expressive emotional excess, sensationalism, perverse sexuality, violence, misogyny and pornography. However, in recent decades with the reassessment of the aesthetic and politics that had characterised studies of national cinemas, it has become possible to rethink connections between film history, its modes of production and reception, and through critical writings on them blur taxonomic boundaries between canonical, auteurist and popular forms involving genres, affective styles and audience engagement.

Academic writings on Italian cinema have until recently largely leaned towards elite art forms and neglected or misrecognised popular forms (see Frayling, 1981; Koven, 2006; Nerenberg, 2012). Though some of the Spaghetti Westerns and horror films were shown in the first-run (*prima visione*) movie houses, many found their home in neighbourhood (*terza visione*) movie theatres. In characterising these popular films, Mikel J. Koven and Ellen Nerenberg find the designation 'filone' or 'school' better terms than 'genre' to account for the *giallo* that 'spans varied cinematic genres as well as locations of production' (Nerenberg, 2012: 73–4). Nevertheless, the filiations between art and popular cinema can be seen in a shared fascination with visual technology, the cinematic body, modernity, spectacle and perception. Mikel J. Koven distinguishes the *giallo* as being 'vernacular', rooted in local practices, as incorporating elements from folk, middlebrow and high culture, and as addressing 'the experiential dimension of cinematic people's lives' (2006: 28–9). The treatment of narration and form is most likely hybrid and allows for a flexible conception of genre production.

Here I explore how Argento's films violate boundaries between elite and mass culture, feeling and thinking, fiction and history, to offer a version of politics and aesthetics that resists reduction by introducing uncertainty and potentially the possibility of *thinking* about cruelty and violence. Similar to the Italian Westerns, his films are eclectic in form and content, override national (Italian) boundaries, and incorporate experimental and formulaic forms. The cult status of his films and their hybrid character does not disqualify them from an engagement with aesthetics as well as politics that involves the uses of folklore, cinema history, the relation of cinema to the other arts, and formal experimentation, as well as the inevitable but hard-to-define invocation of their operations through the cinematic lens of sensory reception.

The Argento Syndrome enlists the contemporary viewer in engaging with problems posed by historical transformations in media linked to altered social and historical realities. In order to identify these realities and the cinematic language in which they are couched, I locate formal aspects of crime detection and of the supernatural in operatic, folkloric, commonsensical and legalistic language examined in the cultural writings of Italian philosopher and political activist Antonio Gramsci. His attentiveness to popular language, even in its most stylised and formulaic terms, provides an understanding of the many-layered and contradictory dimensions of culture and politics pertinent to Argento's form of filmmaking. I also discuss writers and artists from the 1920s, such as the Surrealists, especially Jean Vigo, Luis Buñuel and Antonin Artaud, who undertook a self-conscious exploration of sensation and perception in cinema through their portrayals of violence and death. In discussing select Argento films – *Profondo rosso/Deep Red* (1975), *La sindrome di Stendhal/ The Stendhal Syndrome* (1996), *Non ho sonno/Sleepless* (2001) and the Three Mothers trilogy – I call on the contemporary writings of Gilles Deleuze on allegory and on the Baroque as illuminating Argento's aesthetics of cruelty.

Antonio Gramsci and the Literature of Crime Detection

In his *Prison Notebooks*, Antonio Gramsci (1891–1937) commented on the popularity of foreign crime detection fiction in Italy, exemplified by Victor Hugo, Arthur Conan Doyle and G. K. Chesterton (1977: 368–9). Rather than deride such works, he emphasised their popularity with the public and recommended their study to account for the effects of popular forms on the spectator. One aspect of Gramsci's analysis of popular expression involves the 'operatic conception of life', in which 'the baroque and the operatic appear as an extraordinarily fascinating way of feeling and acting, a means of escaping . . . what they consider low, mean and contemptible in their lives and education . . . in a writing style of many people . . . modelled on a repertory of clichés' (Gramsci, 1977: 378). The operatic conception and its repertory of clichés, however, emerge from the everyday world, the institutions that disseminate them and from the singular responses of the people who affirm or resist them.

In further explaining the persistence of this type of expression, Gramsci turns to the language of the law courts, funeral orations, clichés and even academic lectures (Gramsci, 1977: 380) to address popular styles and politics. In particular, he connects popular form to their uses of verbal language and gestural languages, in which can be found:

> A conception of the world and life implicit to a large extent in determinate (in time and space) strata of society and in opposition (also for the most part implicit, mechanical, and objective) to 'official' conceptions of the world (or in a broader sense, the conceptions of the cultured parts of historically determinate societies) that have succeeded one another in the historical process. This folklore is crude, not systematized, and composed of many different and juxtaposed elements. (Ibid.: 189)

In short, Gramsci rejects a simplistic and moral position on folklore and commonsense, regarding the language and form of crime detection and murder texts pertinent to questions of cultural survival and change. For him, the fragmentary signs and symptoms of folklore are not to be understood in totalising fashion and to be studied. His writings were instrumental in directing attention, especially in Italy in the 1960s and 1970s and internationally after his death, to important forms of 'vernacular' expression for addressing residual and modern folklore and its multifaceted relation to social history, cinema history and politics. Similarly, Béla Balàzs (1848–1949), in writing about cinema as the emergence of 'visible man', privileged the importance of fantasy, dreams and the supernatural as characteristic of cinematic art and especially one with a language to awaken sensation.

SURREALISM, CRUELTY AND VIOLENCE

A major text for examining the creation of horror is the Buñuel-Dali film, *Un chien Andalou* (1929), which begins with the slicing of an eyeball, an iconic image in cinematic history. Furthermore, it is an image that evinces different affective responses, evoking fascination, fear or disgust to arouse its viewers. The film resists rigid classification. Is it horrific, bizarrely comedic, satirical, reflective, or all? This image and others throughout the film invite humour and repulsion, but also situate the viewer in a prominent position to look and hence elicit a response. In this respect, the film shares with popular film a serio-comic investment on the part of its viewer by posing riddles about the body and the fragility and permeability of sense perception, especially in its use of instruments of technological visualising, the camera to shoot the images and the process of cutting to create an illusory event of mutilation in close-up.

Filmmaker Jean Vigo commented in 1930 on the violently negative reaction to the image, noting that 'all the horrors men have committed on each other, is put to the severe test when we can't bear the sight of a woman's eye cut in two by a razor on the screen. Is it more dreadful than the sight of a cloud veiling a full moon?' (quoted in Abel, 1988: 61). Vigo insisted on the necessary connection between visions of the horrific and the creation of a social cinema, arguing that '[t]o aim at a social cinema is therefore to underwrite a cinema dealing with provocative subjects, subjects that cut into the flesh' (ibid.: 62).

Argento's films have occasioned similar shock, even disgust, but in defence of his film's focus on violence, he has asserted that '[t]o kill for nothing that is the horror of today. I'm attracted to extreme violence because it's a form of protest – a refusal of established values' (quoted in Jones, 2004: 14). An image from Argento's *Opera* also entertains a striking image of violence, when birds (a direct allusion to Hitchcock) attack the audience in a group display of physical mutilation. Again, extra-diegetic viewers are implicated as passive and potentially endangered spectators to the horror of violence. More striking is the image of the young (female) opera singer forced to watch the killer's act of murdering her boyfriend by pinning her eyes open with needles. If she blinks, her eyes will be mutilated and she will be blinded, but the close-up of her eyes is shocking in ways similar to other images of brutality that we are forced to view. The question is thus raised about the parameters and potential of the horrific through art to make contact with other worlds.

In the Buñuel-Dali film, with the viewing of the slicing of the eyeball the element of shock in the event arises from the spectator's direct frontal experience of the destruction of the physical organ of sight. In Argento's image in *Opera,* the eye is not physically destroyed, though the victim is threatened with blindness if she blinks and refuses to gaze at the murder being perpetrated before her eyes. This episode introduces the element of cruelty attributed to the killer, if not translated to the filmmaker.

In the Buñuel-Dali film the spectator is invited to consider a form of vision

Figure 6.1   Enforced viewing? Betty (Cristina Marsillach) in *Opera.*

Figure 6.2   Crowded allusions to art and death in *The Stendhal Syndrome*.

that requires a radical demolition of conventional sight to ask the viewer to contemplate another, more internalised perception. With Argento the viewer is obsessively and cruelly forced to confront the horror of external violence. The threat not only of being forced to gaze but to gaze helplessly at the brutal destruction of another involves the external viewer who is situated in a related position, if he or she wishes to view the gruesome events or retreat in distaste. This segment not only evokes a consideration of the barbarism of violence and questions of coercion and power through the spectre of cinema. It also raises the question of whether this event is possibly also parodic, invoking cinematic censorship and reductive assumptions of looking as voyeurism and sensationalism instead of more complex responses to seeing and hearing.

The particular character of Argento's films has been described as a brand of scattershot narratives soaked in the blood pouring through past centuries of vicious Italian history, culture and fine art. However, his work can be aligned to the Surrealists' shocking imagery, disorienting perspectives, focus on threatened bodies often through dream and fantasy, and a mistrust of rationality. In his writings, Antonin Artaud shared with the Surrealists the desire 'to metamorphose all perceptions of reality through dream states'. For Artaud, however, dreaming collapses into 'violence and fragmentation, tending toward horror and madness' (Barber, 2004: 14), involving graphic descriptions of torture, rape and bodily decomposition. In his script, *The Butcher Revolts* (1930), the principal figure is a madman, a wildly volatile character who alternates between extreme states of joy and despair. The protagonist sees an animal carcass that falls from a truck and associates it with human flesh. After visiting an abattoir, he is taken into custody by the police. Artaud's penchant for characters and images involves the taste for blood, cannibalistic fantasies, eroticism and cruelty. His conception of cinema entails a violent assault on the senses, but instead of reducing the subjugated spectator to passivity, 'the spectator remains firmly grounded in the tactile world. Aware of what the film is subjecting them to, and also incited to react, in simultaneously physical and revolutionary ways' (ibid.: 25), the viewer actively confronts life through the theatre of cruelty.

Similarly, Franju's Le sang des bêtes/Blood of the Beast (1949) approximates to Artaud's conception of cinema where the spectator is placed 'at the very extremes of visual experience, exposed to a multiple crisscrossing of expulsive forces which necessitate a transformation of the conditions and nature of visual perception, and impel a resistance toward society and cinema itself' (ibid.: 28). Artaud inveighs against representation as being inextricably linked to social and religious institutions, and, therefore, dangerous for life in annihilating alternative perceptions of the world. His ruminations on cinema are predicated on a necessary bond with spectators, engaging them through a visual contact with bare flesh, a sight that threatens the integrity of conventional responses. This form of interaction is a significant dimension of Argento's focus on flesh, torture, violence, mutilation and death as dissections of the nature and potential effects of the cinematic image in contact with bodies. For Artaud, 'flesh' means above all an 'apprehension, hair standing on end, flesh laid bare with all the intellectual profundity of this spectacle of pure flesh, and all its consequences for the senses, that is the sentiments' (Artaud, 1976: 111).

PROFONDO ROSSO: THE FORMULAIC AND THE AESTHETIC

Argento's thrillers (gialli) such as L'uccello dalle piume di cristallo/The Bird with the Crystal Plumage (1970), Il gatto a nove code/The Cat o' Nine Tails (1971) and 4 mosche di velluto grigio/Four Flies on Grey Velvet (1971) share certain characteristics: though filmed largely in Italy they employ non-Italian actors in key roles; include animals and insects; invoke science and/or the world of art; evince ambivalent attitudes towards the police; show amateur detectives drawn into crime detection not as professionals but often for personal reasons; and show an ambiguous attachment of victims and detectives to early traumatic experiences. The films share a codified visual language in relation to the murderer, involving disguises as part of the legacy of horror, figured in literature and film: black gloves; a mask, a cloth, a stocking or a floppy hat covering the face; a long black coat; and often shot from the rear or from the view of the victim, but not from the viewer, until exposed.

This clothing serves to blur the identity, particularly as gendered, of the killer. Disfigurement, decomposition and decay are largely inherent to a milieu that suggests a baroque fascination with mortality. In these film conceptions of the human and the 'normal', of subjectivity and objectivity, art and commonly held conceptions of science are explored. As Elena Past indicates, the science of crime is ambiguous, if not treated critically (2012: 212). Argento gives us killers as victims and victims as killers, and 'illustrates his enthusiasm for bringing ... ethical questions [such as genetics in *Il gatto a nove code*] into the popular realm' (ibid.: 213). His treatment of animals includes aggressive human–animal parallels, though in his treatment of Jennifer in *Phenomena* (1985) there is an apparent bond of affection and intuition with a chimpanzee. *Profondo rosso* adopts many of the codes and conventions of these films but links them self-consciously and tightly to issues of visual perception and memory to raise questions about the tenuous character of seeing and remembering. The issue of trauma and the relation between killers and their murder victims assumes second place to the complex focus on how to respond to what is seen and heard. Throughout this film, editing tricks and special effects undermine the spectator's complacency about what is shown, compelling them to hover between bewilderment and a refusal to look, but a compulsion to see, thanks to the uses of colour, camera position and uses of space.

The film begins with the sounds of a children's song and the shadows of two people, one stabbing the other, and a bloody knife falling to the floor by a child's leg. Abruptly the scene returns to interrupted credits and seems to begin again in a church where jazz musicians are rehearsing (in this film Argento has shifted from Ennio Morricone to the music of Goblin) where the leader of the group, Marcus Daly (David Hemmings), urges them to strive for more earthy music. The transitions between the earlier shadowy scene of murder and this one are disjunctive, but the viewer familiar with crime detection and especially with Argento's films anticipates a hybrid agenda in which surprise and ambiguity prevail.

The rehearsal scene blends into a theatre where a lecture is taking place, in which the camera movement changes to include an unknown presence and to montage editing that entails a relay of shots from an uncertain position from behind curtains, a balcony, from the rear of a head, images of black gloves, close-up of an eye, running water and hand-washing, intercut with scenes of the stage, the lecturer and the audience to a talk that concerns telepathy. The non-Italian speaker, Helga Ulman (Macha Méril), establishes her credibility in clairvoyance (to the cinematic audience) when she identifies the presence in the building of a killer that the viewer familiar with the uses of sound in Argento's films can recognise. She later reveals to the psychologist and his colleague (overheard by the killer) that she is aware of the killer's identity, marking her as a victim and setting in motion the involvement of the two amateur detectives, Marcus and Gianna (Daria Nicolodi), another link to the external viewer in relation to sharing an investigation.

What remains of this prologue is the realisation of the anticipated murder and Marcus's involvement in seeing it take place, and in his confusion about having seen a painting that he believes is important to unravelling the crime. Visual memory emerges as a major problematic to implicate knowledge through the senses. Helga's murder introduces other unsettling elements involving history through the images of the menorah in her room as well as that of a Star of David, her connections to Eastern Europe, and finally her burial in a Jewish cemetery. Thus, the question of her Jewishness and what she knew appears as a clue to understanding the violence, though the film will not explore this historical position but move on to include other lines of investigation.

The trope that captures the evanescence of the image and of memory is that of liquid: water and blood. The unseen killer is first identified with water flowing from a sink. The suffocation of author Amanda Righetti (Giuliana Calandra) is a composite of previous images – childhood toys, a bird, a naked rubber baby doll – but the significant aspect is the flowing hot steaming water from the bath tub that leaves a clue to the murderer's identity (and causes the death of Professor Giordani who deciphers the message). Flowing water is another revelation of the film's investment in the moving image and also of the cruelty of passing time. In this sense, Argento's films merge the familiar with the nightmarish (Cooper, 2012). This death and its spectacle of violence will vie with the elaborateness and intensity of the murders to follow, namely Giordano's, and ultimately Marta's (Clara Calamai), the murderer (seen in the mirror that earlier Marcus mistook for a painting). The film ends with Marcus gazing at his own reflection in a pool of blood, thus undermining confidence in conventional and uplifting conceptions of truth and justice.

While visual memory is an overarching concern in Argento's *gialli* and supernatural films including the Three Mothers trilogy, his treatment of sexuality has been controversial. Most notably, sexual ambiguity as well as misogyny has been a commonplace criticism of Argento's cinema. In *Profondo rosso*, according to Giorgio Bertellini, 'sexual ambiguity . . . is both part of, and a metaphor for, a larger Argentian theme, that of the perpetual elusiveness associated with the cinematic image', and that this is 'particularly stunning when applied to the narrative combination of murder mystery and sexual identity' (2004: 216). Jacqueline Reich argues rather that the focus in Argento is on male castration anxiety and that women are regarded as 'object rather than subject in the symbolic order' (2001: 102). However, an overview of Argento's filmmaking indicates that his murderers and victims are male *and* female, masculinised *and* feminised, and violence is inherent both as spectacle and more often as a means of investigating its existence, affects and effects. The film, rather than enlisting gendered identifications, unsettles them through ambiguity, misrecognition and also humour to create uncertainty or questioning for the viewer.

Sexual antagonism is handled humorously in *Profondo rosso*: the character of Gianna is developed through her playful insistence on games with Marcus involving dominance (arm wrestling) and insistence on combining business with pleasure, thus taunting and exposing his uncertainty about sex and bonding. Humour recedes as the police fade into the background when the investment of the two amateur detectives, Marcus and Gianna, in sleuthing exceeds professional objectives and endangers their lives. The ambiguity of sexuality and violence comes to the fore dramatically in *Profondo rosso* through the enigmatic figure of Carlo, associated with addiction to alcohol, indifference to crimes witnessed, and through the specific identification with being gay.

Carlo offers clues to the killer that Marcus (and the viewer) does not comprehend until the final segments of the film, when the identification between him and the child in the reiterated crime scene is finally made. While the antique dealer in *L'uccello dalle piume di cristallo* and Carlo in *Profondo rosso* are assumed to be gay, it does not follow that Argento is targeting them as social symptoms. The director is not averse to stereotyping, but more often as false clues to the crime. In this way Koven has observed that the 'sexually confused killer in giallo cinema is a frequent, but by no means *typical*, character' (2006: 109). More pertinent to these traumatised figures is an evocation of history, if often indirect, to the fascist past. The 'real past trauma is a historical one: the defeat and emasculation of Italy in the war and under fascism: And this trauma has been haunting Italians ever since' (ibid.: 109).

In *Profondo rosso*, the ghosts of history are in its recollection. History is invoked by misdirection and through a range of brief allusions. These allusions start a process of dispersing a range of images that enigmatically evoke memories of a past, possibly the war, fascism, the Holocaust – and even classical Rome by the fountain where Marcus meets his friend Carlo (Gabriele Lavia). Further to this, an ancient house is critical to the crime and potential identity of the murderer; and a photographic display of Carlo's mother as an actress during the fascist era offers another layer of memory and history. All these allusions muddle conventional interpretation of criminality and guilt through emphasising the uncertainty of recollection that also implicates the film viewer in what s/he sees to incite uncertainty about causes but not effects.

Also reminiscent of *Profondo rosso*, the later *Non ho sonno* returns to childhood trauma in which a dwarf accused of murder was himself murdered (or committed suicide) and, after twenty years, mysteriously appears to return. The film brings the operatic into film with its emphasis on prophecy, witches, ghosts, folklore, and madness also suggests an operatic conception of life inherent to popular culture as described by Gramsci in his discussion of folklore (1985: 378). The clues involve drawings of farm animals, a children's poem, puppets and a murder reminiscent of the butchering of animals.

Ulisse Moretti (Max von Sydow) is a retired policeman who was on the case of the 'dwarf murders' when young Giacomo (Stefano Dionisi) witnessed the brutal killing of his mother, and Moretti promises he'll find the killer even at the expense of his own life. Giacomo, now an adult bent on solving the crime, is not a professional detective and, further, has an emotional investment in solving the crime. Thus, the relationship between the two amateur detectives is bonded through memory, age difference, lack of professional motivation and having been witnesses to the initial crime.

Through the uses of art forms such as children's songs, poems and paintings (*Profondo rosso*, *La sindrome di Stendhal* and *Non ho sonno*), opera (*Opera* and *Il fantasma dell'opera*/*The Phantom of the Opera*), dance (*Suspiria* and *Non ho sonno*), literature (*Tenebre*), architecture (the Three Mothers trilogy of *Suspiria*, *Inferno* and *La terza madre*), and endlessly manufactured dream landscapes, Argento's films explore the horrific through invoking the cinematic as a medium that has the potential to engulf other media, even television. Intertextual references animate the images of perverse sexuality and extreme violence, and disrupt any sense of continuous internal space, interrupting the flow of the narrative reminiscent of Buñuellian optics that are unstable and threatening. The viewer moves between surface and depth, works of classical and popular art that lose their shapes, their borders, the boundaries between the real and the imaginary, the subjective and objective, and, like the characters, becomes prey to the terrors of a constantly altering modern and visible world.

LA SINDROME DI STENDHAL: OCULAR DESTRUCTION

In *La sindrome di Stendhal*, the characters move into a world where the quotidian is metamorphosed into nightmare through images derived from classical paintings that involve the viewer's responses to art derived from French writer Stendhal's (Marie-Henri Beyle, 1783–1842) description of his disturbing experiences with painting and architecture. The syndrome evokes a response to art that can be deadly, even destructive – conducive to altered states of feeling, rapid shifts of affect and blurred boundaries between life and death, ecstasy and abjection.

Stendhal wrote in 1817 after a visit to the Church of Santa Croce: 'My emotion was profound, aspiring to pity. The gloomy religiosity of this church, its timbered ceiling, the unending façade, all spoke intensely to my soul' (Gallant, 2001: 136). Stendhal described his disturbed physical and psychic response to the church as 'initial confusion, followed by a sense of suffocation, nausea, fainting, high fever, depression' (ibid.: 130). The film takes this disturbed state further by appropriating it to investigate the effect of art on his protagonist and, by extension, on viewers.

The protagonist in the film, Anna Manni (Asia Argento), is a policewoman afflicted by a 'malady' traceable to the Stendhal syndrome after a traumatic rape at the hands of a brutal and maniacal killer, Alfredo (Thomas Kretschsmann), who is also addicted to art (which acts as his bond with Anna). The syndrome is introduced through the psychiatrist Dr Cavanna (Paolo Bonacelli), who treats her after she exhibits symptoms derived from the trauma of brutal rape. Based on his readings to her from the text by Stendhal on his responses to the church and by the vertiginous symptoms described by him, the concept allows Argento to pursue his examination of connections between the appreciation of high and religious art to the mundane experiences of threatening encounters with the unknown and with a world of violence that afflicts commonplace characters. Indeed, the Botticelli, Caravaggio, Brueghel and Rembrandt paintings, as well as Anna's own paintings, serve to dramatise Anna's metamorphosis into a killer. They provide a language to visualise Anna's terror, confusion and rage inaccessible in the formulaic terms of everyday language but possibly understood through art.

Allegory in the Walter Benjaminian sense is evident throughout: in the choice of classical paintings to visualise Anna's vulnerability before and following the rape, her hair-cutting, her blonde wig, vaginal paintings and the image of the animated Devil with erect penis as she lies pinioned in the cave after the brutal rape. The final image of Anna overcome by the police and carried like a *Pietà* (an icon of the body of Christ) through the street, crowns the allegory, ambiguously positioning her as both killer and victim, and the viewer as partner to grief and mourning. Connections with the other arts, particularly cinema and painting, facilitate a retreat from story forms and a focus on the relationship between art and violent cruelty.

The Stendhal syndrome itself, interpreted and analysed by Graziella Magherini (1989) in her psychoanalytic study of art, is thus instrumental for Argento in his investigation of the relationship between visual art and violence. Anna's rape plays a critical role as a potent source of her derangement, one that involves her in further encounters with painting – her own and those of others. The two rape scenes of Anna and of the other victims are lurid and cruel. The spectator is forced to confront the sight of rape through the lens of sexually charged images of sadism and murder from the close range of the perpetrator, the victim and the viewer.

These scenes of cruelty similar to the image of Betty's (Cristina Marsillach) pinioned eyes in *Opera* implicate the viewer in looking at the sight of violence. As if portrayal of a rape is not enough to compel the spectators to shield their eyes, the raw scenes of torture with a razor, the grotesque shooting of the faces of the victim at the point of the rapist's orgasm, and the vaginal penetrations coupled to the copious amounts of spewing blood would qualify as being what Argento described 'as the most brutal movie I ever made' (Jones,

2004: 230). Argento asserted that he tried to 'engender the same accumulation of weird sensations and unsettling emotions in the audience that Anna is feeling' (ibid.: 230). The brutality of the film, involving rape, the uses of his daughter Asia and the bloody gruesome deaths, pales alongside the unanswered questions that the film raises concerning viewing the existence and sight of torture and violence. The cruelty as articulated in Artaud's writings involves acknowledging visions of the intolerable to produce sensations other than identification in confronting the intolerability of what is seen through unsettling perceptions.

ALLEGORY AND THE BAROQUE: THE THREE MOTHERS TRILOGY

In *Suspiria* (1977), one his most innovative, beautiful and successful films (Schneider, 2007: 96–7; Cooper, 2012: 75), Argento adopted a gothic supernatural form that continued in *Inferno* (1980) and culminated in *La terza madre/Mother of Tears* (2007). Allegory plays a significant role in the films. Argento draws on a range of sources: fairy tales, folk tales, English literature (notably De Quincy's *Confessions of an English Opium Eater*), Disney films, *La commedia/The Divine Comedy*, and expressionist art with its emphasis on extreme affect and violence, and generative of anxiety defined in Eugenie Brinkema's words as 'the creeping of the flesh' that she identifies 'as something that is a nothing, it is a not-yet nothing that churns' (2014: 187). Anxiety is an affect that is rarely invoked when it comes to the horrific, and yet it is often experienced as unsettling. The lighting in the film and its grotesque dreamlike scenarios are connected to images from history, legend and art as pedagogy of power and perversion. More than the other two films, *Suspiria* is reminiscent of German expressionism in its architecture, landscape, décor, and also in its emphasis on science and magic.

The casting of the teachers at the dance school is characteristic of Argento's use of famous actors in his films: in *Suspiria*, Joan Bennett of Hollywood fame, and the Italian star Alida Valli (also in *Inferno*), also identified with Hollywood cinema and with Alfred Hitchcock (in *The Paradine Case*, 1947). Argento's penchant for young protagonists is also evident in the trilogy, with Suzy Banyon (Jessica Harper) in *Suspiria*, Sarah (Eleanora Giorgi), Rose (Irene Miracle) and Mark (Leigh McClosky) in *Inferno*, and Sarah Mandy (Asia Argento) in *La terza madre*, suggesting a familiar generational divide in his films. The location of the three films is diverse: Germany, the United States and Italy. The phenomenon of witchcraft is further associated with the lower depths reminiscent of Dante's *Divine Comedy* but also allegorically of the human body (Cooper, 2012) and with this body is its violent destruction identified with the evil mother, the bad witch.

Argento's maternal figures, teachers and witches are brutalising, though they are also brutalised, and in the Three Mothers trilogy Argento includes benign maternal figures and witches. However, the trilogy especially qualifies for some critics as misogynistic wherein horror as a 'body genre' means that 'the body of the spectator is caught up in an almost involuntary mimicry of the emotion of sensation of the body on the screen' (Williams, 1995: 143). The witches in Argento's films are punished as monsters, freaks and castrating threats (Reich, 2001: 90-1), inviting a closer examination of the self-conscious uses of the medium as artifice through the operations of a camera, editing, and attention to clichés through colour, spaces and bodies.

Linda Williams and Jacqueline Reich suggest that the films mimic Argento's misogynist designs on his viewers. This view would reinforce Argento as a purveyor of decadence and sensationalism in his reliance on reproducing conditions of imitation, identification and unself-conscious affect. While such critics are aware of the artifice, special effects and operatic character of horror, their emphasis seems to be on the mimetic dimensions of violence and the material of cinema as real and influential through being fused within the body of woman. This position postulates a cinema that fails to distinguish Argento's distinctive contribution to a mode of cinema that does not merely stimulate emotion but, through formal and aesthetic strategies, incites the viewer to react not only viscerally and reductively but also intellectually.

By contrast to Williams and Reich, Linda Schulte-Sasse (2002) comments on the aesthetics of *Suspiria*'s sheer specularity as invoking a different view that bypasses gendered representation. The film invites a mode other than narrative of viewing as an enactment of movement through space. Throughout this film, as well as the other two of the trilogy, albeit differently in each case, the viewer is held captive by image and sound; each movement from space to space is experienced more aesthetically than in narrative terms (Schulte-Sasse, 2002). The death of the victim, as is the case in the student Pat's (Eva Axén) death in *Suspiria*, vies with the graphic design of the art deco architecture. The intensity of her (and the viewer's) emotion 'is subsumed by the laws of aesthetics that literally *reduce* her to an *objet d'art*, and our reception shifts wildly from the closeness of identification to the pleasure of aesthetic distance – a pleasure that is disinterested in a very different sense than that meant by Kant' (Schulte-Sasse, 2002).

I infer this disinterest as contributing to Artaud's violent reaction against representation and his call for 'ocular destruction' as a social act that seems to inhere in the Argento syndrome. The milieu of the trilogy belongs, as indicated above in, conceptions of the baroque, or of the 'neo-baroque' as characterised by Deleuze in *The Fold* as a fusion of the 'most diverse environments and periods of time' (Deleuze, 1993: x), and by Walter Benjamin as an obsession with the pervasiveness of evil, the 'blackness of the soul . . . the literal hell which haunts Baroque reflexes' (Benjamin, 1977: 18). Benjamin's *The Origins of German Tragic Drama* offers variants on the world of the tyrant through theatrical forms. In Argento, the assaults on cinematic representation function to radically de-realise inherited images of the world. The Argento syndrome is a theatre of cruelty to attack commonplace reality, challenging the spectator to participate in, not merely passively view, the nature and consequences of torture and death. His experimentations with cinematic forms are akin to 'baroque effects to render death and terror visible' (Canova, 2003: 108).

The viewer is invited to be attentive to the images of violence projected rather than becoming immersed in them. The film thrusts the viewer into the interior of vision in which images overflow, dilate or explode. This implosion produces uneasiness for the spectator concerning space and time, an essential element of the baroque 'which is less in the film itself than in the analyst's eye' (Thoret, 2002: 111). The attribution of the gaze tends to fractionate among the different elements, camera position, distance, lighting and conflict between instruments and body parts. The experience of viewing emanates from the numerous folds of space, time, décor, tableau and hallucination.

Argento's treatment of milieus in this trilogy can be compared to Deleuze's description of the experience of the baroque as 'neither falling into nor emerging from illusion but rather *realizing* something in illusion itself' (Deleuze, 1993: 125). The baroque protagonists are 'prey to the giddiness of minute perceptions, they endlessly reach presence in illusion, in vanishment, in swooning, or by converting illusion into presence . . . but that presence is hallucinatory' (ibid.: 125).

The persistence of close-ups of eyes in Argento's films is not merely another instance of self-referentiality but intimately connected to challenges to prevailing conceptions of the world purveyed through art and other contemporary media technologies, most notably through cinema but also in television. However, for Argento, 'television is the literal nightmare of cinema' (Thoret, 2002: 130), not only in its censoring practices but even more its mundane view of the world, emblematic 'in the murderous figure of the television talk show as well as in the censuring role of formulaic fixed patterns' (ibid.: 129–30). The brutality of his cinema addresses a world that has become exceedingly violent and clichéd and that reductively blames media for this state of affairs. Hence, Argento's allegories insert gore into the world both of sitcoms and of popular psychology to unsettle commonsensical theories about sadistic voyeurism and the assumption that the viewer cannot distinguish between art and life (Cooper, 2012).

CONCLUSION

Rather than presenting himself as a filmmaker who remains committed to traditional cinema by waging a war against incursions by new technologies,

Argento's experimentation with special effects by way of digital technology is situated in an interface between cinematic and digital modes, with his fascination for 'special effects' as a dominant feature of his balancing act between spectacle and reflection. Commenting on surrealism as an earlier form of treating internal states and his use of computer graphics, Argento has said:

> Surrealism used to be hard to put on film properly. Although I was reti-cent about it at first, computer graphics allow me to depict my extreme dreams and dark fantasies. Exploding heads, slicing up bodies – it's all easy to show today. It's hard to come to terms with the thought that you are only limited by your imagination when it comes to what you can achieve visually using today's technical tools. (Jones, 2004: 230)

Digital technology enables Argento to probe the boundaries between the real and the fantasmatic on behalf of reconfiguring history and memory. His emphasis on an excess of vision is enhanced through the opportunities afforded by the union of cinema and digital media, furthering his commitment to a Pasolinian cinema of poetry that has marked his work (Koven, 2006: 156–7). The poetic potential of digital effects in *La sindrome di Stendhal* is evident in the painterly composition of the scenes that portray Anna's dis-turbances, but also in the dark and cruel poetry of her role as victim, then as aggressor. His work with SFX specialist Sergio Stivaletti does not strive for realism. His special effects invite the spectator to experience art in another dimension through foregrounding the potential of the image to reimagine the world rather than to reanimate realism.

The Argento sublime does not fall into the utopian or dystopian forms common to critical writings on the technological sublime. They are investiga-tions of cinema – television at times – animating and unsettling institutional and cinematic clichés concerning violence and wanton brutality in all its forms. Argento's uses of media are predicated on the importance of actively engaging his viewers in experiencing and contemplating the horrors displayed. Through riddles, deadly games, he fuses older cinematic forms with current digitalised ones, conventional genre forms and avant-garde styles, and nightmares of sex-uality and violence in the midst of everyday banality gone amuck. His baroque sensibility as identified by critics (as well as by himself) might be understood as existing in a fourth world where thoughts of infinity give rise (not always felici-tously) to reflections on the body, on the senses, on organic and inorganic life, and on violence and power evoked through experimentation with the changing properties of media and their effects.

BIBLIOGRAPHY

Abel, R. (1988), *French Film Theory and Criticism: A History/Anthology*, Princeton: Princeton University Press.

Artaud, A. (1976), *Antonin Artaud: Selected Writings*, Berkeley: University of California Press.

Barber, S. (2004), *Artaud: The Screaming Body*, London: Creation Books.

Benjamin, W. (1977), *The Origin of German Tragic Drama*, London: Verso.

Bertellini, G. (2004a), 'Introduction', in Bertellini, G. (ed.), *The Cinema of Italy*, London: Wallflower, pp. 1–9.

Bertellini, G. (2004b), 'Profondo Rosso/Deep Red', in Bertellini, G. (ed.), *The Cinema of Italy*, London: Wallflower, pp. 213–25.

Bondanella, P. (2009), *A History of Italian Film*, New York: Continuum Press.

Brinkema, E. (2014), *The Forms of the Affects*, Durham, NC: Duke University Press.

Canova, G. (2003), 'La sindrome del sublime: Poetica dell' eccesso e deriva del sguardo, L'ultimo Argento', in Carluccio, G., Manzoli, G. and Menarini, R. (eds), *L'eccesso della visione: Il cinema di Dario Argento*, Turin: Lindau.

Cooper, L. A. (2012), *Dario Argento*, Urbana: University of Illinois Press.

Deleuze, G. (1986), *Cinema 1: The Movement-Image*, Minneapolis: University of Minnesota Press.

Deleuze, G. (1993), *The Fold: Leibniz and the Baroque*, Minneapolis: University of Minnesota Press.

Frayling, C. (1981), *Spaghetti Westerns: Cowboys and Europeans from Karl May to Sergio Leone*, London: Routledge & Kegan Paul.

Gallant, C. (2001), *Art of Darkness: The Cinema of Dario Argento*, Godalming: FAB Press.

Gramsci, A. (1985), *Selections from Cultural Writings*, Forgacs, D. and Nowell-Smith, G. (eds), Cambridge, MA: Harvard University Press.

Gramsci, A. (1977), *Quaderni del carcere*, 4 vols,Turin: Einaudi.

Hawkins, J. (2000), *Cutting Edge: Art Horror and the Horrific Avant-Garde*, Minneapolis: University of Minnesota.

Hughes, H. (2011), *Cinema Italiano: The Complete Guide from Classics to Cult*, London: I. B. Tauris.

Jones, A. (2004), *Profondo Argento: The Man, The Myths & the Magic*, Godalming: FAB Press.

Knee, A. (1996), 'Gender, Genre, Argento', in Grant, B. K. (ed.), *Dread of Difference: Gender and the Horror Film*, Austin: University of Texas Press, pp. 213–30.

Koven, M. J. (2006), *La dolce morte: Vernacular Cinema and the Italian Giallo Film*, Lanham, MD: Scarecrow Press.

Landy, M. (2008), *Stardom Italian Style*, Bloomington: Indiana University Press.

Magherini, G. (1989), *La sindrome di Stendhal*, Florence: Ponte alle grazie.

Nerenberg, E. (2012), *Murder Made in Italy: Homicide, Media, and Contemporary Italian Culture*, Bloomington: Indiana University Press.

Past, E. (2012), *Methods of Murder: Beccarian Introspection and Lombrosian Vivisection in Italian Crime Fiction*, Toronto: University of Toronto Press.

Powell, A. (2012), 'Dario Argento and Deleuze's Cinematic Sensorium', in Allmer, P., Brick, E. and Hurley, D. (eds), *European Nightmares: Horror Cinema in Europe Since 1945*, London: Wallflower, pp. 167–81.

Reich, J. (2001), 'The Mother of all Horror: Witches, Gender, and the Films of Dario Argento', in Jewell, K. (ed.), *Monsters in the Italian Literary Imagination*, Detroit: Wayne State University Press, pp. 89–109.

Ricci, S., *Cinema and Fascism: Italian Films and Society, 1922–1943*, Berkeley: University of California Press.

Schneider, S. J. (2007), *100 European Horror Films*, London: BFI.

Schulte-Sasse, L. (2002), 'The "Mother" of all Horror Movies: Dario Argento's *Suspiria* (1977)', *Kinoeye: New Perspectives in European Film,* Vol. 2, Issue 11, 10 June 2002, www.kinoeye.org/02/11/schultesasse11.php.

Smuts, A. (2002), 'The Principles of Association: Dario Argento's *Deep Red* (1975),' *Kinoeye: New Perspectives in European Film*, Vol. 2, Issue 11, 10 June 2002, www.kinoeye.org/02/11/smuts11.php.

Thoret, J. B. (2002), *Dario Argento: Magicien de la peur*, Paris: Cahiers du cinéma.

Wagstaff, C. (1996), 'Cinema', in Forgacs, D. and Lumley, R. (eds), *Italian Cultural Studies: An Introduction*, Oxford: Oxford University Press, pp. 216–33.

Williams, L. (1995), 'Film Bodies: Gender, Genre, and Excess', in Grant, B. K. (ed.), *Film Genre Reader II*, Austin: University of Texas Press, pp. 15–34.

Wood, M. P (2005), *Italian Cinema*, New York: Berg.

7. SCRAP METAL, STAINS, CLOGGED DRAINS: ARGENTO'S REFUSE AND ITS REFUSALS

Karl Schoonover

It is a cliché to title a critical account of horror with a list of things.[1] Things such as those that precede the colon in my title announce the uncanny role given to them and the expressive hyperbole granted objects by horror diegesis. What I find interesting about this titular evocation of horror's things is that the books and essays they announce rarely address these objects themselves. Instead, horror's things are pretexts for a discussion of the unique affective registers of horror or its exuberant corporeality. This essay will attempt to account for things in the *giallo* and horror films made by Dario Argento during the first decade of his directorial career, widely regarded as his canonical period. In what follows, I largely bracket the infamously wasted bodies of those iconic films in order to allow the matter that populates Argento's *mise-en-scène* to come to the fore. I argue that this imagery in Argento is ecological, if by ecology we mean the study of the interplay of organisms, things and the world, or – as the Garzanti dictionary puts it – 'science that studies the relations between living beings and the surroundings in which they live'.[2]

Is there not something ecological in Argento's camera lingering on still spaces marked by the presence of their former occupant? Objects describe the past life of these places, like the ground level close-up of a cigarette butt in an abandoned city square in Argento's 1971 slasher thriller *Quattro mosche di velluto grigio/Four Flies on Grey Velvet*. Or the limp streamers and confetti in a theatre trashed by a party that has just ended in the same film. The camera discovers this latter detritus only moments before fixing on a dead body strewn among it. So then a sense of the ecological emerges not just in the actual image of waste but also in its treatment, in the camera's refusal to treat it as refuse. This ecological awareness is signalled in the discussion of polluted waters in the film's scene at the fishing shack, and moreover in the seemingly odd prominence given to the shack's patchy walls, which come to dominate the frame for a few seconds and which are later echoed in the grime-stained city wall. The management of things as a form of mere waste management is in this sense refused by Argento's imagery. Another example: the floor of a laboratory mottled by marks from shoes and accumulated dirt in Argento's 1971 *Il gatto a nove code/Cat o' Nine Tails*. The lighting accentuates black scuffs, a compositional emphasis that equally reflects the overuse and institutionalised neglect of these spaces and also allows the random graphic patterns of these marks to take up space in the centre of the frame. In *Il vicino di casa/The Neighbour* (1973), a short film produced as part of the series *La porta sul buio/Door into the Darkness* made for RAI television, the discovery of a large stain that comes to dominate the otherwise empty walls of a vacation rental confirms the fears of its new occupants that the general dirtiness of the place is both insanitary and an indication of something gone deeply wrong.

Argento's imagery not only aestheticises waste; his films depend upon waste to make their images cinematic. After Argento's more famous trademark blood and gore, this attention to filth and grime grants the images of these films their cinematic quality. Take, for example, the field of smudged fingerprints revealed by backlighting a windowpane (*Il gatto a nove code*) or the spirals of petrol on wet black pavement revealed in an aerial shot of a car leaving a parking lot in *La bambola/The Doll* (another episode of *La porta sul buio*). In both instances, residue takes visual prominence in the image. It does so for the purposes of narrative evidence and formal experimentation; residue furthermore reveals a lived relationship between things and humans. Residue confronts us with the odd reality in modernity that things dominate humans; humans are servants to things. The Argento image confronts its viewer with that reality (often by leaving that viewer to contemplate scenes of the aftermath of a human life subjugated to things). In doing so, his films are ecological to the degree that they engage with the material impact of human life on the world, as well as in how they reveal domination of the environment leading to the eventual contraction of human living. While never overtly political, these films nevertheless provoke a political thinking by way of confronting their viewer, through a re-formation of that viewer's perspective on the physicality of the world via a kind of aesthetic agitation.[3] By subtly and persistently asking their viewers to experience the skewing of the presumed hierarchy between humans and things, these films point to the consequences of what we now call the anthropocene, prompting a series of questions, not the least of which is: Is it ever possible to live cleanly, purely, without a trace?

With these examples in mind, I ask what Argento's filmic engagements with debris would look like if film theory took seriously horror's meditations on matter. What would his waste imagery mean if we were to regard his images of waste as nothing more than and nothing less than stuff? In other words, what if we were to take their stuff as stuff? In what follows, I embark on that project. It means a departure from how objects have been treated in much horror theory, but it also involves an extension of some of the better critical engagements with Italian horror cinema. Mikel J. Koven argues that Italian horror is marked by 'an ambivalence toward modernity' (Koven, 2003). The genre expresses this ambivalence via its *mise-en-scène*, particularly in its equivocal depictions of 'modernity's accoutrements and creature comforts' (Koven, 2003), or what we might call modernity's things, its stuff. The fact that *giallo* killers often appropriate everyday objects as brutal weapons is, for Koven, an example of how the genre turns 'modernity's stuff back onto its consumers'. While Koven's approach could be enhanced by greater attention to contextual detail, I am intrigued by how his polemic suggests that in order to understand these films as more than simply reactionary or regressive texts, we must remain attentive to how they 'open up a discursive space wherein modernity itself can be discussed and critiqued'. What goes unremarked upon in Koven's approach, and what is worth emphasising here, is how the sites of this opening up in horror more generally are typically *mise-en-scène* elements: otherwise innocent objects acquiring a nefarious prominence (candlestick, kitchen knife), backgrounds that stop being only backgrounds (walls come to life, cobwebs in the face), environments glowing with force (latent historical repressions, toxic waste). Argento's films cite these generic conventions of *mise-en-scène* while amplifying the vitality and agency of the inanimate even more so than is typical for the genre. At first glance, stuff appears both over-accumulated in the Argento image and over-burdened by that image. It exceeds narrative economy: there is too much of it and it means too much.

Taking a closer look at these films' infatuation with detritus, the peculiar materialism of the late twentieth century comes into focus, one that marks a shift in the perceived relationship of human living to the material world, a consequential reordering of the give and take between life and things. This is why it is crucial for us to understand Argento's imagery as persisting in its depiction of things as *things*, as opposed to things as symbols, metonyms or totems. His imagery also anticipates the new materialism of contemporary theory, and it does so by exploring the inaccessibility of truly clean surfaces, the impossibility of absolute emptiness, the unobtainability of visual quiet. It does all of this by way of twentieth-century modernity's quintessential documentarian: the cinematic image. As if in response to consumer capitalism's own increasingly cluttered *mise-en-scène*, the Argento image opens itself to a different profilmic by focusing on waste as the site in the *mise-en-scène* able to respond to the illusory security offered by *il boom*, 'the economic miracle' or period of post-war prosperity when the standard of living and quality of life appeared to improve for the majority of Italians. A politics of waste thus emerges in Argento's films from this period. This politics of waste complicates conventional accounts of Italian horror as favouring hyper-stylisation over substantive content, or as one recent BBC Four documentary would have it, as making all else 'totally subordinate to style'.[4] Giorgio Bertellini writes that critics and scholars have regarded Argento's 'sumptuous cinematic virtuosity as something of a stylistic exercise unworthy of in-depth analysis'.[5] Working against such dismissals, I will argue that in these films waste registers a shifting relationship between the human and the non-human worlds.

This short essay should be understood to offer provocations rather than final conclusions about Argento. It hopes to prompt a fuller accounting of how his films potentially register a historically specific account of the socio-political nature of materiality. In this spirit of provocation, I offer eight tenets to describe what waste does *for* Argento's film image. I have posed each of these tenets in the negative for two reasons. On the one hand, I want to differentiate Argento's image of waste from other modernist and post-modernist appropriations of refuse, and in particular from the conventional means of reading those appropriations. These tenets each respond to (and unsettle) what I see as a different conventional means of reading images of waste, refuse, the leftover, the neglected surface, the soiled space.

On the other hand, proceeding by negation responds in kind to the challenge posed by Argento's image of waste. If we accept that challenge, I argue, then we must resist our urge to see waste's meaning as immediately graspable and assignable to the world as it is known and lived. That challenge is only distinct in its meanings when we accept its refusals of the known world and that world's accounting of value. Here waste's value (or negative values) does not arise from an autonomous realm outside the film and the film's aesthetic realisation. Encountering the world through negation is then what Argento's image of waste asks us to do. Argento asks us not to decide in advance how to assign meaning to difference. My process of definition through negation attempts therefore to contend with Argento's aesthetic intervention by negation into the politics of how lives, things and even matter itself are organised in the latter days of the anthropocene.

1. *Waste in Argento is not a passageway to a modernist abandonment of representation.*
Quattro mosche di velluto grigio ends by slowing down the movement of a gruesome car accident. In its exuberantly aesthetic meditation on the formal properties of the shattering of glass and crushing of metal, this decelerated crash would seem to offer the viewer a harrowing glimpse of modernity's consequences for the human subject. Debris comes to crowd out the image,

consuming the human form, fracturing compositional cohesion, and obstruct-
ing the recognisability of things as things, objects as useful items. This
sequence echoes one of art cinema's most modernist passages from two years
prior: the detonation montage in Michelangelo Antonioni's *Zabriskie Point*
(1970), which begins with the repetition of explosions from the demolition
of a luxury modernist home and then proceeds slowly through the explosion
of various household objects (a refrigerator, groceries, television sets). Like
Quattro mosche di velluto grigio, Antonioni's film emphasises its protracted
engagement with shattered stuff by using a non-diegetic choral orchestration.

It would be easy to read Argento's similarity to Antonioni here as evidence of
a hyper-formalism growing in Italian cinema across the 1960s and 1970s.[6] This
perspective is anticipatory (and I would argue, presumptive) of the art cinema
image's modernism. According to many standard accounts of the aesthetics
of this period's cinema, the film image pulls away from the representational
imperative of photographic media and towards an abstraction that is more
painterly or expressionist. Auteur theory, another dominant critical paradigm
of the late twentieth century, and one often used in concert with or to support
the modernist thesis, would regard these moments as flourishes that index the
individual genius of an artist. Argento's excess would be said to proclaim
the director's status as more than just a work-a-day horror director guided
by commercial interests: his explosion instead would be seen to piggyback
on Antonioni's demolition aesthetics, borrowing not only Antonioni's style
but also his status as an auteur. For these accounts, things are anything
but things.

As I have argued elsewhere about waste in Antonioni, however, the introduction of debris into the image is as much about political engagement with
the nature of materiality as it is a move away from figuration or stylistic icono-
clasm (Schoonover, 2012). And if our hermeneutics continue to lean on one
or both of these two dominant perspectives – modernist or auteurist – then we
risk losing track of an emerging dialogue in post-war Italian film, a dialogue
about value and use in late capitalism that gets articulated in the images of
these films.

*2. Waste is not about excess in any typical fashion in Argento. Its presence in
the image denotes neither a surfeit of style nor an overindulgent aestheticism.*
Kristin Thompson's pioneering account of excess in cinema suggests excess
exists in all films but is by nature something that we don't see at first because
traditional narrative systems ask us to look past anything irrelevant to story,
making us inattentive to anything lacking a narrative role (Thompson, 1986).
Finding excess, a critical viewing practice Thompson endorses for insight
it can offer to scholars of film style, thus requires watching the same film
several times. Once we are acclimatised to a film's story, the narrative system's

hold on our attention is loosened and we can see other facets of the film's aesthetics.

In Thompson's definition, excess is in tension with story. Form therefore remains subservient to content. Things are messier in Argento. His excesses are not so easily reined in by story, which is itself often opaque in its structure. His excesses would in fact be hard to miss even in a first viewing. This unruly or exuberant formalism mixed with an intensely expressive *mise-en-scène* is termed by one account as 'operatic excess', which the same critic goes on to define as Argento's nearly 'pornographic' stylisation of violence and his 'expressionist' style which is 'symbolic . . . at the expense of cinematographic realism' and characterised by 'extreme colours and overwrought images' that are 'over-the-top' (Gracey, 2010: 20–1). This begs the question: in films where form and content are already loosened from the strictures of classical Hollywood narration, is it fair to label his image excessive?

In his important analysis of *Tenebre* (1982), Michael Siegel argues that Argento's images formally interrogate space in a way that 'persuades us to take Argento's rather schlocky genre films seriously as a form of social critique' (Siegel, 2015: 4). Siegel reads *Tenebre* 'as a *socio-spatial* artefact, that is, as a text that is thoroughly marked by the whole set of shifting social, economic, and geographic realities of its contemporary moment . . . the particular moment [that] we now commonly refer to as neoliberalism, a new global order of capitalism that would repurpose the progressive values of mid-century social movements' (Siegel, 2015: 3). Siegel, however, is more precise than Koven in describing how the film enacts its critique of modernity. He provides an exposition of this 'artefact' and its historiographical interventions; in doing so he retains the cinematic image's specificity. What interests him is the exactitude of the image's contents, 'not what it states through metaphor or misdirection but what it draws our attention to in its very actuality and particularity' (Siegel, 2015: 2).[7] Siegel concludes that Argento's films 'can be usefully seen as histories of the present in that they make visible certain emergent or even pre-emergent aspects of actively lived, contemporaneous experience' (Siegel, 2015: 4). The point here is not simply that the film supplies precise 'histories of the present' but also that the present requires a precise kind of history to be told (Siegel, 2015: 4). From this perspective, *Tenebre* and Argento's other films of this period testify to the profound shifts that result from the market economy's infiltration of all areas of life and its totalising desire to reconcile all to its system of value.

3. *Argento's waste image does not manifest the post-modern sublime.*
Over the last ten years many humanities scholars have found in wastelands the site of a post-modern sublime. In a special issue of *PMLA* on garbage, for example, Patricia Yaeger writes '. . . trash has become a material for

enacting the exultations of an older sublime. The feelings of aesthetic election that used to come from excursions through the Simplon Pass now come from confronting residue' (Yaeger, 2008: 330–1). Yaeger goes on to describe the aestheticisation of trash in late twentieth-century art and literature as 'the sublime never-endingness of spent objects' (336). This is a sublime in which the unfathomable scale of waste in the landscape overwhelms the subject as a form of affective assault.

In an essay on Argento subtitled 'the poetics of excess', film scholar Gianni Canova hails Argento's aesthetic as the 'new frontier of the sublime', describing the affective impact of his images on the viewer in terms very similar to Yaeger's post-modernist sublime of the trash heap (Canova, 2003: 106). Argento uses images, he writes, 'not so much for their meaning, as for the phonetic and rhythmic effects that they evoke. It is impossible to think of submitting Argento to a "realistic" reading: his hyperrealism is by now so extreme and – at the same time – so extoled, so far from any even vague notion of "verisimilitude", as to make his cinema a ludic device for the production of unrelenting jolts and agitation' (Canova, 2003: 106).

In both accounts the disruptive sublime grounds the subject's sense of her apartness from the image, which even in its impact seems removed from her world. This apartness offers the optical equivalent of a *cordon sanitaire*. Argento's work offers a crucial corrective here. His objects of waste never appear spent and his piled debris is rarely shown contained. Trying to identify boundaries between stuff and humans in Argento is a futile endeavour. Like the stain in *Il vicino* mentioned above, the never-ending explosions of Victoriana and art nouveau accoutrements in *Suspiria* (1977) or the visually symphonic clouds of dust from encrusted air vents in *Inferno* (1980), wasted matter never appears fully dead; it is inexhaustibly contaminating. Its potency cannot be banished or abjected. In Argento's worlds, a *cordon sanitaire* is not an option.

4. *Waste is not refused by Argento's optic. It is not the repressed that returns.* Slavoj Žižek argues that most in the Global North live within an optique, or a perceptual regime, that vigilantly removes trash from our view through both infrastructural and illusory (ideological) means. According to Žižek,[8] before we even see refuse it has been refused for us. A major achievement of modernity has been its ability not just to transport our trash away from our bodies, homes and cities, but moreover to fully absent the true spectre of our trash heap from what is discernible in the world. In a sense waste has never gone away. It is around us always and yet we can't see it.

Argento's visual narration behaves in the opposite manner of the optic that Žižek describes. Waste in Argento's world is defiantly visible. It refuses to go unnoticed, and for that reason we might align Argento's camera with the task that Siegfried Kracauer sets for the medium of cinema: the redemption of physical reality through the reorientation of sight toward those things and views otherwise cast aside. For Kracauer the cinematic medium enacts its true essence when its images confront us with sights we are otherwise predisposed not to see. Interestingly, Kracauer chooses our visual relationship to garbage to explain cinema's redemption of reality. Under the heading 'The Refuse', he writes: 'Most people turn their backs on garbage cans, the dirt underfoot, the waste they leave behind. Films have no such inhibitions; on the contrary, what we ordinarily prefer to ignore proves attractive to them precisely because of this common neglect' (Kracauer, 1996: 54). For Kracauer, the camera's promiscuous love for all things, its inability to filter as Žižek's subject's gaze would, is reflected in the indexical images that it creates. Argento's camera is not immune to the automatic registration of contingencies unintended to be recorded. It picks up dust and debris inadvertently as most photographic lenses do. Argento's lens promiscuously loves the physical world as much as Kracauer's mythic cinematic apparatus. Yet the most 'intentioned' elements of Argento's images also work to refuse the optique of refuse. The most stylised and famous of Argento's images appear to bask in an unwillingness to separate the useful and vital from the wasted and inert. Waste is not simply that which is refused, and diegetic looking rarely seems able to evade waste's presence.

Argento's films work to make the viewer feel the unfamiliarity of both what is all around us and what is just underfoot. In the words of the film *Inferno*: 'The key is under the soles of your shoes.' The everyday is the location of horror. And yet in Argento's films, waste does not proclaim the indexical features of the image any more than does any other image. Waste does not point to some fuller profilmic reality that has been overlooked by our habituated patterns of seeing.

Tenebre opens with the narration reading from the pages of a new *giallo* novel just published in the fictional world. This narration sets the terms for the film, suggesting that for the psychopath violence supplies a means of psychological relief. Killing offers an apparent liberation from internal and external sources of oppression.[9] The film's title, which references a Holy Week service involving the extinguishing of candles, when considered alongside this opening narration raises the issue of transcendence: can redemption be achieved through annihilation? However, as the film progresses we discover such transcendence remains elusive. Violence appears as a ritual that aims at annihilation but always fails to achieve total disposal. Through exuberant spectacles of violence, including set pieces depicting messy eruptions of the insides of bodies and walls sprayed with expressionist splashes of blood, the film forces its spectators to confront the impossibility of the psychopathic murderer's plans for cleaning up. Even as its body count rises quickly in the final scene, and as we begin to sense that the film will eliminate every character we have met, the film also reminds us of how complete disposal remains impossible. This refusal of negation joins metaphysical injunction to political intervention. Siegel thus finds in the film's 'quantity and intensity of violence . . . a kind of political allegory at play[,] where the terrifying, random excess . . . actually figures the opaque, esoteric structures of unleashed global capitalism under neoliberalism' (Siegel, 2015: 12). The film's most striking images aren't simply gore-for-gore's-sake or flamboyant overindulgences of style; instead these images visualise the hubris of any individual's attempt to fully sweep away the world, to barricade themselves against the relations of lived existence.

Another self-reflexive narration is spoken in a scene leading up to *Tenebre*'s bloody conclusion. The film's protagonist, best-selling *giallo* novelist Peter Neal, is discussing his theory of murder investigation with a police detective. As he continues, he quotes *The Hound of the Baskervilles*: 'When you've eliminated the impossible, whatever remains, however improbable, must be the truth.' A moment later Neal continues, paraphrasing, 'So weird, unbelievable but possible. That's what we have to find. Truth is always possible.' Of course, Neal is flirting with danger here, taunting the investigator to discover clues to his own identity as the killer. So perhaps he proposes this approach as a red herring, and yet narrationally these statements ring true, perhaps confirming the viewer's suspicion of his guilt. This guidance is not unrelated to the optical imperatives of waste. For Neal's Doyle, truth resides in the overlooked, the neglected and the remainder. This epistemology thus echoes the idea of detritus's unwillingness to remain hidden, its refusal to be refuse. If we compare these two competing mottoes that the film narrates (standing as bookends of the narrative), one is about the truth of the remnant, and the other asserts the insanity of thinking it is impossible to get past the remnant. The improbability of that truth makes it all the more persistent and important.

5. Waste in Argento signals neither imagistic fullness nor total emptiness.
Many Argento films use waste to raise the question of the film image's representational capacities. However, what look like empty corners, lonely alleys, abandoned locations and barren wastelands are not always as vacant or as unstructured as they may first seem. In her work on British cinema, Charlotte Brunsdon proposes a history of cinematic empty spaces, suggesting that they 'are places of both narrative and analytic possibility' (219). Brunsdon apprehends emptiness in specific sites: 'urban wastelands' and 'bombsites: cleared ground, ruined houses, debris' (221, 225). Her key examples are post-war and post-industrial urban London locations in films from the second half of the twentieth century. Italian film history offers obvious parallels, whether by way of neorealism's bombed-out cities or Antonioni's toxic swamps. Landscape in many horror films also echoes

atomic disaster and the wounds of post-industrialism.[10] Argento's films are no exception.

However, Brunsdon also understands these empty spaces as historical in a very specific sense. They are not simply historiographic in a conventional sense of evidencing past traumas and neglect. Empty spaces carry an 'unregulated, liminal quality [. . .] unidentifiable and transitory' (220). For Brunsdon, emptied landscapes address the post-war spectator as spaces of immanence, since they appear devoid of things, people and governmental control (228). One of their allures is that they offer places where 'ordinary rules don't quite apply' (224). Thus, cinema renders these places as spaces ripe for a new order, whether neoliberalising or even simply property development. Brunsdon suggests how emplacement participates in (and is determined by) what we might call a political economy, and she calls our attention to the role played by emptiness in this system. Emptiness can be seen as both a space that needs controlling and governing, and as a space of opportunity. Emptiness becomes a ripe space. Rather than geographically open to anything, it is instead receptively open(ed) to a predetermined set of particular possibilities. It is this context of double immanence that I would suggest Argento's aesthetics addresses. His imagining of waste asks whether there can ever be a truly unregulated image, a proper emptiness without the anticipation of value lost, restored and capitalised upon. His films attempt to *image* a kind of empty space without immanence. Such a space, consciously designed or not, might allow for a rethinking of post-war economics.

Given the many examples of emptiness in Argento, including the barrenness of many of his compositions and their refusal to provide narrative information, we might initially mistake such shots as attempting to figure the empty image. Instead they are working towards two rather different, opposite but concurrent goals. First, Argento's nearly emptied images pose metaphysical questions: Can nothingness be imaged in a photographic image? Can any image be truly empty and still be an image? Can the cinematic image hold emptiness? As Brunsdon notes, empty spaces bear the mark of 'hesitation in the cinematic image' (221). With Argento's waste image, this becomes amplified and thus directly raises questions about the nature of cinematic image-capture: what can be held in the image? What should be and should not be included within cinema's frame? It asks what it means to take something ineffable in the world and make it *matter*. Second, Argento's nearly emptied images raise questions, as Brunsdon's arguments might suggest, about the politics of offering up space as empty. By raising the question of what it means to capture something in the image, Argento's waste begins to propose an *ethics* of the image. It asks what it means to grasp otherness, without trying to reconcile it to a known value system or render it useful.

6. Otherness surfaces in waste, but waste itself refuses to perform as otherness, per se.

The opening of *Inferno* operates almost as a collection of horror film's expect-ant gestures of peeling back surfaces. Entering the cluttered space of an antique shop, looking beneath a curtain, going under the stairs, descending into a cellar, exploring the city's underground spaces. As in gothic horror, surfaces almost always give way in *Inferno* to the waking world's underbelly. Ordinarily, in the horror film, when the camera overtly confronts a solid surface, that surface eventually gives way. The typical surface in horror introduces the uncertainty of the unknown, the heaviness of its otherness – like all those walls of book-shelves in *Scooby Doo*. But as with that programme's familiar bookshelves, that which is behind and/or beneath often gets explained as less menacing or unsettling than was first imagined. A hidden passage is revealed, opening to a space already known to us or whose character is, whether banal or significant to the narrative, in any case far from supernatural. As many historians describe it, Italian horror and *giallo* may seem to draw on the gothic but their horror derives from the everyday.[11] We can see this in the following of a leak as the opening scene of *Inferno* continues. Unlike in *Scooby Doo*, though, the revela-tion of the quotidian doesn't insulate the viewer from the menacing qualities of otherness. In this sense, following the path of the leak may have more in common with Antonioni's methodical long takes that follow water leaking from an abandoned water barrel during the experimental ending of *L'eclisse/ L' Eclisse* (1962). It is the upending and unmooring of movement from narra-tive agency or meaning that makes these sequences so disruptive. Even the final revelation of a tangle of horrific floating corpses in the *Inferno* sequence, while climactic, doesn't add up to much narratively.

7. Argento's waste image isn't a critique of consumerism's apocalyptic after-math but of its central gestures of acquisition and accumulation, such as owning, needing, monetising and hoarding.

Late capitalism's totalising prevalence makes it difficult to recognise the utility in things that don't have market value, in qualities that don't amount to any profit, in experiences that can't be measured, and in relations that can't be monetised or reproduce what is monetisable. Any object, experience or desire without a price tag and therefore a payoff remains illegible and almost unrec-ognisable. We are perpetually discouraged from granting such phenomena any space in our lives. They should be ignored, disavowed, abjected, left behind, quarantined or simply tossed away.

The conventional discourses of waste partake in the process that blinds us to value other than exchange value. Argento's waste imagery offers an interim step between recognising alternative sites of value and being able to account for them outside the terms of an exchange economy. This imagery doesn't offer a substitute value system, or even an alternative semantics per se. It does offer an experience, a set of fixations, spectacles, affects and interrogations that work towards opening up an affective space in our imaginations where the presently non-useful might regain its utility, a space from which new systems of value might therefore emerge.

The afterlife of stuff in Argento is not simply a screed against our impending peril at the hands of a materialist world. It is more importantly an exploration of the consequences of a kind of possessiveness, of holding onto something too long, of trying to own the other. And as with *L'eclisse*'s ending, *Inferno* uses abandoned things, soiled surfaces and stains to remind us of the consequence of incessant grabbing and of what that grabbing forecloses. Is there a way to grasp (apprehend) the other without grabbing or capturing it? Without demanding its possession? The films of both Antonioni and Argento can be seen as posing these questions alongside their pursuit of an antipositivist mode of making photographic images. In other words, can one make images without capturing something?

8. *Crucially, however, the otherness of Argento's waste does not raise the spectacle of absence that psychoanalysis associates with gender/sex difference.* Queer bodies populate Argento's films in ways that a cursory critical consideration might deem homophobic. The figure of the queer emerges as a stand-in for waste itself. *Profondo rosso* draws concordances between a queer and garbage in brutal fashion, as when the long mechanical retrieving hook of a refuse truck accidentally grabs onto the film's homosexual Carlo and then drags him along the road to his death like just another piece of the truck's scrap metal load. This positioning of sex/gender otherness as waste can be troubling to encounter in these films. Queer bodies, such as the one at the end of *Profondo rosso,* may in fact be shown to be interchangeable with refuse and with other things deemed useless by the diegetic world. But as we have seen, detritus is not exactly equivalent with the absence of worth in Argento's universe.

Tenebre poses the question of homosexuality as a form of waste when, in the film, a literary critic asks the protagonist, Peter Neal, about his book's focus on perversion. The critic himself is coded by the film as gay, and his articulation of the words like 'deviant' and 'perversion' suggest an ironic inflection. Responding to the critic's (mis)reading of his book as a conservative warning against the destructive force of perversion, Neal explains that the psychopath his book describes kills to eliminate 'corruption' but Neal goes on to question what exactly constitutes 'aberrant behaviour'. To pose the spectacle of an obsessive and psychotic elimination, Argento's film seems compelled to employ figures of queerness as both victims and perpetrators of the cleansing violence. The figures of queerness across Argento's films make visible the qualities of excess that culture earmarks for elimination, but the films do not endorse that elimination. Sexual and gender otherness may be associated with waste and excess in Argento's image, but that association does not condemn those non-patriarchal sex/gender identities to a position of menacing lack in the narration.[12]

It's not hard to see Argento partaking in the sexual exploitation and the objectification of bodies. However, the interchangeability of people and objects in his films isn't rendered only along lines of sexual difference: all genders of people are mistaken for things. Take for example the 'portrait' in *Profondo rosso/Deep Red* (1975) or *Inferno*'s floating corpses reanimated by disruptions in the water. In both examples, questions about the cinematic image's representational capacity are raised alongside the question of how to image the value of a human life. How can cinema grasp the worth of living in all its diversity? This overt objectification (via the waste image) comments on the tyranny of a system, mentioned above, where all must be assigned value in order to be useful. Might this then explain why his films from this period continually gravitate towards sexualities? Is it possible that these differently sexed bodies represent a resistance to this tyranny? After all, these sexualities reproduce in ways that cannot accumulate value.

As Bertellini puts it, 'sexual ambiguity is both part of and a metaphor for a larger Argentian theme, that of perceptual elusiveness linked to the cinematic apparatus' (Bertellini, 2004: 21). If disruptions to gender and sex norms so often go hand in hand with spectacles of waste, then any evocation of 'perceptual elusiveness' they introduce also carries the political weight of ecological matters discussed throughout this essay. Argento's waste image proposes a relationship to difference that operates without being reconciled to the value and use determined by markets, which poses a threat to most systems of value within which moderns live. Like trash, queer bodies reveal modernity's compulsive need to construct and to manage anything that is other to commodity capitalism.

It is sensible to hesitate before reclaiming Argento's films for queer politics.[13] Nor should queer sexualities be seen as existing outside of capitalism or in spite of its ugly modes of production, such as neoliberalism. However, I remain intrigued by Argento's images of waste for the ways they encapsulate how disruptions to sex and gender norms can undo traditional systems of value by making waste in and of the world as it is known. A paradigmatic network of images in *Il gatto a nove code* link sex with an overage that refuses to lead to reproduction: gay nightclubs (where both cisgender performance and the desiring gaze appear unhinged), genetic experimentation (lots of loose sex chromosomes are mapped out on laboratory walls), and a post-coital aftermath (the camera metonymically fixes on milk spilled from small cartons). Queerness can be found revelling in unaccounted spaces and in the shadowy realm of the unmonetisable. It threatens to expose the uselessness of exchange value and the fallacy of its reproduction. Queers are then not the exclusive vehicles of negation (in Edelman's vocabulary); they are, however, one part of a larger aesthetic working to bring a different optique into practice. This aesthetics (in this essay Argento's image of waste) asks its viewer to encounter difference differently: to resist the urge to assign value immediately, and pause before those sights (sites) whose worth is not immediately recognisable as significant, productive or useful. The commensurability of queers and garbage is not an expression of either one of these spectacles' otherness as lack, the sublime or menacing emptiness. Instead, these two stand together at the edge of what the current system can recognise as valuable, worthwhile, gainful or productive. When they appear in Argento's image they ask the viewer to experience that limit point, to recognise a different affective orientation to the world, and to remember kinds of value that we all may already have at our disposal but don't have the means to express.

If we no longer have the ability to recognise the worth of things that do not proclaim their practical, commodified or monetised value, what would allow us to see differently? If Argento's films have a politics, it is allowing us to see differently, if even just for a moment. In other words, a politics becomes apparent in the affective encounters that these films stage with waste and in the questions that follow from them. A politics emerges from experiencing what it feels like to see without applying late capitalism's relentless assignment of value to all things, lives and experiences. This could be put another way. One of the principal challenges of arguing against the reigning orthodoxies of political economy is confronting the limits of what we are collectively willing (able) to see of this world. Such a confrontation will only lead us to an encounter with the matter of waste, and this may be what Argento's cinema is good for.[14]

NOTES

1. To name a few: Clover (1993); Grant & Sharrett (2004); Guins (2005); Hunt (2004); McDonagh (2010).
2. *Dizionario Garzanti di Italiano*, Garzanti Editore s.p.a., (1994: 413). All the translations from Italian are made by the author.
3. At the opening of *La porta sul buio*, Argento speaks to the audience directly, saying that what makes the short films of the series similar is that they share a common atmosphere. In describing that atmosphere, he uses the term 'inquietudine', a word that at once evokes restlessness, anxiety, unease, worry and concern.
4. 'Horror Europa with Mark Gatiss', Tuesday 30 October 2012 at 21:00, BBC Four.
5. 'Regularly excluded from scholarly publications [. . .], Argento's films have been regarded as lacking cultural (read political) and artistic consistency – products of a fanatically cinéphilic and thus disengaged and solipsistic filmmaker lost in his own nightmarish obsessions' (Bertellini, 2004: 213).
6. Links to Antonioni abound in the Argento archive. David Hemming, the central actor in Antonioni's 1966 *Blow-Up*, plays the protagonist in Argento's 1975

Profondo rosso. The two directors both used cinematographer Luciano Tovoli on some of their canonical films, including Antonioni's *The Passenger/Professione: reporter* (1975) and *Il mistero di Oberwald* (1980), as well as Argento's *Suspiria* (1977) and *Tenebre* (1982).

7. Siegel's point here is broader. Argento's film is unlike most traditional cinema that uses 'landscape-as-expression' to '*generalise* and *abstract*'. Thus, Argento's practice of *mise-en-scène* resists conventional appropriations of landscape for figurative operations (metaphor, allegory or metonymy) that must downgrade the importance of the 'topographic or sociohistorical specificities of a given site'. For Siegel, *Tenebre* refuses this conventional tendency, aiming 'to introduce Peter as a *specific* kind of urban subject inhabiting a *specific* kind of urban space' (2).

8. Žižek's interview in *Examined Life* (Astra Taylor, 2008). Žižek's commentary can be found in this clip on Youtube: http://www.youtube.com/watch?v=iGCfiv1xtoU [accessed 15 July 2015.]

9. The opening narration includes this passage from the novel: '. . . ogni ostacolo umano, ogni umiliazione che gli sbarrava la strada poteva essere spazzato via da questo semplice atto di annientamento: l'OMICIDE.'/'. . . every human obstacle, every humilation that barred his way could be swept away by that simple act of annhilation: HOMICIDE.'

10. See, for example, Adam Lowenstein's essay in this book.

11. See, for example, Della Casa.

12. So while often reliant on outmoded typing of gay men as recognisable for their effeminacy, decadent style, shame or teeth-sucking cattiness, these queers carry special access to the truth when all other avenues of investigation have failed. The investigatory impulses of *Quattro mosche di velluto grigio* carry queer cadences; pursuit of knowledge requires delving into the world of gay men and following the trail of the homosexual private investigator whose beat is mostly constituted by locations that gays are meant to haunt (a posh florist, the apartment of a fan-loving, cackling queen, dark public bathrooms). Gay informants are found in other films, such as *La bambola*. With their special relation to knowledge, gay characters figure a deductive epistemology forwarded in *Tenebre*.

13. Knee offers an extensive analysis of gender and homosexuality in Argento. McDonagh argues that the censored versions of his films distributed abroad occluded Argento's sympathy for gay characters and led to misapprehensions of homophobia by Anglophone critics (103). For a broader discussion of lack and non-normative sexual identity in horror, see Halberstam. For an equally canonical account of how 1970s and 1980s horror films link their explorations of surplus to non-normative sexual identities, see Wood.

14. This essay was helped by the critiques and suggestions of Michael Pigott, Rachel Moseley, Lloyd Pratt, Helen Wheatley, Louis Bayman, Stefano Baschiera, Ivan Girina, Adam Lowenstein, audiences at King's College London and the graduate students in my 'Waste and Its Aesthetic Management' seminar.

BIBLIOGRAPHY

Bertellini, G. (2004), 'Profondo Rosso/Deep Red', in Bertellini, G. (ed.), *The Cinema of Italy*, London and New York: Wallflower, pp. 213–22.

Brunsdon, C. (2007), 'Towards a History of Empty Spaces', *Journal of British Cinema and Television*, 4:2 (1 November 2007), pp. 219–34.

Canova, G. (2003), 'La sindrome del sublime: Poetica dell'eccesso e deriva dello sguardo: L'ultimo Argento', in Carluccio et al., pp. 105–36.

Carluccio, G., Manzoli, G. and Menarini, R. (eds) (2003), *L'eccesso della visione: il cinema di Dario Argento*, Turin: Lindau.

Clover, C. (1993), *Men, Women, and Chain Saws: Gender in the Modern Horror Film*, Princeton, NJ: Princeton University Press.

Della Casa, S. (2001), 'L'horror', in Miccichè, L. (ed.), *Storia Del Cinema Italiano*, Vol. X, Marsilio: Edizioni di Bianco & Nero, pp. 368–99.

Gracey, J. (2010), *Dario Argento*, Harpenden: Kamera Books.

Grant, B. K. and Sharrett, C. (eds) (2004), *Planks of reason: essays on the horror film*, rev. edn, Lanham, MD: Scarecrow Press.

Guins, R. (2005), 'Blood and Black Gloves on Shiny Discs: New Media, Old Tastes, and the Remediation of Italian Horror Films in the United States', in Schneider, S. J. and Williams, T.(eds), *Horror international*, Detroit: Wayne State University Press, pp. 15–32.

Halberstam, J. (1995), 'Bodies That Splatter: Queers and Chainsaws', in *Skin shows: gothic horror and the technology of monsters*, Durham, NC: Duke University Press, pp. 138–60.

Hunt, L. (2004), 'Boiling Oil and Baby Oil: Bloody Pit of Horror', in Mathijs, E. and Mendik, X. (eds), *Alternative Europe: Eurotrash and Exploitation Cinema since 1945*, London: Wallflower, pp. 172–80.

Kracauer, S. (1997/1960), *Theory of film: The redemption of physical reality*, Princeton: Princeton University Press.

Koven, M. J. (2003), '"La dolce morta": space, modernity and the giallo', *Kinoeye*, 3:12, 27 October 2003, http://www.kinoeye.org/03/12/koven12.php [accessed 12 July 2015].

Knee, A. (1996) 'Gender, Genre, Argento', in Grant, B. K. (ed.), *The Dread of Difference: Gender and the Horror Film*, 1st edn, Austin: University of Texas Press, pp. 241–59.

McDonagh, M. (2010), *Broken Mirrors/Broken Minds: The Dark Dreams of Dario Argento*, Minneapolis: University of Minnesota Press.

Siegel, M. (forthcoming 2015), '*Tenebre*, or, Neoliberalism and Everyday Violence', in Kannas, A. (ed.), *The Films of Dario Argento*, London: Wallflower.

Schoonover, K. (2012), 'Antonioni's Waste Management', in Rhodes, J. D. and Rascaroli, L. (eds), *Michelangelo Antonioni: Centenary Essays*, London: British Film Institute/Palgrave Macmilllan, pp. 235–53.

Thompson, K. (1986), 'The Concept of Cinematic Excess', in Rosen, P. (ed.), *Narrative, Apparatus, Ideology: A Film Theory Reader*, New York: Columbia University Press, pp. 513–24.

Weiner, R. G. and Cline, J. (eds) (2010), *Cinema inferno: celluloid explosions from the cultural margins*, Lanham, MD: Scarecrow Press.

Wood, R. (2002), 'The American Nightmare: Horror in the 70s', in Jancovich, M. (ed.), *Horror, the Film Reader*, London: Routledge, pp. 27–32.

Yaeger, P. (2008), 'The Death of Nature and the Apotheosis of Trash; or, Rubbish Ecology', *PMLA*, 123: 2 March 2008, pp. 321–39.

8. THE *GIALLO*/SLASHER LANDSCAPE: *ECOLOGIA DEL DELITTO, FRIDAY THE 13TH* AND SUBTRACTIVE SPECTATORSHIP

Adam Lowenstein

How Italian is the American slasher film? How American is the Italian *giallo* film?

I begin with these questions not because they have never been asked, but because the answers that are usually offered have not encouraged us to take the relationship between these two important horror film sub-genres as seriously as we should. By examining a seminal Italian *giallo*, Mario Bava's *Ecologia del delitto/The Ecology of Murder* (1971, also known as *Antefatto, Reazione a catena, A Bay of Blood, Carnage, Last House – Part II* and *Twitch of the Death Nerve*) alongside a phenomenally popular American slasher film that bears an uncanny resemblance to it, Sean S. Cunningham's *Friday the 13th* (1980), I will argue that we have more to learn about these well-known sub-genres than we might have imagined. More specifically, the centrality of natural landscape to both films suggests that the *giallo* and the slasher film can cross-pollinate to enable what I will call a 'subtractive spectatorship' that challenges some of our conventional assumptions about what watching graphic horror is all about.

Most scholars and viewers have a fairly well-defined sense of what they mean when they talk about the Italian *giallo*, the American slasher film and the relationship between them. Indeed, one of the appealing aspects of these two sub-genres seems to be the relative clarity about what constitutes their core semantic/syntactic elements and most influential examples, even if deeper questions concerning their similarity to or difference from related types of films remain unresolved.[1] The Italian *giallo* takes its name ('yellow') from the colour of those books issued by the Milanese publisher Mondadori that featured mystery and detection elements associated with authors such as Agatha Christie and S. S. Van Dine.[2] Although the books began appearing in 1929, it was not until the 1960s that the *giallo* gained a pronounced cinematic presence with the release of Bava's *La ragazza che sapeva troppo/The Girl Who Knew Too Much/The Evil Eye* (1963) and *Sei donne per l'assassino/Blood and Black Lace/Six Women for the Murderer* (1964). Dario Argento's *L'uccello dalle piume di cristallo/The Bird with the Crystal Plumage* (1970) placed *giallo* on the international map while inspiring an intensive burst of Italian production of *gialli* that peaked during the early and mid-1970s but continues even today among directors like Argento, Lamberto Bava (Mario's son) and the French filmmakers Hélène Cattet and Bruno Forzani. The *giallo* tends to feature a particular sort of narrative structure as well as certain stylistic devices and visual emphases. The plot, as Mikel J. Koven observes in his valuable study of the *giallo*, involves 'an innocent person, often a tourist' who 'witnesses a brutal murder that appears to be the work of a serial killer. He or she takes on the role of amateur detective in order to hunt down the killer, and often succeeds where the police fail' (Koven, 2006: 3–4). In terms of style, the graphic horror and meticulous, imaginative orchestration of the multiple murders usually override their narrative significance; the killer is often masked, with black leather gloves, coat, and hat to obscure his or her identity; the victims include representatives of both sexes, but special attention is lavished on the deaths of beautiful, often partially unclothed, women; and subjective camerawork, particularly point-of-view shots that seem associated with the unseen killer, heighten the films' pervasive sense of threat from inside and outside the frame.

The American slasher film, like the Italian *giallo*, has its roots in the films of Alfred Hitchcock. Bava already nodded to Hitchcock's *The Man Who Knew Too Much* (1934/1956) in the title of his *La ragazza che sapeva troppo*, while Argento owes enough to Hitchcock to have been dubbed 'the Italian Hitchcock'.[3] For Bava and Argento, but even more so for the American slasher films, Hitchcock's *Psycho* (1960) is an inescapable point of reference. *Psycho* gathered the slasher film's essential ingredients and combined them to such electrifying effect that a formula took shape: what Carol Clover, in her brilliant study of gender and the modern horror film, calls 'the immensely generative story of a psychokiller who slashes to death a string of mostly female victims, one by one, until he is subdued or killed, usually by the one girl who has survived' (Clover, 1992: 21). Many key elements of the slasher film are, as Clover notes, already present in *Psycho*: 'the killer is the psychotic product of a sick family, but still recognizably human; the victim is a beautiful, sexually active woman; the location is not-home, at a Terrible Place; the weapon is something other than a gun; the attack is registered from the victim's point of view and comes with shocking suddenness' (Clover, 1992: 23–4). Two films that managed to channel their debts to Hitchcock in especially successful and influential ways for future slasher efforts were Tobe Hooper's *The Texas Chain Saw Massacre* (1974) and John Carpenter's *Halloween* (1978). These films revised and expanded what is a more minor role in *Psycho*: the active, resourceful woman who senses the killer's presence, survives his attacks, and outwits or sometimes even kills him herself. Clover calls her the 'Final Girl' and she has been at the heart of American slasher cinema ever since *Halloween*, which precipitated an initial wave of slasher films that crested in the early and mid-1980s. But the popularity of the slasher formula, particularly in the series of sequels, remakes and even parodies spawned by *Halloween*, *Friday the 13th* and *A Nightmare on Elm Street* (Wes Craven, 1984), has proven remarkably durable and lives on in the present.

These thumbnail histories of the *giallo* and the slasher film are by no means exhaustive, but they set the stage for my discussion of *Ecologia del delitto* and *Friday the 13th*.[4] Before turning to those films, there is still the matter of how the relationship between the *giallo* and the slasher film has usually been described. In short, this is a relationship that has been noted by many scholars, but analysed by very few. Most critics mention the influence of Hitchcock on the Italian films as well as the influence of the *giallo* on the post-*Halloween* slasher films, but then let these statements stand matter-of-factly, as if they speak for themselves and demand no further scrutiny or elaboration. For example, Adam Rockoff's detailed history of the slasher film acknowledges Bava as 'the godfather of Italian horror' and Argento as 'Italy's supreme fearmaker' (Rockoff, 2002: 31), but when it comes to examining what these directors' films might actually mean for the American slasher tradition, this is all that is offered: 'Today, [*Ecologia del delitto*] is best-known, however mistakenly, as the film which served as the inspiration for the *Friday the 13th* series' (Rockoff, 2002: 38). Even Koven, who contributes the most thoughtful account of the *giallo*/slasher relationship, minimises its significance. Although he admits that the *giallo* has influenced American slasher films and vice versa, he insists that 'in the majority of cases, Italian filmmakers are influenced by American models, and influence from Italy on Americans is still not the norm' (Koven, 2006: 168). In my discussion that follows, I will seek to illuminate the relationship between the Italian *giallo* and the American slasher film in ways that enable us to see it for what it is: a truly transnational vocabulary for the experience of horror in its most spectacular forms.

ECOLOGIA DEL DELITTO

The murder that begins *Ecologia del delitto* seems like a textbook *giallo* set piece: the rich Countess Federica Donati (Isa Miranda) meets her violent, masterfully choreographed fate at the hands of an unseen, black-gloved killer. But then this killer is revealed to us rather than remaining hidden – it is her husband, Filippo Donati (Giovanni Nuvoletti) – and then he himself is killed. By whom? We do not find out until much later, but Bava's opening sequence has already suggested that the cast of characters who populate *Ecologia del delitto* are there to be depopulated, not to serve as amateur detectives or witnesses to carnage that will eventually be explained and resolved. What unites these characters is not so much a mystery or even a story but a place: the Countess's vast, idyllic bayside property that seems ripe for lucrative commercial development. The interested parties include: Frank Ventura (Chris Avram), an architect and businessman; Laura (Anna M. Rosati), his lover and assistant; Renata Donati (Claudine Auger), the daughter of Filippo Donati; Albert (Luigi Pistilli), her husband; Simon (Claudio Volonté), the bastard son of the Countess who ekes out a living as a fisherman on the bay; Paolo Fosatti (Leopoldo Trieste), an entomologist; and Anna (Laura Betti), his occultist wife. By the film's end, all of these characters and others are dead, slain not by a mysterious murderer who is unmasked at the conclusion but by each other. In *Ecologia del delitto*, almost anyone is capable of murder, many kill, and nearly all die.

Ecologia del delitto is firmly embedded within the *giallo* tradition, yet it departs from the typical *giallo* formula in several important respects. This is most likely due to the fact that the film was conceptualised not just as another *giallo*, but as a critical dialogue with *giallo* conventions by the man who all but invented the form for cinema at a time when his claim to that title was being challenged by the success of newcomer Argento. Indeed, *Ecologia del delitto* had its genesis in meetings Bava had with producer Dino De Laurentiis, who wanted Bava to help him make a *giallo* of his own that would replicate Argento's enviable box-office results. It was De Laurentiis who connected Bava with screenwriter Dardano Sacchetti, who had recently finished work on Argento's latest *giallo*, *Il gatto a nove code/The Cat o' Nine Tails* (1971). Bava and Sacchetti wrote the story of *Ecologia del delitto* together, effectively ensuring that questions of *giallo* form, and in particular Argento's use of that form, would structure the film's production from the very beginning – one of the film's shooting titles was actually *La baia d'argento/The Bay of Silver* (Lucas, 2007: 848–9).

Ecologia del delitto eschews the *giallo* convention that just a few central figures should serve as the killer(s) and the amateur detective(s); instead, nearly everyone does some killing and some detecting. It kills off not some but *all* of the featured characters, so there is no one left to benefit from the knowledge of who murders whom and why; instead, an all-encompassing frenzy of violence subsumes questions of motive and mystery. The film's final deaths come when Renata and Albert are shot by their own small children, young 'innocents' who are playing with a real gun and do not even realise what they (or their murderous parents) have done.

But the most significant departure from *giallo* conventions is what is most essential to *Ecologia del delitto*: its setting. The *giallo* is almost entirely an urban form, with cities nearly always providing the backdrop for the bloody mayhem and its investigation.[5] *Ecologia del delitto*, as even its title foregrounds, is an exception. The bayside property of the Countess, with its water, forest and teeming insects, favours the natural world rather than the urban one.[6] The ecology of murder that this film explores is a matter, first and foremost, of natural landscape.

Why would the Rome-based Bava go through the trouble of substituting country for city on *Ecologia del delitto*, especially when the film's budget, like nearly all of Bava's projects, was extremely limited? All evidence points to Bava's decisions regarding the film's aesthetics, including its setting, to be carefully considered ones. Bava, who was born in 1914 and died in 1980, had a remarkably long, successful career in cinema that traversed designing optical effects in the 1930s under his father, the accomplished cinematographer Eugenio Bava; working as a celebrated cinematographer in his own right in the 1940s and 1950s; and then finally directing his own films in the 1960s and 1970s. His directorial debut, the hauntingly atmospheric *La maschera del demonio/The Mask of the Demon/Black Sunday* (1960), was a major success at home and abroad and is still routinely mentioned as one of the greatest horror films ever made. Despite all of these experiences, Bava was famous for belittling his own cinematic achievements, so much so that his biographer Tim Lucas describes his rare attempts at publicity as 'self-deprecating to the point of self-sabotage' (Lucas, 2007: 307–19). But here again, *Ecologia del delitto* is an exception. The film's release prompted Bava to grant his lengthiest and only career-spanning interview (published in the French film journal *Positif*), where he even confessed to being 'rather pleased' with *Ecologia del delitto* and 'very enthusiastic about some of the film's photographic details'.[7] Bava also committed to supporting the film with an exceedingly uncommon in-person appearance at France's 1st Festival International d'Avoriaz du Film Fantastique, although he failed to appear at the last minute. But perhaps most tellingly in terms of Bava's personal investment in *Ecologia del delitto*, he served as his own cinematographer and insisted that the screenwriter Filippo Ottoni accompany him to scout locations for the film. Bava's choice for the film's most important setting, the bayside landscape, turns out to be a fascinating one: Sabaudia, a small coastal town on the Tyrrhenian Sea roughly 50 miles southeast of Rome (Lucas, 2007: 862, 849, 856).

Sabaudia came into existence in 1933 through the draining of the malaria-infested Pontine Marshes, one of fascist Italy's most ambitious and significant public works projects. Indeed, Benito Mussolini's ideology of *bonifica* (reclamation) was exemplified by the Pontine Marshes plan, so Sabaudia was prominently located within discourses of ideal fascist land for ideal fascist citizens.

As historian Ruth Ben-Ghiat explains, 'land reclamation merely constituted the most concrete manifestation of the fascists' desire to purify the nation of all social and cultural pathology' (Ben-Ghiat, 2001: 4).[8] In a 1934 address celebrating the reclamation of the Pontine Marshes, a zone that had been referred to previously as '*la mortifera palude*' (the death-inducing swamp), Mussolini declared he had accomplished his goal to 'redeem from water and death a great area of territory belonging to the Italian motherland' (Caprotti & Kaïka, 2008: 618, 623). This address, like so many made by Mussolini, was captured in a state-sponsored newsreel and circulated as compulsory viewing in Italy's extraordinarily popular cinemas during the 1930s. In fact, one archival study found seventy newsreels and nine documentaries devoted specifically to the Pontine Marshes project from 1930 to 1939, often featuring Mussolini himself and produced through the national media propaganda organisation L'Unione Cinematografica Educativa (Istituto LUCE) (Caprotti & Kaïka, 2008: 615). The Pontine Marshes also figured notably as the setting in a number of Italian fiction films that resonated with fascist notions of reclamation, such as Alessandro Blasetti's *Sole/Sun* (1927) and *Terra madre/Mother Earth* (1931).[9] Bava would have been particularly aware of the Pontine Marshes project, as well as its representation in newsreels and fiction films; he worked for the Istituto LUCE himself and likely served as an uncredited special-effects artist on Blasetti's fascist-influenced epic *La corona di ferro/The Iron Crown* (1941).[10]

So for Bava to select Sabaudia as the central location for *Ecologia del delitto* is tantamount to performing a reclamation project of his own: restoring death and impurity to a landscape Mussolini had 'redeemed' from death for agricultural fertility and purified fascist productivity. *Ecologia del delitto* might also be seen as refiguring the modernised, urban spaces that characterise the *giallo*. If most *gialli* fetishise 'jet-setting' modern travel and tourism as appealing markers of Italianness (however ambivalent the films ultimately may be towards ideas of modernity), then *Ecologia del delitto* reminds us that Italy's post-war 'economic miracle' cannot be exorcised from its earlier fascist modernisation.[11] Although Sabaudia is never named explicitly within the film, a number of prominently placed clues alert viewers to the geographical setting of the reclaimed Pontine Marshes. First, the distance between the city (assumed to be Rome) and the country is underlined by those car trips undertaken and gas stations visited by Frank and Laura when they move between the film's urban and rural locations. Second, the bay is composed of saltwater, not freshwater – a distinction driven home in graphic fashion by the squid Simon fishes out of the bay, an animal that later wraps itself around the corpse of Filippo Donati to unforgettably nauseating effect. Since squid can only live in saltwater, the bay is consequently linked more closely with marshland than the freshwater lake it could be mistaken for; Sabaudia's well-known Lake Paola is just such a saltwater lake and may well have doubled for the bay in the film. The squid also evokes Antonio Gramsci's famous metaphor for the 'Southern question', that regional divide between North and South at the heart of Italian national identity: 'the North concretely was an "octopus" which enriched itself at the expense of the South [. . .] its economic-industrial increment was in direct proportion to the impoverishment of the economy and the agriculture of the South' (Gramsci, 1980: 71). Sabaudia, although usually considered part of Central rather than Southern Italy, was nonetheless eligible for those dubious special incentives for Southern economic development issued by the Italian government in the 1950s and 1960s.[12] Third, the entomologist Paolo warns Renata and Albert that any plans to develop the bay commercially are 'doomed to fail' because 'the bay is full of insects'. By invoking the chief motivating factor in the reclamation of the Pontine Marshes – to purify it of the insects that carry malaria and death – Bava connects the death-defying fascist landscape of the past with the death-strewn capitalist landscape of the present.[13]

I am not arguing that *Ecologia del delitto* is an antifascist or anticapitalist film in any straightforward sense (Bava himself remained apolitical throughout his life [Lucas, 2007: 73]), but that its treatment of landscape and death intersects with horror spectatorship in ways that may teach us something new about how the aesthetics and politics of horror function. In other words, I am arguing that *Ecologia del delitto* invites viewers to participate in subtractive spectatorship: a desire to subtract or erase human beings from the landscape, to leave it empty. Subtractive spectatorship provides a means to explain what has left so many critics of the slasher film mystified, threatened, or embarrassed; namely, the pleasure for spectators in witnessing the brutally graphic mutilation of a series of the killer's unfortunate victims. For example, Clover reaches a telling dead end in her analysis of the slasher film's audience when she notes that spectators express not just the expected fear when confronted with images of graphic horror, but also an unexpected 'uproarious disgust', a sort of wild delight beyond the bounds of identification with the film's characters or narrative. A slightly puzzled Clover declines to elaborate on what this sort of spectatorship might mean: 'Just what this self-ironizing relation to taboo signifies, beyond a remarkably competent audience, is unclear' (Clover, 1992: 41). I have offered my own explanation elsewhere for this mode of horror film spectatorship by describing how it accompanies films characterised by 'spectacle horror': 'the staging of spectacularly explicit horror for purposes of audience admiration, provocation and sensory adventure as much as shock or terror, but without necessarily breaking ties with narrative development or historical allegory' (Lowenstein, 2011: 42). *Ecologia del delitto* and *Friday the 13th* certainly qualify as examples of spectacle horror, but they also present something else to the spectator.

SUBTRACTIVE SPECTATORSHIP

Subtractive spectatorship should be understood as a subset of spectacle horror, but its emphasis on subtraction rather than addition complicates what has often been assumed to be the fundamental appeal of slasher films: the body count's escalation, the multiplication of more and more artfully slayed corpses. The body count is indeed integral to the slasher film, but more as a matter of counting down rather than adding up. What matters most in terms of specta- tor pleasure is not so much the bodies accumulating, but the human presence dwindling. In subtractive spectatorship, the desire is for a depopulated or empty landscape, a natural state uncoupled from human life and its attendant tensions. In short, the slasher film's pleasures might ultimately depend just as heavily on something like what Sigmund Freud called the death drive as on a cinema of attractions.[14]

Freud's controversial formulation of the death drive in *Beyond the Pleasure Principle* (1920) stems from his own analytic dead end: when faced with the mass destruction of the First World War, how could the pleasure principle remain the foundation for explaining mental life? If the pleasure principle usually governed our thoughts and actions on the basis of maintaining an internal equilibrium by decreasing unpleasurable stimuli and increasing pleas- urable ones, then how can we reckon with those phenomena that appear to reverse this logic? Freud was thinking here not simply of the postponement of immediate gratification made possible by the reality principle, but of the increase in unpleasure and decrease in pleasure detectable in the compulsive repetition of traumatic memories characteristic of shellshocked soldiers. Such phenomena cause Freud to theorise the existence of death instincts beyond and before the pleasure principle: 'we shall be compelled to say that "*the aim of all life is death*" and, looking backwards, "*inanimate things existed before living ones*"' (Freud, 1989: 46). The death drive does not eradicate or replace the pleasure principle for Freud, but it does make the life instincts and their invest- ments in wish-fulfilment, self-preservation, self-assertion and mastery both less primary and less primal. The death instincts reveal a different kind of pleasure, an older and perhaps deeper one based on desires to become inanimate and inorganic, to revert to an earlier and simpler state of being.

One thinker profoundly influenced by Freud's notion of the death drive was the surrealist and sociologist Roger Caillois, whose own concept of mimicry provides the connective tissue between the death drive, landscape and the pleas- ures of subtractive spectatorship at work in *Ecologia del delitto* and *Friday the 13th*.[15] In 'Mimicry and Legendary Psychasthenia' (1935), Caillois studies instances of mimicry in the animal kingdom (particularly among insects) to suggest that it is not, as is often assumed, a primarily defensive phenomenon. For Caillois, imitative acts performed by animals are understood best not as camouflage that protects the organism, but as a desire on the organism's part for self-erasure, for a removal of the distinctions between itself and its surrounding environment. Caillois' mimicry is not an instinct for self-preservation but for self-abandonment, an often dangerous attraction towards 'depersonalization through assimilation into space' (Caillois, 2003: 100). These aspects of self-erasure and depersonalisation cause Caillois to align animal mimicry with the psychasthenic psychology of human beings, or 'disorder in the relationship between personality and space' (Caillois, 2003: 100). The animal or human organism engaged in mimicry or its psychasthenic variants is seduced by 'a veritable lure of space' where the organism 'is no longer located at the origin of the coordinate system but is simply one point among many' (Callois, 2003: 99–100).

The desire to lose oneself, to become assimilated into the surrounding environment rather than control that environment, links mimicry's self-abandonment to subtractive spectatorship's drive towards a depopulated landscape. In *Ecologia del delitto*, the film's tensions are set into motion by human greed and its demand to alter the natural landscape and profit from it; those tensions are relieved by violently removing those humans from the landscape, one by one, until only two children remain. The film's final image frames those children as tiny specks in an extreme long shot that restores the dominance of the landscape itself: it is the natural ecology of the bay, the forest and the sky that persists, while the human ecology of murder has all but disappeared. Stelvio Cipriani's ostentatiously upbeat score that accompanies the film's concluding shots certainly seems to indicate an ironic, even absurdist black humour at play on Bava's part. But there is also the fact that Bava has managed to deliver, against all odds in a film built on unforgiving and unrelentingly graphic horror, a happy ending. As spectators, we got what we wanted.

So what exactly do we want from *Ecologia del delitto* and how do we get it? In terms of subtractive spectatorship, we are able to indulge in those pleasures aligned with the death instincts and mimicry – we 'become landscape', in that we are abstracted from and unencumbered by life's tensions and revel instead in the self-abandonment that comes from a sensory union with landscape itself as inanimate space. Or at least non-human space, as Bava, like Caillois, is particularly attentive to the animal (and especially insect) dimensions of landscape. In fact, the film's very first casualty is not human, but insect: after establishing shots of the bay's environs, we occupy an unseen bug's flying 'point of view' (POV) as it buzzes through the trees and then descends, dead, into the bay.

It is instructive to dwell on this insect POV for a moment, because it precedes and informs the film's later uses of POV. Like so many of the *gialli* before it, as well as the slasher films that follow it, *Ecologia del delitto* includes suspenseful POV shots from an unseen source that convey the presence of a killer without revealing the killer's identity. Some critics have lamented this aspect of slasher films as an insistence on the spectator to sympathise with or even become the killer perceptually.[16] But as this insect POV makes clear, the film uses POV not to have us become whatever is behind it (someone or something that is not usually revealed right then anyway), but to merge with the landscape that anchors that POV in the first place. The landscape predates human presence and is all that remains once that landscape has been emptied of human presence – it is what we revert to, what we abandon ourselves to. The fact that many of the film's killings (moments of Freudian disequilibrium for the spectator) are book-ended by shots of the landscape in beautiful, undisturbed stillness (moments of Freudian equilibrium for the spectator) highlights this point. The victims may come and go, the killer may have one identity or another, the POV may belong to someone or something we can or cannot discover, but in the end as in the beginning, it is the landscape that persists and absorbs us. That is where our vision resides. It is also where our own bodies will return when we ourselves are dead – an essential if often forgotten meaning for landscape that *Ecologia del delitto* and its slasher brethren recall for us.[17]

In *Ecologia del delitto*, the pleasures of subtractive spectatorship work in tandem with those of spectacle horror. Bava teaches us this by reminding us that his gory spectacles are both sensationally present and artificially absent: they are images to feel in the flesh as well as compositions to contemplate in the abstract. For example, one killing involves two copulating lovers impaled by a spear that cuts through them both simultaneously. In a sequence soon after, Anna spies an insect Paolo is studying pinned to a board and writhing in a nearly identical manner. So we perceive the death of the lovers not only as the shocking spectacle it is, but also as a figuration and frame composition that can be applied equally to humans or insects – a gesture of style as well as an act of violence.

Subtractive spectatorship, as I have argued elsewhere with regard to spectacle horror, need not preclude audience engagement with history and may well encourage it (Lowenstein, 2011: 50–8). In the case of *Ecologia del delitto*, subtractive spectatorship's invitation to become landscape carries particular connotations belonging to the Italian post-war context. If two structuring discourses of post-war Italian cinema and society have been the politics of modernisation and the national growth known as 'the economic miracle', both often deployed to overlook or overwrite fascism's history, then *Ecologia del delitto* returns to the scene of the crime: land reclamation as economic engine.[18] By revisiting the geographical centre of fascist land reclamation but replacing fascist purity with horrific impurity, fascist fertility with horrific death, and the tamed landscape of fascist progress (insects abolished) with the wild landscape of murderous ecology (insects unleashed), *Ecologia del delitto* invites us to merge with not just any landscape, but with the landscape built by fascism and inherited by capitalist Italy specifically. What are the political implications of this encounter with landscape for spectators that Bava's aesthetics make possible? Perhaps counter-intuitively we may be in a better position to answer this question by turning to *Friday the 13th*.

FRIDAY THE 13TH

Despite a nearly decade-long interval between their release dates and their different countries of origin, there is little doubt that *Friday the 13th* borrows consciously and liberally from *Ecologia del delitto*. Several factors make this assertion less far-fetched than it may seem at first glance. First, Bava's film was much more successful in the US than in Italy, thanks to exposure at grindhouse and drive-in cinemas where it played for years on double bills with horror films like *The Last House on the Left* (Wes Craven, 1972), which was producer Sean Cunningham's most notable success prior to *Friday the 13th*.[19] Second, Hallmark Releasing Corporation, the small independent distributor of *The Last House on the Left*, acquired *Ecologia del delitto* for a 1972 stateside release and retitled it *Carnage*. Another distributor made the association with *The Last House on the Left* even more explicit by issuing the film as *Last House – Part II* for a 1977 release. Finally, Martin Kitrosser, the script supervisor on the first two *Friday the 13th* films and a screenwriter on the third and fifth entries in the series, also happened to be a dedicated fan of Bava's films (he named his son Mario Bava Kitrosser!) who loaned Cunningham and screenwriter Victor Miller his own 16 mm print of *Ecologia del delitto* to study during *Friday the 13th*'s preproduction (Lucas, 2007: 868).[20]

Given these factors, it is not at all surprising to see a number of the most spectacular killings in *Ecologia del delitto* reprised in *Friday the 13th*: the axe splitting the face, the full-frontal beheading, the chase through the woods culminating in a throat-slitting, the impaled lovers.[21] In fact, these killings are so skilfully staged in both *Ecologia del delitto* and *Friday the 13th* that the special-effects make-up artists on each of the films (Carlo Rambaldi on the former, Tom Savini on the latter) would go on to high-profile, even auteurist careers of their own; so one significant legacy shared by the two films is contributing to the birth of the special-effects artist as gore-auteur. What is more surprising than Cunningham's decision to reprise Bava's killings, however, is his choice to revisit Bava's setting: a remote forest beside a large body of water.

Of course, *Friday the 13th* is set in the US, not Italy, so it trades in the Pontine Marshes for rural New Jersey.[22] But a sense of place is just as vital to *Friday the 13th* as it is to *Ecologia del delitto*, since both films must be seen as body-count movies where 'doing the numbers' means counting down in the manner of subtractive spectatorship. Indeed, even *Friday the 13th*'s title should be understood not only as an obvious *Halloween* knock-off (another 'holiday'-themed slasher film that clearly inspired Cunningham), but as an incorporation of the numbers logic that rules *Ecologia del delitto*.[23] 'Thirteen characters, thirteen murders!' is how Bava summarised *Ecologia del delitto*, and the man knew what he was talking about; this was the director, after all, of the previous 'death by numbers' films *Sei donne per l'assassino* and *5 bambole per la luna d'agosto/Five Dolls for an August Moon* (1970).[24] *Friday the 13th*'s trailer, a crucial ingredient in its stunning box-office success, even promises something akin to Bava's thirteen murders: an ominous voice counts from one to thirteen over clips of implied violence from the film.[25] So the number thirteen presides over both *Ecologia del delitto* and *Friday the 13th*, even if Bava makes good on his bloody promise and Cunningham breaks his (with only ten killings). But the significance of numbers in *Friday the 13th*, as in *Ecologia del delitto*, is ultimately more about subtraction than addition.

Friday the 13th begins in 1958, in the picturesque summertime setting of Camp Crystal Lake. The idyll ends when a mysterious assailant murders two young counsellors in the midst of their make-out session. The film then jumps ahead to the present of June 1980, when a local man named Steve Christy (Peter Brouwer) has renovated the 'cursed' camp and is now welcoming his new counsellors in the hectic final days before the campers arrive. But one by one, the counsellors fall victim to a murderer who stalks them, until only the intrepid Alice (Adrienne King) survives. Alice learns the identity of the murderer: Mrs Voorhees (Betsy Palmer), the mother of a young boy named Jason (Ari Lehman) who drowned at Camp Crystal Lake in 1958 due to what she perceives as neglect by the counsellors. She has been wreaking vengeance in Jason's name ever since, and even ventriloquises her dead son's voice when she pursues her prey (in a blatant riff on *Psycho*, yet another film to which *Friday the 13th* is heavily indebted). Alice succeeds in killing Mrs Voorhees and then passes out in a canoe on the lake. When she awakens the next morning, the police have arrived and her rescue seems assured. Suddenly, Jason rises from the lake and pulls Alice under. She regains consciousness in a hospital room, where she is told that she is the sole survivor and that no traces of Jason have been found. 'Then he's still there', Alice says, and the film's final shot returns to the lake, its surface now placid.

Friday the 13th, like *Ecologia del delitto*, begins and ends with the natural landscape. In both films, what transpires in between should be understood as a form of subtraction. Those humans whose lives disturb the landscape are methodically removed, until only the landscape itself and a token living (or perhaps undead) presence remain. The pleasures of subtractive spectatorship, where this spectacular process of violent depopulation urges the audience to integrate themselves with the landscape as a matter of sensory positioning, are nearly as stark in *Friday the 13th* as they are in *Ecologia del delitto*. The major difference is that *Friday the 13th* offers more of a remainder. Not only does

Alice (and perhaps Jason) survive, but the signs of a surrounding society can also be detected, however weakly: the police, the hospital staff, the residents of the small town near the camp. With the exception of the Donati children, Bava dispenses with such remainders in favour of foregrounding the landscape alone as the endpoint of *Ecologia del delitto*. *Friday the 13th* weakens this exclusive emphasis on landscape slightly, but the act of violent subtraction in a return to the natural landscape still dominates the film.

So what connotations does the landscape carry in *Friday the 13th*? Just as *Ecologia del delitto* presents important clues about where it is geographically situated, so too does *Friday the 13th*. License plates and signage locate the film in New Jersey, where it was indeed shot (in and around Blairstown, about 65 miles west of New York). Additional specificity is provided by Annie (Robbi Morgan), the camp's young cook, who chats before she dies about providing meals for the 'inner-city children' who will be attending the camp. So this camp in rural New Jersey, not far from the urban metropolis of New York, is being prepared to host children from the city, not the country. Annie's comment evokes long-standing social welfare programmes such as those associated with The Fresh Air Fund, a non-profit organisation founded in 1877 and dedicated to allowing 'children living in low-income communities to get away from hot, noisy city streets and enjoy free summer experiences in the country'.[26]

So what haunts the landscape at Camp Crystal Lake is not just a killer who is eventually shown, but a milieu that is never shown: the city, the poor, the non-white. By 1980, decades of post-war suburbanisation and urban decay had taken a severe toll on many US cities, with the result that poor urban populations (often predominantly non-white, largely African-American) were left behind in what historian Thomas Sugrue calls 'the urban crisis' (Sugrue, 1996). Initiatives like The Fresh Air Fund aim to address the urban crisis, to offer a means of 'escape' for those poor urban children left behind. But as commendable as such programmes are, they cannot really offer solutions. By delivering death to the idyllic landscape intended to function as a utopian respite from the urban crisis, *Friday the 13th* gestures towards how deeply seated the crisis really is and how difficult it can be to find any real solutions.

To get a sense of just how frightening the urban crisis is and what lengths even a horror film like *Friday the 13th* will go to avoid it, consider this missing aspect of the film's landscape: the children. With the exception of some quickly glimpsed campers (white, unharmed, asleep) in their bunks during the film's opening sequence, the only child seen in *Friday the 13th* is Jason. And he is really more of a ghost than a physical presence, the subject of a brief flashback motivated by his unhinged mother and perhaps a hallucination generated by Alice's traumatised psyche. But there is no doubt that in certain ways, Jason is the heart of the film. This is borne out not just by how he becomes the unstoppable killer in all of the sequels to *Friday the 13th*, but in how he has already become part of the landscape before the film even begins.[27] He drowns in the very lake that organises the film's action, then rises from it during the film's climactic scare. When he emerges from the lake, he is still the size of a child despite the twenty-two years since his drowning – time has frozen for him, making him less of an actual child and more of an idea or symbol of childhood.

The image of childhood Jason presents is not innocent or romanticised, but nightmarish. He is deformed and disintegrating like the corpse he should be, a testimony to how he belongs more to the lake and the landscape of death than life and the promise of childhood. In short, he is a child beyond the reach of any possible escape or respite that a summer experience in the country might offer. Jason lacks any explicit markers of poverty or non-whiteness, but he is coded as a child with special needs, one who required more care and attention than the counsellors could devote to him. So Jason still conjures the urban crisis by performing childhood as a problem that cannot be solved simply by trading city for country.[28] He has already become the landscape that was supposed to replace city despair with country hope; that landscape is not a solution, but death.

Becoming landscape in the manner of subtractive spectatorship I have described in both *Ecologia del delitto* and *Friday the 13th* is above all a sensory experience bound to spectacle horror. But this sensory experience also turns out to be a political one, in that becoming landscape in these films also means incorporating as spectators, however obliquely or unconsciously, precisely those things that haunt the landscape. In *Ecologia del delitto* it is the legacies of Italian fascism. In *Friday the 13th* it is the American urban crisis. But these are not films that arrive at their politics through overt critique. Instead, their politics become visible only when looking otherwise at the films, at how horror aesthetics can shape spectatorship as a political experience of the senses. To look otherwise at *Ecologia del delitto* and *Friday the 13th* means looking across them, between them, in the interstices of their Italianness and Americanness, in the aesthetic networks crossing the *giallo* and the slasher film. If we can develop this capacity to look otherwise, I believe we will see important aspects of these supposedly 'obvious' horror sub-genres that we have failed to notice as well as the experiences of spectatorship that underpin them.

Notes

I would like to thank Stefano Baschiera, Stefano Ciammaroni, Adam Hart, Marcia Landy and Sabrina Negri for inspiring discussions related to this essay.

 1. For further discussion of film genre's semantic and syntactic elements, see Rick Altman (1999: 207–26).
 2. My account of the *giallo* that follows draws on Gary Needham (2003) and Mikel J. Koven (2006).

3. On Argento's connections to Hitchcock as well as Bava, see Maitland McDonagh (1994: 7–61).
4. For more thorough coverage of the slasher phenomenon, see Richard Nowell (2011) and Adam Rockoff (2002).
5. See Koven (2006: 45–59). Of course, this is not to say that notable exceptions to the urban predilections of the *giallo* do not exist. For further consideration of such exceptions, see Xavier Mendik (2014). For a fascinating case study of a *giallo* in relation to its urban geography, see Michael Siegel (2011).
6. Although the bayside property emphasises the natural world in a manner unusual for the *giallo* tradition, the attention devoted to the wealth apparent in the Countess's villa and some of the surrounding homes is fully in keeping with the *giallo*'s fascination for the lifestyles of the European jet set. For further discussion, see Stefano Baschiera and Francesco Di Chiara (2010).
7. Tim Lucas, liner notes, *Twitch of the Death Nerve* DVD (Image Entertainment, 2000).
8. See also Lara Pucci (2012).
9. For further discussion of these and related films, see Ruth Ben-Ghiat (2001: 70–92); James Hay (1987: 132–49); and Marcia Landy (2000: 48–71).
10. See Lucas (2007: 71–3, 75–7). For an argument that *La corona di ferro* can be interpreted as registering unease with fascism or even subverting it, see Landy (2000: 72–7).
11. For the modernity of the *giallo*, see Needham (2003: 136) and Koven (2006: 45–59).
12. Although Sabaudia managed to achieve economic success (due in no small part to its proximity to Rome), these incentives were usually failures in Southern Italy. See Vera Lutz (1961: 384) and Paul Ginsborg (1990: 165–7, 216–17). This troubled history of special incentives tied to growing the Southern economy (and by extension, the larger 'Southern question') seems to be alluded to in *Ecologia del delitto* when Frank attempts to bully the Countess into selling the bay based on the 'social obligations' attached to its commercial development.
13. Pier Paolo Pasolini makes a similar point concerning Sabaudia while appearing on Italian television in 1974: that the true fascism is not what the fascists accomplished there architecturally, but what capitalist consumerism has accomplished since then in terms of social conformity. See 'Pasolini on Consumeristic Civilization' (https://www.youtube.com/watch?v=bipWHxTi-3c). I am indebted to Sabrina Negri for this reference.
14. For the influential formulation of a cinema of attractions (one that has shaped my own concept of spectacle horror), see Tom Gunning (1986).
15. My account of Caillois that follows draws on my own previous work. See Lowenstein (2010).
16. For a particularly influential version of this argument, see Roger Ebert (1981).
17. See Robert Pogue Harrison (2002). My thinking on landscape has also been informed by Martin Lefebvre (2006).
18. For further discussion of these discourses, see Noa Steimatsky (2008) and Angelo Restivo (2002). These accounts, which do not focus on the *giallo*, can be read usefully alongside Karl Schoonover (2012), who connects the violence in *gialli* with that in Italian neorealist films (see 2012: 219–22).
19. For a detailed account of the distribution history of *Ecologia del delitto* in both the US and Italy, see Lucas (2007: 860–2). For a related discussion of Bava's films as 'intercultural', see Karola (2003). For more on *The Last House on the Left*, see Adam Lowenstein (2005: 111–43). Interestingly enough, Bava's film *Cani*

arrabbiati (*Rabid Dogs*, 1974) appears to have been inspired in part by *The Last House on the Left*!

20. Cunningham has never openly admitted that he was directly influenced by *Ecologia del delitto* on *Friday the 13th*, but he has said, 'Certainly anybody who was making horror films in the '80s owed an awful lot to Mario Bava': see Lucas (2007: 26).

21. It is worth noting that Cunningham tones down Bava's imagery in almost every case, especially the impaling which now involves just one post-coital lover and an attack from beneath the bed rather than above it (although an impaling even more similar to the one in *Ecologia del delitto* appears in *Friday the 13th Part II* [Steve Miner, 1981]). This relative restraint exercised by Cunningham adds credence to Richard Nowell's well-supported argument that *Friday the 13th* needs to be understood as a youth film (with cousins including such lighthearted fare as *Meatballs* [Ivan Reitman, 1979] and *Little Darlings* [Ronald F. Maxwell, 1980]) as well as a horror film. See Nowell (2011: 107–47). Cunningham himself was clear that he did not want *Friday the 13th* to resemble the brutally graphic *Last House on the Left*: 'I knew *Friday the 13th* had to be totally different from *Last House on the Left*, which was a very raw, painful, cynically-edged film. I wanted to make a roller-coaster ride; a trip to Magic Mountain in a movie theater': see David Grove (2005: 13).

22. As a New Jersey native myself, I feel the need here to clarify that I do not see the much-maligned state as just one more 'death-inducing swamp'. I am open to arguments to the contrary, however.

23. Cunningham admits that the influence of *Halloween* was central to *Friday the 13th*: 'Obviously, from a financial standpoint, which was the most important factor at the time of making *Friday*, the success of *Halloween* was the main inspiration': see Grove (2005: 11). It is worth noting that *Halloween*, although set in a small suburban town rather than the country, also traffics in subtractive spectatorship. Consider, for example, the haunting shots near the end of the film, where a montage of the spaces once populated by the killer Michael Myers and his prey appear again; but this time they are empty, animated only by Michael's breathing. In other words, the American (and Canadian) slasher film's predilection for suburban or country settings rather than urban ones signals the centrality of subtractive spectatorship for a large number of slasher films, not just *Friday the 13th*.

24. Lucas, liner notes, *Twitch of the Death Nerve* DVD.

25. See Nowell (2011: 143). The *Friday the 13th* trailer strongly resembles the American ad campaign for another *giallo*, Dario Argento's *Il gatto a nove code/The Cat O' Nine Tails* (1971). See McDonagh, (1994: 20–1).

26. http://www.freshair.org/history-and-mission [accessed 23 June 2014].

27. Clover, who does not address the *giallo* influence on the slasher film, relegates the fact that *Friday the 13th*'s killer is female rather than male to the status of a 'noteworthy anomaly'. But Mrs Voorhees looks much less anomalous when the *giallo* context is taken into account, since female killers as well as more aggressive and sexualised versions of the Final Girl are more common in *gialli* than American slasher films. See Clover (1992: 29).

28. The fact that Jason rises from the lake using imagery that recalls the dreamed conclusion of *Deliverance* (John Boorman, 1972), where a ghostly hand rises from the water where the film's dead bodies, dirty secrets and economic exploitation lay buried, suggests that the image of Jason's resurfacing may also carry associations with the Vietnam War. For the relation of *Deliverance* to Vietnam, see Lowenstein (2005: 129–36). Tom Savini has repeatedly insisted that his own military experiences in Vietnam are inseparable from the look of his make-up effects. See, for example, Grove (2005: 21).

BIBLIOGRAPHY

Altman, R. (1999), *Film/Genre*, London: British Film Institute.

Baschiera, S. and Di Chiara, F. (2010), 'Once Upon a Time in Italy: Transnational Features of Genre Production 1960s–1970s', *Film International*, 8:6, December, pp. 30–9.

Ben-Ghiat, R. (2001), *Fascist Modernities: Italy, 1922–1945*, Berkeley: University of California Press.

Caillois, R. (2003), 'Mimicry and Legendary Psychasthenia', in Frank, C. (ed.), *The Edge of Surrealism: A Roger Caillois Reader*, trans. C. Frank and C. Nash, Durham, NC: Duke University Press, pp. 91–103.

Caprotti, F. and Kaïka, M. (2008), 'Producing the Ideal Fascist Landscape: Nature, Materiality and the Cinematic Representation of Land Reclamation in the Pontine Marshes', *Social and Cultural Geography*, 9:6, September, pp. 613–34.

Clover, C. J. (1992), *Men, Women, and Chain Saws: Gender in the Modern Horror Film*, Princeton, NJ: Princeton University Press.

Ebert, R. (1981), 'Why Movie Audiences Aren't Safe Anymore', *American Film*, March, pp. 54–6.

Freud, S. (1989), *Beyond the Pleasure Principle*, ed. and trans. J. Strachey, New York: Norton.

Ginsborg, P. (1990), *A History of Contemporary Italy: Society and Politics, 1943–1988*, New York: Penguin.

Gramsci, A. (1980), *Selections from the Prison Notebooks of Antonio Gramsci*, ed. and trans. Q. Hoare and G. Nowell-Smith, New York: International Publishers.

Grove, D. (2005), *Making Friday the 13th: The Legend of Camp Blood*, Godalming: FAB Press.

Gunning, T. (1986), 'The Cinema of Attraction: Early Film, Its Spectator and the Avant-Garde', *Wide Angle*, 8, Fall, pp. 63–70.

Harrison, R. P. (2002), 'Hic Jacet', in Mitchell, W. J. T. (ed.), *Landscape and Power*, Chicago: University of Chicago Press, pp. 349–64.

Hay, J. (1987), *Popular Film Culture in Fascist Italy: The Passing of the Rex*, Bloomington: Indiana University Press.

Howarth, T. (2002), *The Haunted World of Mario Bava*, Godalming: FAB Press.

Karola (2003), 'Italian Cinema Goes to the Drive-In: The Intercultural Horrors of Mario Bava', in Rhodes, G. D. (ed.), *Horror at the Drive-In: Essays in Popular Americana*, Jefferson, NC: McFarland, pp. 211–37.

Koven, M. J. (2006), *La Dolce Morte: Vernacular Cinema and the Italian Giallo Film*, Lanham, MD: Scarecrow Press.

Landy, M. (2000), *Italian Film*, Cambridge: Cambridge University Press.

Lefebvre, M. (ed.) (2006), *Landscape and Film*, New York: Routledge.

Lowenstein, A. (2005), *Shocking Representation: Historical Trauma, National Cinema, and the Modern Horror Film*, New York: Columbia University Press.

Lowenstein, A. (2010), 'Interactive Art Cinema: Between "Old" and "New" Media with *Un Chien andalou* and *eXistenZ*', in Galt, R. and Schoonover, K. (eds), *Global Art Cinema: New Theories and Histories*, Oxford: Oxford University Press, pp. 92–105.

Lowenstein, A. (2011), 'Spectacle Horror and *Hostel*: Why "Torture Porn" Does Not Exist', *Critical Quarterly*, 53:1, April, pp. 42–60.

Lucas, T. (2007), *Mario Bava: All the Colors of the Dark*, Cincinnati, OH: Video Watchdog.

Lucas, T. (2000), liner notes, *Twitch of the Death Nerve* DVD, Image Entertainment.

Lutz, V. (1961), 'Some Structural Aspects of the Southern Problem: The

Complementarity of "Emigration" and Industrialization', *PSL Quarterly Review*, 14:59, pp. 367–402.

McDonagh, M. (1994), *Broken Mirrors/Broken Minds: The Dark Dreams of Dario Argento*, New York: Citadel Press.

Mendik, X. (2014), 'The Return of the Rural Repressed: Italian Horror and the *Mezzogiorno Giallo*', in Benshoff, H. M. (ed.), *A Companion to the Horror Film*, Oxford: Wiley Blackwell, pp. 390–405.

Needham, G. (2003), 'Playing with Genre: Defining the Italian *Giallo*', in Schneider, S. J. (ed.), *Fear Without Frontiers: Horror Cinema Across the Globe*, Godalming: FAB Press, pp. 135–44.

Nowell, R. (2011), *Blood Money: A History of the First Teen Slasher Film Cycle*, New York: Continuum.

Pucci, L. (2012), 'Remapping the Rural: The Ideological Geographies of *Strapaese*', in Dalle Vacche, A. (ed.), *Film, Art, New Media: Museum Without Walls?*, New York: Palgrave Macmillan, pp. 178–95.

Restivo, A. (2002), *The Cinema of Economic Miracles: Visuality and Modernization in the Italian Art Film*, Durham, NC: Duke University Press.

Rockoff, A. (2002), *Going to Pieces: The Rise and Fall of the Slasher Film, 1978–1986*, Jefferson, NC: McFarland.

Schoonover, K. (2012), *Brutal Vision: The Neorealist Body in Postwar Italian Cinema*, Minneapolis: University of Minnesota Press.

Siegel, M. (2011), 'The Nonplace of Argento: *The Bird with the Crystal Plumage* and Roman Urban History', in Rhodes, J. D. and Gorfinkel, E. (eds), *Taking Place: Location and the Moving Image*, Minneapolis: University of Minnesota Press, pp. 211–31.

Steimatsky, N. (2008), *Italian Locations: Reinhabiting the Past in Postwar Cinema*, Minneapolis: University of Minnesota Press.

Sugrue, T. J. (1996), *The Origins of the Urban Crisis: Race and Inequality in Postwar Detroit*, Princeton, NJ: Princeton University Press.

9. KINGS OF TERROR, GENIUSES OF CRIME: *GIALLO* CINEMA AND *FUMETTI NERI*

Leon Hunt

Italians first of all fear sudden and violent death ... The world of vice also demands its daily victims. Street-walkers are found dead with silk stockings wound tight around their necks or knives stuck in their ribs, on their unmade beds or in country lanes ... (Luigi Barzini, *The Italians*, 1968: 107)

IL *GIALLO A FUMETTI*

Any attempt to nominate this or that film as the 'first' *giallo* has to negotiate the question of which version of this notoriously slippery term is being used – the *giallo* in its more inclusive Italian sense, 'a metonym for the entire mystery genre' (Koven, 2006: 2), or as a more particular B-movie *filone* that surfaced intermittently in the 1960s, blossomed more fully in the early to mid-1970s and has continued to appear sporadically, particularly in the films of Dario Argento.[1] Either way, Mario Bava's *La ragazza che sapeva troppo/ The Girl Who Knew Too Much* (Italy, 1962; refashioned as *The Evil Eye*, 1964) and particularly *Sei donne per l'assassino/Blood and Black Lace* (a co-production involving Italy/West Germany/France, 1964) are often accorded seminal status in teleological accounts of the *giallo* as a cinematic cycle. Both have at various times had the distinction of being identified as the first 'proper' *giallo*; the former with its tourist-eyewitness heroine and the latter with its bodycount narrative, eroticised violence and overheated visual stylisation. However, neither film clearly belonged to a contemporaneous cinematic cycle, or at least not an Italian one, at the time of their original release. As a West German co-production, *Sei donne per l'assassino* could equally be seen as a *krimi*, the prolific cycle of German mystery films often seen to anticipate and overlap with the *giallo*.[2] According to Tim Lucas, the film (a commercial disappointment that failed to recover its investment costs) performed best in West Germany and Austria (2007: 560). The *giallo* doesn't start to look like a proper *filone* until a series of sexed-up woman-in-peril thrillers starring Carroll Baker and Jean Sorel, starting with *Il dolce corpo di Deborah/The Sweet Body of Deborah* (Romolo Guerriri, 1968) and paving the way for the screen personas of Edwige Fenech, Dagmar Lassander and others. Dario Argento's *L'uccello dalle piume di cristallo/The Bird with the Crystal Plumage* (1970) would subsequently cement the iconography and narrative tropes of the most recognisable type of *giallo*, while Ken Hanke reminds us that it also qualifies as a *krimi*, distributed by German co-producers CCC as a Bryan Edgar Wallace adaptation (2003: 122).

As Gary Needham puts it, the *giallo* is 'constructed out of various associations, networks, tensions and articulations of Italian cinema's textual and industrial specificity in the post-war period' (2003: 138), but some of these associations and networks are transnational and transmedia ones. I want to explore here its connection to what might be seen as a *filone* and another iteration of the *giallo* in another medium, namely the cycle of Italian comics that became known as the *fumetti neri* (black comics). This allows us to see *Sei donne per l'assassino* in the context of contemporaneous Italian popular culture, rather than simply being either a spiced-up *krimi* or a film 'ahead of its time' (anticipating Argento but failing to find the audience or have the immediate influence that his films did). This in turn opens up another network of associations, in this case between Italy and France. The post-war relationship between Italian and French cinema is well known; much of what we think of as Italian or French cinema in the 1960s is in fact Franco-Italian (Betz, 2009). France was one of the co-financiers of *Sei donne per l'assassino* but what I am more concerned with here is a Franco-Italian exchange that produces what I shall call the 'Fantômas gene', the rearticulation of the figure of the masked criminal-killer as the embodiment of terror (the 'Lord of Terror' is one of many fearful names given to the antagonist of the Fantômas novels). While the *giallo*'s connection to Anglo-American detective/mystery fiction is well established, its illogicality, gratuitous sensationalism and evocation of terror might equally be derived partly from French pulp fiction.

The years of production for Bava's first two *gialli* (1962 and 1964) are significant ones for Italian popular culture. November 1962 saw the publication of the first *fumetto* aimed at adults (the words *per adulti* appeared on the cover of early issues). *Diabolik* was created by two Milanese sisters, Angela and Luciana Giussani. The story goes that they took their inspiration from a discarded *Fantômas* novel left on a train, the inspiration both for a similar character and a pocket-sized format that could be read on public transport (the 12 x 17 cm digest format would be used by all of its imitators). The name of the character has some interesting possible origins. 'Diabolic' had been the name of a character in a 1957 *giallo* novel called *Uccidevano di notte* ('They killed by night') by 'Bill Skyline' (the pseudonym of writer Italo Fasan) (Gaspa, 2012: 32). 'Diabolich' had also been the signature on a series of anonymous letters to the police regarding the murder of a Turin factory worker in 1958 (ibid.). But early issues of *Diabolik*, a figure who would later mutate into a combination of Fantômas and James Bond, plagiarised the 'Lord of Terror' extensively, as authors Marcel Allain and Pierre Souvestre had already borrowed from earlier French *feuilleton* characters such as Rocambole and particularly Zigomar. The first issue is entitled *'Il Re del Terrore'*, the King of Terror, and follows the plot of the first Fantômas novel quite closely while adding some imaginative suspense sequences of its own, such as Diabolik disguising himself as a scarecrow in a wheatfield while being pursued by Inspector Ginko (a variation on Inspector Juve from Allain and Souvestre's novels).[3] In 1964, the *fumetti neri* would explode into a comic-book cycle. *Kriminal, Satanik, Fantax* (subsequently *Fantasm*) and *Mister X* all made their debuts, followed the year after by *Sadik, Zakimort, Spettras, Demoniak* and the oddly named *Jnfernal*. Not all of these were Fantômas-like criminals. Some, like Fantax/Fantasm and Zakimort, were vigilantes, even though Fantasm looked virtually identical to Kriminal with his skull mask and skeleton bodystocking. *Satanik* sometimes pushed towards horror, its anti-heroine a disfigured scientist who develops a potion to turn herself into a beautiful but evil *femme fatale*. In one issue, she encountered a vampire called Count Wurdalak, a nod to Bava's *I tre volti della paura/Black Sabbath* (1963). The 'K factor' in so many of the names has been much commented on (Burratini, 2012; Gravett, 2012) – 'an alien intrusion' by a letter not in the Italian alphabet (Dumontet, 1998: 11) and possibly a nod to the *krimi*. But the *fumetti neri* were widely promoted as comic-book *gialli*. *Diabolik*, the only one of these *fumetti* still in regular publication, still carries the tag *'Il giallo a fumetti'*, while *Kriminal* was known for a time as the *Supergiallo settimanale* (weekly super*giallo*). While the *giallo* label was undoubtedly meant in its literary generic sense, the *fumetti neri* also had many of the qualities of the cinematic *filone* that Bava's films anticipated.

While *Diabolik* was tamer than *Fantômas*, whose first victim has her throat cut so deeply that she is nearly decapitated, the *fumetti neri* published from 1964 upped the violence and also threw a lurid sado-eroticism into the formula. The first issue of *Sadik*, *'Il castello del terrore'*, looks like the close relation of Massimo Pupillo's trashy torture-film *Il boia scarlatto/Bloody Pit of Horror* (Italy, 1965). Its opening pages show its masked antagonist whipping a black female victim (he calls her *'sporca negra'* – dirty negress) in the dungeon of his castle, a castle that also contains a pool filled with crocodiles. When the *nero* cycle extended to the *fotoromanzo* (photo-comic), its sadism moved closer to softcore pornography. *Killing*, first published in 1968, was ostensibly another *Kriminal* clone but offered pages of black-and-white photos of underwear-clad models being tortured by the gleeful antagonist. Starting in 1965, there was an extensive media campaign against *fumetti neri*, culminating in several publishers being put on trial the following year. In 1967, these publishers were fined and those comics that survived (*Kriminal* and *Satanik* would run until 1974) were substantially toned down (Burratini, 2012: 88–91). As Simone Castaldi argues, the *fumetti neri* can be seen as a particularly spectacular manifestation of Italy's *miracolo economico* (1958–63), which had fuelled an explosion in popular media as well as some significant shifts in cultural mores: 'the relaxation of censorship brought to the surface a large section of the collective imagination that had been deeply repressed' (2010: location 287). As we can see from *Sadik*'s racism, the 'return of the repressed' isn't always the liberating force we might like it to be. Misogyny, albeit mixed in with more ambivalent representations of female sexuality and agency, also pervades a significant number of *fumetti neri* and *gialli*; the 'independent, sexually uninhibited and substantially evil' female protagonists are seen by Castaldi as an exorcising of the female emancipation that the economic miracle helped bring about (ibid.: location 306).

If *Sei donne per l'assassino* seems like a film whose *filone* had yet to appear, the *fumetti neri* would seem considerably less like *gialli* on their way to the big screen. Their passage to the cinema took two forms. Interestingly, their notoriety is best seen in several multi-director *episodi* films (all of them produced by Dino De Laurentiis, who would later produce Bava's *Diabolik* [Italy/France, 1968]) that refer to the scandal of the 'black comics'. The earliest is *Thrilling* (Carlo Lizzani, Gian Luigi Polidoro and Ettore Scola: Italy, 1965), whose second episode 'Sadik' (directed by Polidoro) weaves black comedy out of Dorian Gray's obsession with *fumetti*, leading to her insisting that husband Walter Chiari dress up as '*il signore del crimine*' and menace her as she sleeps. The episode ends in *fotoromanzo* mode, with onscreen dialogue bubbles. In '*Una sera come le altre*', Vittorio De Sica's episode in *The Witches/Le streghe* (Luchino Visconti, Mauro Bolognini, Pier Paolo Pasolini, Franco Rossi and Vittorio De Sica, 1967), Silvana Mangano also undermines her husband (Clint Eastwood) in sexual fantasies about *fumetto* characters (one of them Sadik), while in one of the more quotidian scenes she berates him for allowing their son to read *Diabolik* and *Kriminal*, reminding him of the damning things being said about them on TV. Finally, in Mario Monicelli's '*La bambinaia*' episode from *Capriccio all'Italiana* (Mauro Bolognini, Mario Monicelli, Pier Paolo Pasolini, Steno, Pino Zac and Franco Rossi, 1968), Mangano plays a nanny shocked to find her young charges reading *Diabolik*, *Kriminal* and *Satanik*. In a sly comic twist, her attempt to distract them with a Charles Perrault fairy story reduces them to terrified tears. The other form that the *fumetti neri* took onscreen was a series of adaptations that coincided more or less with their printed counterparts being put on trial: *Kriminal* (Umberto Lenzi, 1966), *Il marchio di Kriminal* (Fernando Cerchio, 1967), *Mister X* (Piero Vivarelli, 1967), *Diabolik* (Mario Bava, 1968) and *Satanik* (Piero Vivarelli, 1968). And yet, one would never guess from any of these films that these characters had generated such outrage in Italy. International cinema had by this point established a default approach to adapting comics: tongue in (cowled) cheek. An earlier attempt by producer Tonino Cervi to film *Diabolik* with Jean Sorel (soon to be one of the *giallo*'s most prolific stars) and Elsa Martinelli had stalled, and by the time Bava adapted it for De Laurentiis, the character was already on his way to being more of an anti-hero than the King of Terror. The style of the *fumetti neri* in their pre-censorship period is easier to find not only in *Sei donne per l'assassino* but also *Il boia scarlatto*, whose masked bodybuilder-torturer (Mickey Hargitay) embodies the cruelty of Kriminal, Sadik and Killing (see Hunt, 2004). The film even features the most plagiarised of *fumetto nero* outfits, the skeleton bodystocking and skull mask, worn by one of the characters for a *fotoromanzo*-like photo-shoot featuring a character called Skeletrix.

I'm not the first person to link *Sei donne per l'assassino* to the *fumetti neri*. Rolando Caputo sees the film as Bava's 'first attempt to introduce the fumetto style into his work' (1997: 58), while Piselli et al. include the film in their book on the *cinefumetto* (2008: 18), and speculate that it might have been an influence on the *fumetti neri* (the Wurdalak's cameo in *Satanik* certainly suggests that writer Max Bunker/Luciano Secchi and/or artist Magnus/Roberto Raviola had seen other Bava films). The film was released in Italy in March 1964 (Lucas, 2007: 542), while *Kriminal* (the *fumetto* that most resembles Bava's film) was first published in August of that year. Roberto Curti goes further when he observes that the notorious fifth issue of *Kriminal*, '*Omicidio al riformatorio*' ('Murder at the reformatory', December 1964) 'almost looks like a novelization (of Bava's film) set in a reform-school!' (2002). Whether such an influence was a direct one is open to speculation (and raises the question of why Bava's film had seemingly so little impact in Italy when something so similar was flourishing in comic-book form). But first, we need to return to Fantômas.

THE FANTÔMAS GENE

The *giallo* and the *fumetto nero*'s eroticisation of the mystery genre can be seen as an ambivalent response to the *miracolo economico*, particularly its transformative effect on social and moral values. This is most evident in its mixture of the permissive and the punitive, and never more so that in its representation of female sexuality. The next cycle of *fumetti per adulti* plunged more emphatically into pornographic territory, notably in such erotic horror titles as *Jacula* (1969–82), *Zora La Vampira* (1972–85) and *Sukia* (1977–86). On the other hand, the emphasis on terror and a dwelling on violent detail that pushed the mystery-thriller towards the generic terrain of horror have a much earlier source. When the first *Fantômas* novel (1911) was published in Italy in 1912, its impact can be measured by it generating a stage adaptation in Naples later that year, the first dramatisation of the character anywhere, pre-dating Louis Feuillade's film serials by a year (Castelli, 2011: 61). The character would transfer to *fumetti* after the war, with a five-album series *Fantomas ritorna* in 1946 and an adaptation of the first novel in the Venice weekly *GialloNero* in 1947 (ibid.: 87). In 1963, the year following *Diabolik*'s debut, the novels were reissued monthly by Mondadori in their *Gialli Mondadori* format (ibid.: 62–3). These were modified translations by the novelists Carlo Fruttero and Franco Lucentini, even bearing new titles (the first novel reissued as *Il Terrore Mascherato*, 'The Masked Terror'). The comic Fantômas films of the 1960s would be French-Italian co-productions (as would the Bava-De Laurentiis *Diabolik*). Interestingly, as Fantômas himself was being played for laughs in France, his Italian offspring would take his reign of terror into a more permissive cultural context.

The 'Lord of Terror', then, was sewn into Italian popular culture virtually from his origin, and in the 1960s was being deployed as a prototype for a new type of comic book while being editorially revised for a contemporary audience by the publisher who had created the *giallo* format in the first place. The *fumetto nero* approached the *giallo* less as a genre of detection and deduction (although one of the central characters is often a policeman) than one of sensation, shock and sadism, and it arguably passed the 'Fantômas gene' on to the cinematic *filone* that would later pick up on those generic tropes taking shape in Bava's first two contemporary thrillers.

The first characteristic of the Fantômas gene is a masked criminal who spreads, even embodies, terror. In the most quoted passage of the first *Fantômas* novel, a dialogue exchange between two unnamed characters, one asks what the 'Genius of Crime' *does*, and receives the reply, 'Spreads terror!' (Allain and Souvestre, 1986: 1). He is opposed and pursued by an indefatigable police nemesis, and accompanied by a female companion who may have some misgivings about his criminal methods. His activities leave a trail of bodies, often killed in highly imaginative and gruesome ways. Not all of this is applicable to the *giallo* more generally, but fits *Sei donne per l'assassino* quite well in most respects. Its 'faceless' killer spreads an almost supernatural terror through the fashion house setting (he even seems to disappear before the very eyes of one character at one point). Inspector Silvestri is a more dispassionate figure than Juve, Ginko or *Kriminal*'s Inspector Milton – the killer is a mystery to be solved, not a nemesis who has become a personal obsession. However, another Fantômas/*nero* trope is present, the criminal couple. Just as the Lord of Terror has Lady Beltham, Diabolik has Lady Eva Kant (as much of an icon in Italy as he is), Kriminal has Lola Hudson and Sadik has Loona, Bava's two killers are lovers; Massimo Morlachi (Cameron Mitchell) and Countess Cristiana Cuomo (Eva Bartok). Morlachi kills cruelly and without remorse while donning what would become the iconic *giallo* outfit of black raincoat, wide-brimmed hat, black gloves and mask, while Countess Cristiana kills out of romantic devotion and with some evident distaste. Nevertheless, like Eva Kant (another aristocrat with a taste for crime), she has already dispatched her husband and now kills to provide an alibi for her lover, held in custody after the first four murders.

Secondly, there is a mystery surrounding the identity of this criminal, his crimes prompting the question less of 'Whodunnit?' than 'Who are you?' (a celebrated *Diabolik* story is entitled '*Diabolik, Chi Sei?*' – 'Diabolik, who are you?'). This is partly a matter of his appearance. The *giallo* killer wears a mask to conceal his/her identity. Fantômas, Diabolik and (initially) Kriminal, on the other hand, in addition to their signature masks, don an array of disguises so that their presence becomes nearly impossible to detect and a source of terror (he could be anyone in the room). Fantômas's costume, Tom Gunning suggests, aspires to invisibility (black bodystocking, black hood or cagoule), embodying 'the radical eradication of identity', generating a 'terror spawned by uncertain vision and unreliable identity' (2008: 28). In *Sei donne per l'assassino*, an eyewitness tells the police that the killer 'has no face' – as Roger Sabin argues, his 'facelessness' is a particular source of terror in the film, 'an empty canvas upon which we project our deepest fears' (2008: 32). Robin Walz suggests that the Fantômas novels frequently require the villain 'to be anyone and anywhere, at any time, in order to sustain the character' (2000: location 719), sometimes seemingly in two places at once (a possible consequence of Allain and Souvestre's rapid turnover and practice of writing alternate chapters to divide the workload). As is also the case with the *fumetto nero* antagonists, these 'fundamental incoherencies of time, space and character' (ibid.: location 721) are aided by the many disguises. The *giallo* must find other 'swerves', as Walz calls them, to conceal the identity of the killer. *Sei donne per l'assassino*'s swerve is having two killers; 'masks and identities', Walz says of the Fantômas novels, 'are interchangeable, continually changing, and essentially equal' (location 701).

Thirdly and finally, there is a psychological 'flatness' in favour of what Robin Walz calls 'pure pulp carnival, a mishmash of flat characters, stilted dialog and cheap thrills', an 'endless, yet predictable, string of murders, thefts, disguises, pursuits, traps, confrontations, arrests, and escape – and none of it plausible' (ibid.: locations 496, 499). Reader satisfaction derived not from 'sophisticated literary construction' but 'the exploits and details that filled a highly melodramatic form' (location 553). Thus the *giallo* as a *filone* was perfectly suited to the viewing context of the *terza visione* (third-run) cinemas described by Christopher Wagstaff, an audience offered 'a nightly appointment where it would receive a series of discrete gratifications that were part of a longer-term sequence' (1992: 254). Similarly, one might imagine the reader of *fumetti neri* getting discrete gratifications (sex, murder, escape) on the journey to and from work. Just as the *giallo* is often remembered more for its set pieces than its narrative, early surrealists played a game of someone calling out the title of a *Fantômas* novel while the others would have to remember the murders from that particular book (Walz, 2000: location 817).

France in the early twentieth century and the Italy of the economic miracle were experiencing both exciting and disorientating collisions with modernity – seemingly the strongest contextual link between the *feuilleton,* the *fumetto nero* and the *giallo*. In the final section, I shall examine the dialogue between the latter two.

SEI DONNE PER IL RE DEL DELITTO: FROM BAVA TO BUNKER

A young woman, described as being 'as beautiful as Venus' but implicated in the world of crime, sneaks off to meet her older lover (who incidentally is the local mayor). As she undresses, neither of them notices a cowled figure watching them through the window. She unfastens her suspenders and one of her stockings starts to slide down her leg. After sex, she makes her way back through the snow, eager for her absence to go unnoticed. But that masked figure is following her. When he grabs her, there is a struggle, and she escapes by biting his hand. He gives chase, but she manages to reach the gates of the reform school she has absconded from. However, as she climbs over the gate, he grabs her leg, she slips and is impaled on the spikes on the gate. Some of the other girls hear her cry and run out, barely covering their flimsy nighties with their semi-fastened coats. 'Che orrore!' ('How horrible!') one of them cries as she sees the corpse. But we are offered a more particular view of the body from the other side of the gate; skirt hiked up, effectively bent over the gates, the girl's underwear and stockings displayed for our gaze.

On paper, this might sound like a deleted scene from *Sei donne per l'assassino*, perhaps the one where Bava went just a little bit too far for the censors in making a spectacle of violent death and the eroticised female body. But in fact, it's the most notorious sequence from perhaps the most infamous issue of *Kriminal*, '*Omicidio al riformatorio*'. Unlike Bava's film, the institution filled with beautiful bad girls isn't a fashion house (*L'atelier della morte* was the shooting title of the film) but a reform school. As in *Sei donne per l'assassino*, there are two shadowy figures menacing these girls, one of them the titular 'King of Crime'. Each of the *sei donne* in *Sei donne per l'assassino* ('Six women for the killer'),[4] too, is implicated in something compromising. The film's first victim, Isabella, is a blackmailer who knows the terrible secrets of the other five, each of them glancing anxiously at her crimson diary when it is later discovered. After Isabella's death, the killer drags her body away and her skirt, like Carol's (the impaled girl in '*Omicidio al riformatorio*'), is lifted to display her suspenders and bare thighs. Bava will contrive to give us glimpses of lingerie in most of the murders that follow; Nicole's top being torn as she is pursued, Greta struggling in a black slip as she's suffocated with a pillow, Tao Li drowned in her semi-transparent underwear, the towel around her waist removed as she sinks into the bathtub. This lascivious detail, tame compared to the nudity and softcore sex of later *gialli*, was new in *Sei donne per l'assassino*, something that Bava had not included in the more Hitchcockian, more playful and less violent *La ragazza che sapeva troppo* and certainly not something one would expect to find in the *krimi* cycle. But this titillating aspect was something that it shared with the *fumetti neri*, again making the film's comparative lack of commercial success in Italy hard to account for.

Kriminal, like Bunker and Magnus's other *fumetto nero Satanik*, has come to be recognised as a cut above its peers. Filippo Scozzari, for example, characterises their work as 'innovative and rebellious . . . ribald and belligerent' (quoted by Castaldi, 2010: location 260). The artwork in the *nero* comics generally ranged from the professionally competent to the frankly inept, but Magnus/Raviola's was as stylish in its way as Bava's camerawork. It bore some resemblance to the American EC Horror Comics of the 1950s, taking the edge off the violence with a slightly cartoonish style that suggested black humour more than outright gore.[5] Castaldi characterises this style as a mixture of 'artsy realism' and the 'cartoonish style of children's comics', characterised by 'heavy blacks, and sensual round, thick lines promising mischief and forbidden thrills' (ibid.: location 552). Those 'forbidden thrills' are most evident in the women he drew; voluptuous bad girls, usually clad in either their underwear or flimsy nightwear. According to Paolo Ferriari, 'the female body is the true protagonist' of "Omicidio al riformatorio"' (2010: 255). Some are hapless victims akin to Bava's *Sei donne per l'assassino*. Overhearing an 18-year-old girl tell her older fiancé that she'd rather die a virgin than give up her honour before marriage, Kriminal pushes her out of a window (ripping off her skirt in the process), quipping that she has got her wish (#3, '*Il museo dell'orrore*', 1964). Others are *femmes fatales* akin to Satanik, such as the marvellously named Patty Gaylord, whose suspenders look like inverted crucifixes and who at one point whips Kriminal across his bare chest (#53 '*Bramosia d'oro*', 1966). Bunker/Secchi brought not only a dark humour to these 'black' comics, but an ingenuity in plotting and a tendency towards ongoing continuity that is still unusual in mainstream Italian comics. Secchi has dismissed Diabolik as a 'soft character', while Kriminal 'became a symbol for sexual freedom' (1998: 4), but as we can see, this was a predominantly masculinist conception of sexual liberation. Even so, female sexuality, ambivalently represented, is a key agency, as it will become in the cinematic *giallo*.

The first issue of *Kriminal* ('*Il re del delitto*' – 'The King of Crime', 1964) works as a *giallo* structured around a mystery. The mystery is the identity and motivation of Kriminal, but in fact by the end of the episode we have been provided with answers to both of those questions. Unlike Diabolik and Fantômas, he does have a 'real' name, Anthony Logan, and his main motivation is revenge on those he holds responsible for his father's death. This leads to a series of gruesome murders (a decapitation, an arrow in someone's eye) investigated by Inspector Milton of Scotland Yard (it shares its generic London setting with the *krimi*). The Fantômas gene is at its strongest in this first issue. Kriminal is a figure of dread, his crimes discussed fearfully over dinner by his intended victims (the sort of corrupt wealthy people who populate later *gialli*), and like Fantômas and Diabolik he contrives to have one of his victims wrongly executed. The most Bava-like scene has him strangle the wife of one of his targets with a stocking immediately after sex. In a touch of misogynist black humour, she has just commented that she likes to be treated roughly by the man she loves. The post-strangling scene is framed cinematically from above, Kriminal's discarded mask to the left of her while he stands over her to the right. The third issue, '*Il museo dell'orrore*', places Kriminal in that most iconic of horror-film settings, a wax museum, and is full of suitably *grand guignol* scenes involving a wax-melting furnace. Assorted police officers are dumped in the boiling vat, later found melted down to skeletons (but with uniforms still intact), and when Kriminal himself falls in, he rises from the vat like some supernatural spectre before the terrified gaze of one hapless bobby. One panel of him dragging a police officer's body down the steps to the furnace bears a striking (if probably coincidental) resemblance to a shot in *Sei donne per l'assassino* of Morlachi creeping down the steps to the furnace room where Peggy is tied up waiting to be tortured.

In examining the relationship between *Sei donne per l'assassino* and '*Omicidio al riformatorio*', it is worth summarising their respective narratives. The former follows a series of murders of the models at a fashion house, starting with Isabella, who has kept a diary detailing the vices and vulnerabilities of nearly every other character in the film (drug addiction, an unwanted pregnancy, a bankruptcy, and most importantly murder), most of whom she has been blackmailing. Possession of the diary leads to the deaths of two further models at the hands of the killer. All of the men at the fashion house, including the owner Massimo Morlachi, are detained as suspects, but there is a fourth murder while they are being held. The men are released, and it transpires that

Morlachi killed the first three victims, while the Countess murdered Greta to provide an alibi for him. Isabella had been blackmailing them because she knew that they had murdered the Countess's husband. Morlachi persuades the Countess that she must kill again, making the murder of Tao Li look like a suicide and faking a confessional suicide note. In fact, he is setting up the Countess and frightens her into a fall from a loosened balcony. Nevertheless she survives long enough to shoot her faithless lover.

In 'Omicidio al riformatorio', a replacement doctor arrives at a girls' reformatory school. One of the girls, Carol, is connected to a bank robber named Guld who has stolen £25,000. Carol's lover, the mayor, is also after the stolen money. Kriminal lurks in and around the reformatory and brings about Carol's death, although not deliberately. Another girl, Margie, starts to investigate from the inside, while a third girl, Loren, is smothered with a pillow by a mystery assailant, but it later transpires that she has survived. Margie is menaced both by the mayor and a sinister hunchback, both of whom are killed by Kriminal. Inspector Milton works out that the doctor is in fact Guld, and during a confrontation the director hits Guld hard enough to kill him. He then proceeds to drug Milton because the director is in fact Kriminal, who has escaped with the money (which he then loses when his car crashes).

If there are some striking similarities between these two narratives, there are important differences, too (some of them inevitably matters of format). In 'Omicidio al riformatorio', it is less a question of who the killers are than which disguises they are hiding behind (a question taking us back to Fantômas). Much has been made of the Italian title of Sei donne per l'assassino with its promise of a female bodycount. But if we keep count (and the film invites us to by having the Countess add up the victims on her fingers at one point), it's evident that only five of these are murder victims as such. The sixth is the Countess who is both herself a killer and tricked into her fatal injuries by her partner-in-crime. What the title is perhaps offering is six *potential* women for the killer. 'Omicidio al riformatorio' only delivers one of its women to the 'killer', even though the title page shows him throttling another girl whose breasts are barely covered by her babydoll nightie. But Carol also needs to be seen as part of a longer sequence of such titillating death scenes, starting with Karin in issue one. Margie and Loren (who only appears to meet the same fate as Greta in Sei donne per l'assassino) are women-in-peril who also have some of the qualities of the 'Final Girl' or the amateur detective figure of the giallo. Margie, for example, engages in her own investigation and proves quite able at detecting (even though she needs rescuing by Kriminal at one crucial point). There are in fact more male victims than female in the story, but it's Carol's death that tends to be remembered. 'They even looked sexy when dead!' is Carlo Dumontet's judgement of the female bodies in Kriminal (1998: 9), something that Sei donne per l'assassino seems to be aiming for with its image of

Tao Li floating in the bathtub, nipples and pubic hair partially visible, one of the most frequently reproduced images from the film. But it would be wrong to suggest that *Kriminal*'s women are *only* eroticised in death or that punishment awaits all of these reform school girls. Margie might be as scantily clad as Carol for much of the story, but she is granted a bit more agency than at least five of Bava's six women (the obvious exception being the Countess). '*Omicidio al riformatorio*' is more playful than *Sei donne per l'assassino*, which emphasises what Tim Lucas calls 'the ruination of beauty' (2007: 561) and the physical pain endured by its victims.

In subsequent issues, *Kriminal* will introduce two more regular female characters. The first is Gloria, the policewoman fiancée of Inspector Milton, who is seduced by Kriminal and develops an erotic love-hate fixation on him, even after he has thrown vitriol in her face. She makes a striking return as a vengeful but still infatuated figure in issue 57 'L'invidia corrode' ('Envy corrodes', 1966), menacing Kriminal and Lola, her gloved hand turning off the mains power before she appears clad in Kriminal's own costume. There are shades here of some of Dario Argento's female killers. But it's Lola who will become Kriminal's great love; like Eva Kant in *Diabolik*, humanising the character by adding romance to the formula, what Franco Spiritelli calls *nero-rosa* (1996: 95). Lola makes her debut in '*Dramma in collegio*' (#55, 1966), a virtual remake of '*Omicidio al riformatorio*' – we're back in an institution full of scantily clad girls surrounded by vice, this time a girls' boarding school (Lola herself is a variation on Margie, sexy and active in solving the mystery). The title page, depicting Kriminal chasing a lingerie-clad girl, seems to promise more of the same, but the tone is different and much less like *Sei donne per l'assassino*.[6] Editoriale Corno, the publishers of *Kriminal*, would ask Bunker and Magnus to tone down both *Kriminal* and *Satanik* as the trial loomed in 1966 (Burattini, 2012: 90),[7] but there seemed to be a slight move away from the more outrageous material even before this. The scantily clad girls are still there but the violence has become even more cartoonish (Kriminal hanging someone with an exaggerated tug on the other end of the noose). Kriminal was no longer the outright villain of early issues, the man who threw vitriol in Gloria's face and laughed. He had become noticeably more handsome, too, a rebellious anti-hero to identify with, not the faceless figure of terror of the *feuilleton* or the *giallo*.

The question remains as to why *Sei donne per l'assassino* performed so disappointingly at the Italian box office when it now seems so in tune with developments in popular storytelling *per adulti* of the time, offering the same kind of 'forbidden' thrills. It is possible that the Italian public preferred such stories in comic-book form to seeing them onscreen. By making its criminals rebellious transgressors as much as figures of terror, the *fumetti neri* might have captured the permissive mood of the economic miracle more successfully, whereas the cinematic *giallo* blossomed more fully in the less optimistic times of the 1970s. But it is even more likely that the actual reasons are more mundane than this, unfortunate casualties of distribution or exhibition, about which we still know considerably less than we would like. Comics, moreover, circulate in very different ways from films, and Bava's film may have simply flown under the radar rather than somehow failing to connect with the popular taste of the time. But while we cannot confirm either that the film was a direct influence on *Kriminal*, what is clear is that it is a film that sits at the centre of a number of generic and transnational currents – French (the revival and reiteration of Fantômas), Italian (the rise of the *fumetti neri* and the relaxation of censorship facilitated by economic prosperity) and German (the cycle of *krimi* films that bled into the *giallo* as a prolific *filone*). Its longer-term influence (on Argento, on American slasher films) has rarely been in question, but it is a film that was far from being 'ahead of its time', but rather at the centre of some contemporaneous trends as well as some future ones.

NOTES

1. The *giallo* section in an Italian bookshop is usually pretty much identical to the Crime section in an Anglo-American one, while the *Giallo* TV channel is populated largely by American and British cop shows. In DVD stores, on the other hand (in my experience, at least), you are nowadays more likely to find Argento, Bava and others among the horror films. In English-language accounts, the *giallo* label tends to conjure certain kinds of images and pleasures (black gloves, razors and knives, female nudity) but that is a very particular type of *giallo* that emerged under very particular historical and industrial circumstances. Nevertheless, outside Italy, the term has come to bestow a certain exotic cult capital that the word 'thriller' probably doesn't.
2. The *krimi* cycle ran from roughly 1959 to 1972, adapted mainly from the English mystery writer Edgar Wallace (and later, his son Bryan Edgar Wallace), and set in 'a studio-created England (beefed up with rear-screen stock shots and Hamburg streets passing for London's Soho)' (Hanke, 2003: 111). Three things distinguish *Sei donne per l'assassino* from its German counterparts: its Rome setting (which is also different from the *Roman Holiday*-style Eternal City of *La ragazza che sapeva troppo*), its use of colour and its lurid sexualised violence.
3. *Diabolik* was initially set in France, but later established the geographically non-specific non-place Clerville as its location.
4. Which was also its French title, *6 Femmes pour l'assassin*.
5. Bunker and Magnus's secret agent spoof *Alan Ford* (1968–) bore a resemblance to another EC comic – *Mad*.
6. If 'Omicidio al riformatorio' resembles *Sei donne per l'assassino*, 'Dramma in collegio' is closer to arguably the only 1960s *giallo* to show much resemblance to Bava's film – *Nude . . . si muore* (Antonio Margheriti/Anthony M. Dawson: Italy, 1967). The film stages a series of murders in a girls' school, its characters a mix of victims and plucky amateur sleuths, its female lead a pigtailed heroine not dissimilar to Lola, its killer disguised as one of the teachers. Its titillating title notwithstanding, it's lighter in tone than either Bava's film or the notorious fifth issue of *Kriminal*. Clearly not all of these similarities were coincidental – Tim Lucas reveals that Bava worked

157

on the original script (uncredited in the final film) and was set to direct it (2007: 711–19). The poster for its American release (retitled *The Young, the Evil and the Savage*) makes an inadvertent reference back to 'Omicidio al riformatorio' – 'Behind the spiked gates of this "exclusive" girls' school, live . . . *The Young, the Evil and the Savage!*'

7. In issue 64, 'Il Segreto di Kriminal' (September 1966), Anthony Logan's origin story is revisited to give it a more tragic dimension, completing his transition to anti-hero rather than the gleeful sociopath of the earlier stories.

Bibliography

Allain, M. and Souvestre, P. (1986), *Fantômas*, London: Penguin.

Barzini, L. (1968), *The Italians*, London: Penguin.

Betz, M. (2009), *Beyond the Subtitle: Remapping Italian Art Cinema*, Minneapolis: University of Minnesota Press.

Bruschini, A. and Tentori, A. (2013), *Italian Giallo Movies*, Rome: Profondo Rosso.

Burratini, M. (2012), 'Il fattore K', in Gomboli, M. (ed.), *La Diabolika Astorina: 50 Anni Con Il Re Del Terrore*, Milan: Cartoomics, pp. 85–95.

Caputo, R. (1997), 'Blood and Black Celluloid: Some thoughts on the cinema of Mario Bava', *Metro*, 10, pp. 55–9.

Castaldi, S. (2010), *Drawn and Dangerous: Italian Comics of the 1970s and the 1980s*, Jackson: University Press of Mississippi (Kindle Edition).

Castelli, A. (2011), *Fantômas: Un Secolo di Terrore*, Rome: Coniglio Editore/ Struwwelpeter s.r.l.

Curti, R. (2002), 'The Wild, Wild World of Diabolik and co.: Adults-only comic books on screen in the 1960s', www.horschamp.qc.ca/new_offscreen/fumetti/html [accessed 31 January 2014].

Dumontet, C. (1998), 'Bloody, sexy and scary', in Dumontet, C. (ed.), *Ghosts, Vampires and Kriminals: Horror and Crime in Italian Comics*, London: National Art Library/V&A, pp. 6–20.

Ferriari, P. (2010), 'Belle da morire', in *Kriminal*, Vol. 1, Verona: Mondadori/Max Bunker Press, pp. 252–5.

Gaspa, P. (2012), 'Astorina, una diabolika avventura', in Gomboli, M. (ed.), *La Diabolika Astorina: 50 Anni Con Il Re Del Terrore*, Milan: Cartoomics, pp. 29–49.

Gravett, P. (2012), 'Fumetti Neri: Diabolik and the Italian Comics Connection', *Comic Heroes*, 14, pp. 52–7.

Gunning, T. (2008), 'Making fashion out of nothing: The invisible criminal', in Uhlirova, M. (ed.), *If Looks Could Kill: Cinema's Images of Fashion, Crime and Violence*, London: Koenig Books, pp. 22–30.

Hanke, K. (2003), 'The "lost" horror film series: the Edgar Wallace *krimis*' in Schneider, S. J. (ed.), *Fear Without Frontiers: Horror Cinema Across the Globe*, Godalming: FAB Press, pp. 111–23.

Hunt, L. (2004), 'Boiling oil and baby oil: *Bloody Pit of Horror*', in Mathijs, E. and Mendik, X.(eds), *Alternative Europe: Eurotrash and Exploitation Cinema Since 1945*, London and New York: Wallflower, pp. 172–80.

Koven, M. J. (2006), *La Dolce Morte: Vernacular Cinema and the Italian Giallo Film*, Lanham, MD, Toronto and Oxford: Scarecrow Press.

Lucas, T. (2007), *Mario Bava: All the Colors of the Dark*, Cincinatti, OH: Video Watchdog.

Needham, G. (2003), 'Playing with genre: defining the Italian *giallo*', in Schneider, S.

J. (ed.), *Fear Without Frontiers: Horror Cinema Across the Globe*, Godalming: FAB Press, pp. 135–44.

Olney, I. (2013), *EuroHorror: Classic European Horror Cinema in Contemporary American Culture*, Bloomington: Indiana University Press.

Piselli, S., Bruschini, A. and Morrocchi, R. (2008), *Cinefumetto: Nerosexy/Fantastique/ Western/Saderotik/Estetica Pop Italiana 1960–1973*, Florence: Glittering Images.

Secchi, L. (1998), 'Introduction', in Dumontet, C. (ed.), *Ghosts, Vampires and Kriminals: Horror and Crime in Italian Comics*, London: National Art Library/V&A, p. 4.

Sabin, R. (2008), 'The Face of Fear', in Uhlirova, M. (ed.), *If Looks Could Kill: Cinema's Images of Fashion, Crime and Violence*, London: Koenig Books, pp. 32–8.

Spiritelli, F. (1996), 'Diabolik, quasi un'antologia', in *Diabolik: L'uomo dai mille volti*, Turin: Lo Scarabeo, pp. 59–60.

Wagstaff, C. (1992), 'A Forkful of Westerns: Industry, Audiences and the Italian Western', in Dyer, R. and Vincendeau, G., *Popular European Cinema*, London and New York: Routledge, pp. 245–61.

Walz, R. (2000), *Pulp Surrealism: Insolent Popular Culture in Early Twentieth-Century Paris*, Berkeley, Los Angeles and London: University of California Press (Kindle Edition).

10. POLITICAL MEMORY IN THE ITALIAN HINTERLAND: LOCATING THE 'RURAL *GIALLO*'

Austin Fisher

This chapter aims to locate a sub-set of what has become known as the '*giallo*' *filone* within its historical contexts, and to ask what significance this relationship might hold for the broader study of Italy's cultural history. Such an undertaking immediately poses methodological questions: what are we looking for when we seek to identify 'history' in such popular cinema; by what models can we best pursue a 'historical' approach to an amorphous, frequently unruly cinematic format like the Italian *filone*? Certainly, such films can offer insights into how discourses about the past have been represented and consumed within particular registers of historical address. John Foot concludes his study of Italy's 'divided memory' by stating that, for the historian:

> [Italy] provides a rich and complicated kaleidoscope of debates over the past. Our task is not to look for overarching theories or outcomes that suppress these competing visions and narratives, but to understand, explain, and study how the past has been experienced and narrated over time. (Foot, 2009: 206)

Foot's central thesis places the nation's history in an osmotic relationship with a contested 'public memory': a relationship that ensures that the past is continually constructed and narrated anew in the negotiated, organic shaping of the present. By thus repudiating perceived boundaries between notions of (empirical) 'history' and (subjective) 'memory', Foot seeks to examine heterogeneous 'lived experiences' of a people's relationship with their national past: analysing not mere 'facts', but the differing ways in which perceived facts have been understood and utilised (Foot, 2009: 5–6). In essence, this approach seeks to appraise 'history' on its audiences' terms, to take account of the cultural options open to them for its interpretation and negotiation in a given moment.

Such an approach is brought into particular focus when we consider Italy's 1970s: a decade notable for schismatic preoccupations with the national past,[1] which presents an array of cinematic registers through which such preoccupations were represented. Increasingly, scholarship in this area provides nuanced considerations of how popular formats engaged in historical discourse. Yet, where contextualisation within the specific political and historical conditions of 1970s Italy is concerned, gaps remain surrounding the diverse category of the *giallo* thriller. In seeking partially to fill these gaps, my subject matter comprises a small group of films, united by their representations of a parochial rural Italian underbelly: *Non si sevizia un paperino/Don't Torture a Duckling* (Lucio Fulci, 1972), *I corpi presentano tracce di violenza carnale/Torso* (Sergio Martino, 1973), *La casa dalle finestre che ridono/The House of the Laughing Windows* (Pupi Avati, 1976) and *Solamente nero/Bloodstained Shadow* (Antonio Bido, 1978). I shall argue that these films, which for the sake of brevity I shall call the 'rural *gialli*',[2] gaze inwardly to invest in a set of discourses surrounding the nation's past, and thereby offer symptomatic insights into the preoccupations of their own era.

It is first necessary to hold the very category '*giallo*' up to some degree of scrutiny since, though the films that form my central subject matter are usually considered to belong to this *filone*, they are noticeably different from its more widely studied strands (most notably, the films of Dario Argento). Attempts to define the cinematic *giallo*, indeed, are often problematic, full of caveats and acknowledgements of ambiguity. As is well known, the generic appellation derives from Mondadori publishers' yellow-covered murder mystery books, at first translated from Anglophone novels and then localised by Italian writers such as Leonardo Sciascia. As Gary Needham argues, however, the cinematic *filone* that followed constitutes 'a body of films that resists generic definition', so permeable are its perceived boundaries (Needham, 2003: 136). Where tentative definitions are attempted, they coalesce around consistent themes surrounding modernity and cosmopolitanism. The *filone*'s settings and locations, for example, have been described as 'fundamentally contemporary and cosmopolitan' (Bondanella, 2009: 387), 'modern' (Bini, 2011: 63) and 'urban' (Olney, 2013: 104). Accordingly, the *giallo*'s thematic concerns tend to be traced back to one of two 'founding texts': the tourist-in-urban-Italy model of *La ragazza che sapeva troppo/The Girl Who Knew Too Much* (Mario Bava, 1963); and the fashion-house chic of *Sei donne per l'assassino/Blood and Black Lace* (Mario Bava, 1964). Such a broad generic umbrella therefore appears to be of limited use if we wish to appraise the specific concerns of the 'rural *giallo*', whose backwater settings and overt focus on rustic superstition point to an alternative point of origin, also directed by Mario Bava: *Reazione a catena/A Bay of Blood* (1971).

If, however, we put to one side the *giallo*'s heterogeneous semantic accoutrements, and consider instead the thematic preoccupations that characterise this *filone*, the 'rural' variant does have a role to play within a larger generic identity, by providing an important counterpoint to the more celebrated 'urban' examples. Tensions between parochialism and cosmopolitanism, tradition and modernity, and the national and the transnational run throughout both the films and the scholarship that surrounds them. Needham (2003), Koven (2006) and Baschiera and Di Chiara (2010), for example, all emphasise the *giallo*'s fixation on notions of travel, tourism and foreignness, and include instances of the rural *giallo* in a broader narrative pattern in which an outsider figure travels to an alien locale where he or she becomes a witness to or investigator of grisly murders. Koven identifies a consistent association of 'jet-set' cosmopolitanism with violent psychoses, and ties this to feelings of ambivalence towards encroaching modernity in post-war Italy, arguing that *gialli* perform a culturally and historically specific 'vernacular' function on behalf of Italy's *terza visione* audiences by registering their own feelings of unease at the rapid changes underway in their national culture (Koven, 2006: 45–59). For Koven, the rural variant's contrasting depictions of provincial villages whose populations resist the invasion of the modern world provide an introspective manifestation of this same anxiety.

The extent to which the *giallo* can be said to constitute such a culturally specific 'national' or 'local' (Italian) discourse, however, divides opinion. Focusing on the liminality of place and identity, Baschiera and Di Chiara argue that the tension between the local and the global that runs throughout this *filone*, and specifically the rural variant, cuts it adrift from any 'national' moorings (Baschiera and Di Chiara, 2010: 112–19). The ostensible 'Italian-ness' of the rural settings is here read as a performance of exoticism in the construction of a transnational 'tourist gaze' on behalf of international audiences, who formed the primary focus of address for films such as *I corpi presentano tracce di violenza carnale,* which enjoyed considerably greater success in export markets than in Italy itself. The rural *giallo*, they argue:

> copes in a different way with the transnational productive nature of the genre itself. Instead of hiding the national character [. . .] it represents particular local places charged with artistic values, and renders them perfectly understandable and known for every audience thanks to their touristic features. (Baschiera and Di Chiara, 2010: 118–19)

Thus, the provincial underbelly of Italy operates as an object of fascination across perceived national or cultural boundaries, bringing the global to the local through the diegetic intrusion of the 'outsider' figure.

The issue of whether 'cultural specificity' can or should be read into these films is indeed a pertinent one, and raises broader methodological questions for my research. Tim Bergfelder diagnoses a widespread critical assumption that, while US cinema is polysemic, open and international in appeal, European cinematic forms exist within discrete national categories, demanding culturally 'competent' viewers (Bergfelder, 2005: 325). In such a diasporic, supranational arena of distribution and consumption as late twentieth-century Europe, he argues, notions of national 'belonging' should be recalibrated to take account of the fluidity of cultural identities. Given this ambiguity, to what extent can we (or should we) situate rural *gialli* as documents of the historical and political concerns of 1970s Italy, as I am seeking to do here? As the above summary indicates, it is certainly not the case that the validity of such an approach should be assumed, and this *filone*'s transnational aspect goes some way to explaining the relative lack of such contextualisation in the existing literature.

Given its common setting in contemporary Italy, it is for example notable how seldom the wider *giallo* is analysed in relation to the synchronous events of the *anni di piombo*, or 'Years of Lead'. Alongside the *poliziottesco* police procedural, the *giallo* is one of two *filoni* that began to proliferate at the beginning of the 1970s, and then flourished during post-war Italy's most traumatic decade. Both *filoni* commonly revolve around amplified levels of violence in contemporary Italian locales, and both invest in narratives that seek to solve or explain the causes of these irrational and perplexing acts.[3] The *poliziottesco* is increasingly studied for its commentary on the politically motivated violence of its time and place.[4] Such analyses of the *giallo*, however, are rare. One such study, from Andrea Bini, argues for a link between this *filone*'s disquiet towards modernity and a growing sense of unease and insecurity in Italian society as indiscriminate acts of violence were becoming more frequent in the 1970s (Bini, 2011: 63–72). This kind of reading seeks to identify political or historical significance arising from a direct relationship to the material conditions that surround the cinematic medium: an approach more often applied to the *poliziottesco*, which overtly represents the terrorist acts and related conspiracies of Italy's 1970s. While arguing for the rural *giallo*'s status as an historical 'document', however, I also seek to demonstrate that it operates within a different mode of address: one that registers preoccupations, confusions and ambiguities arising from its cultural moment. If notions of 'cultural specificity' are rendered problematic by the complexities of the films' socio-political surroundings, it is through their very polysemy that they register negotiated, transitional identities within their cultural moment.[5]

For obvious reasons, it is common to focus on notions of 'violence' when looking at the Years of Lead and their processes of cultural representation. Given that the presence of homicidal acts is usually seen to be integral to the *giallo*'s generic identity, it might seem logical to focus (as does Bini) on this aspect if one is seeking to locate this *filone* in its historical contexts. I would like to suggest, however, that in the case of the rural *giallo*, this period of Italian history leaves its mark through more indirect inscriptions and preoccupations to do with the nation's past, which lay behind the intensification of violent acts. The period between the bombing of Milan's Piazza Fontana in December 1969, and the kidnapping and murder of former Prime Minister Aldo Moro in May 1978 provides a key case-study for Foot's analysis of 'divided memory', as an era during which the past and its competing forms of memorialisation were increasingly politicised subjects of dispute (Foot, 2009: 183–203). Foot presents a continuum in post-war Italy, whereby the schisms of living memory persist through continual conflict over the innately disputed details and significance of historical 'truths'. In the 1970s, this intensified cognitive and physical battleground over both the 'facts' of the past and their resonance in the present centred on memories of events both decades old (the War, the Resistance and unresolved grievances between communism and fascism) and recent (the bombings and their disputed culpabilities, the 'accidental' death of the anarchist Giuseppe Pinelli in police custody). The picture of Italy's 1970s painted by Foot's valuable study is therefore one of a forum in which open wounds of the local past were being perpetually exposed anew in an ongoing 'memory war' (Foot, 2009: 150).

By no means was this exclusively an Italian phenomenon, since similar processes of divisive preoccupation with the living past and over how that past should continue to be interpreted were evident across Western Europe in the 1970s. It is a well-studied[6] phenomenon that, as the unprecedented prosperity of the post-war boom began to wane, tensions that had festered since the War began once more to rise to the surface, and this was particularly acute in those former Axis countries where the extent of denazification remained a hot topic of debate. Mark Mazower, for example, writes that the terrorism and retaliatory police repression of 1970s West Germany 'raised the spectre of that interwar political extremism and ideological polarization which most of western Europe hoped had been left behind for good' (Mazower, 1999: 324). In a broader sense, therefore, this can be seen as a period of reflection on the rapid changes of the past three decades, as well as one of renewed crisis as untreated wounds of living memory were being opened up to haunt the present. The supranational nature of this phenomenon allows us to observe a process of crisis that fluctuated and responded according to the demands of particular cultural-political (rather than strictly 'national') contexts.

It is when we consider this context of negotiable and fiercely disputed outlooks on the past that the rural *giallo* becomes an intriguing 'historical' document. Each of the films under consideration in this chapter frames tropes common to the larger *giallo* category as entry points into an examination of the local past. The *filone*'s common tension between cosmopolitanism and parochialism, for example, here provides a figurative form of 'time travel', in which a representative of modernity discovers a point of contact with this past, which inescapably haunts or shapes the 1970s present. Each also demands that this 'time traveller' figure delves into the local past to solve a mystery; but in each, the 'facts' of the past are shown to be unstable, so that 'history' becomes a construct of competing memories, be they individual or cultural. In each, therefore, the living past and the unreliability of its facts are presented as objects of intense scrutiny. I do not seek to claim these films as under-appreciated works of political commitment. Nor am I attempting to prove that the filmmakers were necessarily aiming to comment upon their era's schismatic outlooks. Instead, I wish to explore in more detail the relatively obvious point that any act of addressing or imagining a national or local past is an inherently politicised one, and that this was particularly the case in 1970s Italy. Through such modes of representation, these films display one available register through which such discourses were being distributed and consumed at this time.

La casa dalle finestre che ridono is emblematic of this trend. This is due not only to its setting in a parochial, rural Italian locale, but also to the fact that its thematic construction overtly focuses on this setting by examining the tourist veneer of Italy's heritage industry. As the traveller figure Stefano is welcomed into the remote village by Mayor Solmi, it is made clear to him that the image of quaint antiquity must be restored in order for the local economy to recover through tourism. Indeed, this is why Stefano has been called for in the first place: to help maintain the tourist façade by repairing the fresco in an old rural church. The viewer is then presented with various symbols for this peeling veneer, which barely covers up the traumas of the past: most overtly, in the very painting Stefano is here to restore, which acts as a palimpsest as its historical layers and their disturbing meanings are uncovered through the course of the film.

Furthermore, the traumas of the Second World War surface time and again as a past that lurks just beneath the community's present difficulties, haunting the collective memory of this village. The local river can no longer support wildlife because it remains littered with war surplus. The hotel landlady's lie that she is expecting a busload of tourists is exposed when the cleaner tells Stefano 'our last tourists were those German bastards in the 1940s'. Even the church itself acts as a historical palimpsest, since we are told that it was rebuilt after the SS used it as a hideout. The village in Avati's film (in reality Lido degli Scacchi in Emilia-Romagna) is therefore presented as more than just a stereotypically parochial backwater. Alongside this mode of representation runs a constant theme pertaining to the open wounds of the past, and how they continue to flow through the present.

The film is most illustrative of this argument when its plot proceeds to frame the past as an entity in which 'facts' are unstable, their meanings demanding deduction through the examination of collective or individual memories. A pivotal scene comes just after Stefano has found bones buried outside an abandoned building (giving him and the viewer clear evidence of historical murders), and then discovers the dead body of his accomplice Francesca hanging from a hook inside the same building. As he hurriedly returns to the scene with the local *carabinieri* to show them the evidence, both the bones and Francesca's body have mysteriously disappeared. Time and again in this film, such pieces of evidence for the crimes of the past disappear, leaving only their memories (for both Stefano and the viewer): a taped voice is inexplicably wiped; the restored painting is sabotaged; and then these bodies go missing. Stefano is therefore left to construct his story from memory alone, and the meanings he attaches to these memories are more important than the bare facts, which are shown to be unreliable. Indeed, throughout *La casa dalle finestre che ridono*, the narrative of history does not merely consist of the 'facts' of the past, but instead relies on what we make of those facts (Stefano's quest to piece the mystery together from the fragments he has at his disposal forms the entire narrative thrust) and which ones we can see: as the *carabinieri* depart from the suddenly empty mass grave, the camera reveals to the viewer alone that a jawbone had in fact been left behind, but missed during the search. Tantalising traces of the past therefore remain, if only the characters can find them.

The comment contained in the above scene, and in the film more broadly, on the selective construction of history is not particularly sophisticated, and does not necessarily require a more detailed textual deconstruction than that which I have just provided. It should, however, be situated in its cultural-political contexts and appraised for what its particular mode of address can tell us within larger discourses of its era. Firstly, and as already stated, *La casa dalle finestre che ridono* was not alone in sending a representative of contemporary Italy into a primitive rural backwater, or in using this setting as a means to examine the traumas of the past. Indeed, its industrial status as a product of the Italian *filone* system (characterised by formulaic repetition alongside incremental innovation) is palpable when we compare its opening sequence to the almost identical equivalent in *Solamente nero*, made two years later. In both, an urbane young Italian art historian named Stefano and played by Lino Capolicchio arrives from the modern city into a remote, superstitious locale by boat, having just met a female visitor who will later become his accomplice in the investigation of historical murders. In both films, a painting then plays a key role in the unravelling of the plot (itself an echo of *L'uccello dalle piume di cristallo/The Bird with the Crystal Plumage* (Dario Argento, 1970) and

Profondo rosso/Deep Red (Dario Argento, 1975)), and in both the denouement reveals a perverted priesthood to be the source of the psychosis in question. Koven identifies the similarities between these two films as an indication of the *giallo*'s iterative ambivalence towards the encroachment of modernity: the two Stefanos acting as harbingers who are resisted by the local community (Koven, 2006: 57–8).

Entwined within this commentary on the onset of modernity is of course the contrapuntal framing of a residual Italy from a bygone era, whose antiquated mores cause tensions upon the arrival of the cosmopolitan protagonist. Each of the rural *gialli* under consideration here invests in and explores notions of a packaged 'picturebook' Italy, whether by overtly focusing on the tourist trade (as in *La casa dalle finestre che ridono*) or by using locations with resonance to a tourist outlook. Baschiera's and Di Chiara's critique of *I corpi presentano tracce di violenza carnale* examines the film's initial setting in Perugia – a provincial city containing a popular university for foreigners – as an apt space to frame a tension between local and touristic perspectives (Baschiera and Di Chiara, 2010: 116). The locations of both *Solamente nero* (the Venetian islands) and *Non si sevizia un paperino* (the mountains of the Southern interior), meanwhile, possess particular historical redolence of an Italy constructed by the Baedeker guidebook and the *Illustrazione Italiana* magazine.[7]

Such framings of Italy, through an overt focus on location to explore the backwardness of rural or provincial communities, are also to be informed by scholarly debates around the 'heritage film': a genre (if 'genre' we can call it) that is intimately tied to discourses of remembrance around national and local histories. Rosalind Galt takes issue with analyses that view such 'heritage' films as ahistorical myth, celebratory nostalgia or anodyne spectacle, arguing instead that *Nuovo Cinema Paradiso/Cinema Paradiso* (Giuseppe Tornatore, 1988), *Mediterraneo* (Gabriele Salvatores, 1991) and *Il postino/The Postman* (Michael Radford, 1994) possess political significance, not for the few direct references to the ideological schisms of their setting in the immediate postwar years, but through their very mode of address within the conventions of romantic melodrama. Galt's astute analysis diagnoses an exchange between the films' setting (in a moment of possibility and hope just before the foundation of Italy's First Republic) and the political moment of their production (when that same, now corrupted, republic was on the verge of implosion and demise): an exchange whose temporal specificity demanded the 'projection of politics onto romance' (Galt, 2006: 38).

It rather goes without saying that the representations of provincial Italy to be found in the rural *gialli* are of a different tenor to those of the heritage films analysed by Galt: psychotic, nightmarish visions of occult superstition, which would be hard to shoehorn into the category 'romantic'. These *gialli* are also, of course, set in the 1970s present rather than in the past *per se*.

Galt's argument nevertheless provides illuminating methodological context for appraising the mode of popular address through which the rural *giallo* invests in representations of Italy's antiquated underbelly: through the diagnosis of one particular mode as an appropriate register for the concerns of the films' own cultural-political moment. By definition, the 'mystery' narrative format (which, as Russ Hunter points out, is a more accurate implication of the word '*giallo*' in an Italian cultural context than are oft-assumed 'horror' paradigms (Hunter, 2009: 104–6)) demands that a film's plot burrows into the past. When allied to settings that overtly evoke Italy's 'heritage' antiquity, this provides a particularly apt filter for a symptomatic preoccupation with local history at a moment of national crisis, when reflections on the past and its implications for identity were pressing.

Non si sevizia un paperino provides a vivid illustration of this point. Shot mostly in the mountains of Puglia and Basilicata, this film is set in, not only a distinctively Italian locale, but specifically a southern Italian locale, and invests heavily in traditions of representation that have surrounded the south of the Italian peninsula for centuries. The *Mezzogiorno* has long been framed as an archaic frontier land, serving simultaneously as a mirror for Italian national identity and a window into Italy's primitive or feudal past.[8] Since the *Risorgimento*, the South has thereby offered an arena for deliberation around contemporary neuroses of the nation state: what John Dickie terms 'the testing-ground of Italy's modernity, the measure of its claims to civility, and the focus of national solidarity' (Dickie, 1999: 54). Fulci's film utilises this local significance of the setting to provide a stage for a *giallo* murder mystery around a series of child killings, and also one on which to examine a culture clash between a dark, benighted underbelly and the onset of cosmopolitan modernity.

The film's overt focus on the primordiality of its fictional southern village of Accendura is adequately addressed in the existing scholarly literature.[9] The opening shot in particular has received attention for the way in which, in the words of Cosimo Urbano, it 'immediately establishes the film's basic and unresolvable conflict: a modernity fuelled by economic development travers- ing an ancient, almost archaic, rural community, disrupting age-old rhythms' (Urbano, 2007: 74). A long shot of the mountainous landscape of the southern interior straight away pans to the concrete scar of the *autostrada* ploughing through the middle of the rugged natural beauty, providing a clear symbol for this culture clash in twentieth-century Italy. This conflict, indeed, pervades the narrative and the *mise-en-scène*, setting up a series of thematic and symbolic contrasts in the opening ten minutes. The intrusion into the quiet village of the liberated, licentious Milanese woman Patrizia (Barbara Bouchet), for example, provides a counterpoint to the ostracism of the feared witch Maciara (Florinda Bolkan). Patrizia's strikingly modernist house is first seen perching awkwardly above the ancient whitewashed village, and the editing accentuates the juxta-position by cutting straight to the architectural hub of rural community life, the *campanile*. A subsequent scene of gaudily dressed women driving along the *autostrada* and loudly discussing their consumerist lives up north is fol-lowed by one of a mysterious, candle-lit voodoo ceremony. Fulci himself stated that the film's original setting was going to be Turin – a northern industrial metropolis that had seen a large influx of southern migrant workers during and after the Economic Miracle of the 1950s – where he claimed to have seen voodoo ceremonies taking place among factory workers (Palmerini and Mistretta, 1996: 59). The anachronistic incongruity of what were perceived to be southern cultural mores in contemporary Italy was, therefore, the driving theme behind his film's production from the start.

Fulci's 'South' therefore inherits that region's long-established role of holding up a mirror to contemporary Italy as a contrastive means by which to scrutinise the condition of the modern state: a point that is made explicit when the dying, bloodied Maciara, having been savagely beaten by the townsfolk, crawls agonisingly to the edge of the *autostrada*. Her final moments are spliced with images of comfortably well-off tourist families speeding past on their holidays in the picturesque South, oblivious to her suffering and, by extension, to the violence of Italy's underbelly literally lying just inches away from their consumerist dream. Steven Thrower identifies this scene as a key moment of social criticism in the film: 'a devastating vision of the social isolation of these quiet, superficially picturesque backwaters' (Thrower, 1999: 88). As Maciara at last expires, indeed, the scene cuts straight to police officers covering her dead body, and a detective provides an explanation (as if it were needed) for the clear symbolism: 'we construct gleaming highways, but we're a long way from modernising'.

Yet side-by-side with this obvious critique of modernity lies another of the South's traditional cultural functions: that of a window into the past through an exploration of the nation's primal state. This is most manifest in the reso-lutely archaic *mise-en-scène* already mentioned, which situates the viewer and the 'outsider' figures alike in a perceptual time warp: as when Patrizia and Martelli (Tomas Milian) stop their car on a mountain road, and the passer-by they ask about a missing child is on horseback. The focus on a past that is fast disappearing is also woven into the film's thematic construction. The denoue-ment reveals that (as in *La casa dalle finestre che ridono* and *Solamente nero*) the killer is the village priest. As he falls to his death, Don Alberto's motiva-tions for the child murders are explained in a voiceover. Nostalgic flashbacks of his victims' youthful vigour are spliced with shots of the priest's violent demise, as we learn that his intention all along was to prevent the children from falling into sin by freezing them in their innocence. As a plot device, this merely iterates what Koven dubs the *giallo*'s 'pop-culture psychology', whereby the *filone* repeatedly lends itself to 'pat psychoanalytical explanations' for killers' psychoses (Koven, 2014: 206). The decision to ally such a thematic focus on preserving the past in aspic and resisting the progress of time with an empha-sised setting in a stereotypical rural South, however, places Fulci's film within a continuum of cultural representations of the region that are always already implicit commentaries on the past. As Bondanella has pointed out (Bondanella, 2009: 393), Accendura is a pre-modern relic, reminiscent of the anachronistic village described in Carlo Levi's 1945 memoir *Cristo si è fermato a Eboli/ Christ Stopped at Eboli.*

Taken together, the rural *gialli* appraised here can therefore be seen as part of a larger pattern, in part illustrated by Galt, of Italian popular culture turning to modes of representing and negotiating the national past in moments of crisis. Though these *gialli* are all physically set in contemporary Italy, Galt's argument helps us to look at ways in which an engagement with local history and its ongoing political significance does not necessarily have to come through direct references to ideological conflicts, either in the past or the present. A brief, dismissive reference to the hostility of students to the authorities at the start of *I corpi presentano tracce di violenza carnale* is the closest to direct commentary on late 1960s or early 1970s politics as these films get. Instead, we can diagnose a preoccupation with the past that emerges from a film's sub-text, and that possesses a particular power in that film's own cultural moment.

All of which poses the important question of definition surrounding the term 'historical film'. Clearly, if we are to categorise the rural *giallo* thus, this term cannot refer exclusively to films set in or directly 'about' the past. On this point, Marnie Hughes-Warrington argues the following:

> What makes a film 'historical' [. . .] is its location in a timebound network of discussions – more or less explicit – on what history is and what it is for. On this definition, any film may be historical because it is viewed as offering indexical markers – on-screen phenomena seen as capturing or connected with past phenomena – or because it suggests something about how and why histories are made. (Hughes-Warrington, 2007: 191)

Such a definition therefore includes films, such as rural *gialli,* whose settings and themes work together to invite the viewer to contemplate the construction and representation of historical narratives and their relationship to the present. While the point that all films can be seen as 'historical' is valid (in that all films act to some degree as documents of their era), however, it is less clear how such an all-encompassing approach should be applied to the political signifi-cance that is attached to particular cinematic treatments of history. As stated, the rural *gialli* appraised here are not 'political films' in the commonly applied sense of direct 'political commitment' associated with the celebrated auteurs of *cinema d'impegno*. Nor are they seeking to offer direct commentary on the events and controversies surrounding the Years of Lead, in the way that many *poliziotteschi* were. By arguing as I have that they register preoccupations of their political surroundings indirectly, and that this is what makes them symptomatically 'political', I am therefore at risk of applying Hughes-Warrington's approach too broadly, by arguing that all films do this and therefore 'all films are political'. This would lead us down a redundant path whereby equally no films are political in any meaningful sense, and this is not my intention.

Instead, I am arguing that certain periods charge the past with particularly potent political memory, and that Italy's 1970s constitute one such period. This applies when the *anni di piombo* themselves are the subject of historical representation (for example, in the continuing trend of twenty-first-century films that seek to reappraise the significance of the era's events for the present, such as *Buongiorno, notte/Good Morning, Night* (Marco Bellocchio, 2003), *Romanzo criminale/Crime Story* (Michele Placido, 2005) or *La prima linea/ The Front Line* (Renato De Maria, 2009)), but also demands that we appraise the variety of modes in which cinema of the period itself engaged with a past filtered through the outlooks of the 1970s. Such a line of enquiry around the power of a given epoch to shape historical memory is indebted to such seminal philosophies of history as Walter Benjamin's notion of *Jetztzeiten*, or 'now time'. This refers to points in time that are particularly replete with political significance, and remain so as they are remembered and represented throughout subsequent eras, famously defined as 'a past charged with the time of the now which [is] blasted out of the continuum of history' (Benjamin, 1999: 253). As already outlined with recourse to the analysis of John Foot, Italy's 1970s were years in which memory and history were, even more than usual, inherently politicised entities, so that any mode of contemplating the local past and its ongoing negotiation in the present can be seen in this period to possess a degree of political significance.

Furthermore, it has been my intention here to analyse one such mode on its own terms, rather than trying to shoehorn it into ill-fitting theoretical models surrounding more widely recognised registers of political or historical cinema. I opened this chapter by quoting Foot's insistence that 'our task is not to look for overarching theories or outcomes that suppress [. . .] competing visions and narratives, but to understand, explain, and study how the past has been experienced and narrated over time' (Foot, 2009: 206). I have sought to illustrate the relevance for the study of popular Italian cinema of this dictum, which itself has a rich heritage in twentieth-century historiographical debate. Isaiah Berlin, responding to E. H. Carr's argument that impersonal, ideological 'forces' determine human behaviour, insisted that, while such forces do indeed constrain the room for manoeuvre, the historian's job is to identify what that room for manoeuvre was in a given historical or political moment (Ignatieff,

2000: 206). The need to revisit the past, which characterised Italy's 1970s, was enacted in a variety of cultural registers. An apperception of this cultural moment's 'room for manoeuvre' must therefore take this variety into account. The 'rural *giallo*' constitutes one such register, and one cultural option open to Italian audiences at the time for the negotiation of their contemporary condition.

NOTES

1. The ferments that followed the bombing of Milan's Piazza Fontana in December 1969 are well documented. The Italian Ministry of the Interior's bare statistics record 14,591 'politically motivated' acts of violence on people or property between 1969 and 1987, resulting in 491 deaths and 1,181 injuries (Cento Bull & Cooke, 2013: 13). The related intensification of political confrontation during the 1970s revolved around the spectre of fascism returning to haunt Italy's political terrain, with the official cover-up of the atrocity's neofascist culpability being exposed by investigative journalists affiliated with the militant journal *Lotta Continua* in 1970.
2. Xavier Mendik (2014) dubs such films the '*Mezzogiorno giallo*'. My alternative use of the term 'rural *giallo*' seeks to avoid conflating Italy's rural spaces with specific discourses surrounding the nation's southern regions (the '*Mezzogiorno*'), since these films (with the notable exception of *Non si sevizia un paperino*) are mostly set and shot in the north of the country.
3. This is not to say that these two *filoni* adopt identical explanations for such acts of violence. The plots of *poliziotteschi* such as *La polizia ringrazia/Execution Squad* (Steno, 1972) and *Milano trema – la polizia vuole giustizia/Violent Professionals* (Martino, 1973), for example, are engaged firmly with the socio-political moment, leading towards the exposure of official cover-ups lurking behind politically motivated acts of violent crime. In contrast, the best-known *gialli*, such as *L'uccello dalle piume di cristallo/The Bird with the Crystal Plumage* (Dario Argento, 1970) and *Perché quelle strane gocce di sangue sul corpo di Jennifer?/The Case of the Bloody Iris* (Giuliano Carnimeo, 1972), as well as the 'rural *gialli*' examined in this chapter, tend to offer psychological explanations of individual psychosis.
4. See, for example, Uva (2007), O'Leary (2010) and Fisher (2014).
5. One possibly significant point to note, if we are to consider the 'Italian-ness' or otherwise of these films, is that while the majority of *gialli* were international co-productions (and therefore were by definition designed to appeal to more than one national market), each of the films that form my central subject matter in this piece were produced exclusively by Italian companies. These are not, however, grounds to discount Bergfelder's apposite warning, which considers factors outside of production processes.
6. For a particularly detailed analysis of the sense of sudden socio-economic and political stagnation that arose in 1970s Western Europe, see Judt, 2005: 453–83.
7. The *Illustrazione Italiana* was one of a number of Milanese magazines that emerged in the second half of the nineteenth century, which coincided with increasing northern urbanisation and catered for an attendant fascination with 'exotic' areas of the world, including the South of Italy. For a detailed analysis of this publication's modes of representing the South, see Dickie, 1999: 85–111.
8. For close historical and archival analyses of these processes of representing the South of Italy, see Dickie (1999) and Moe (2002).
9. The significance of this film's southern setting is, for example, central to Mendik's

identification of Italy's 'rural repressed', which reveals hidden depths within the national psyche (Mendik, 2014: 399).

BIBLIOGRAPHY

Baschiera, S.and Di Chiara, F. (2010), 'A postcard from the grindhouse: exotic landscapes and Italian holidays in Lucio Fulci's *Zombie* and Sergio Martino's *Torso*', in Weiner, R. G. and Cline, J.(eds), *Cinema Inferno: Celluloid Explosions from the Cultural Margins*, Plymouth, MA: Scarecrow Press, pp. 101–23.

Benjamin, W. (1999), *Illuminations*, trans. Harry Zorn, London: Pimlico.

Bergfelder, T. (2005), 'National, transnational or supranational cinema? Rethinking European film studies', *Media, Culture and Society*, 27:3, pp. 315–31.

Bini, A. (2011), 'Horror cinema: the emancipation of women and urban anxiety', in Brizio-Skov, F. (ed.), *Popular Italian Cinema: Culture and Politics in a Postwar Society*, London: I. B. Tauris, pp. 53–82.

Bondanella, P. (2009), *A History of Italian Cinema*, London: Continuum.

Cento Bull, A. and Cooke, P. (2013), *Ending Terrorism in Italy*, London: Routledge.

Dickie, J. (1999), *Darkest Italy: the Nation and Stereotypes of the Mezzogiorno 1860–1900*, London: Macmillan.

Fisher, A. (2014), '*Il braccio violento della legge*: Revelation, conspiracy and the politics of violence in the *poliziottesco*', *Journal of Italian Cinema and Media Studies*, 2:2, pp. 167–81.

Foot, J. (2009), *Italy's Divided Memory*, Basingstoke: Palgrave Macmillan.

Galt, R. (2006), *The New European Cinema: Redrawing the Map*, New York: Columbia University Press.

Hughes-Warrington, M. (2007), *History Goes to the Movies: Studying History on Film*, London: Routledge.

Hunter, R. (2009), *A Reception Study of the Films of Dario Argento in the UK and Italy*, PhD thesis: University of Aberystwyth.

Ignatieff, M. (2000), *Isaiah Berlin: a Life*, London: Vintage.

Judt, T. (2005), *Postwar: A History of Europe Since 1945*, London: Vintage.

Koven, M. J. (2014), 'The *giallo* and the spaghetti nightmare film', in Bondanella, P. (ed.), *The Italian Cinema Book*, London: British Film Institute, pp. 203–10.

Koven, M. J. (2006), *La Dolce Morte: Vernacular Cinema and the Italian Giallo Film*, Oxford: Scarecrow Press.

Levi, C. ([1945] 2000), *Christ Stopped at Eboli*, London: Penguin.

Mazower, M. (1999), *Dark Continent: Europe's Twentieth Century*, London: Penguin.

Mendik, X. (2014), 'The Return of the Rural Repressed: Italian Horror and the *Mezzogiorno Giallo*', in Benshoff, H. M. (ed.), *A Companion to the Horror Film*, Chichester: Wiley-Blackwell, pp. 390–405.

Moe, N. (2002), *The View From Vesuvius: Italian Culture and the Southern Question*, London: University of California Press.

Needham, G. (2003), 'Playing with genre: defining the Italian *giallo*', in Schneider, S. J. (ed.), *Fear without Frontiers: Horror Cinema Across the Globe*, Godalming: FAB Press, pp. 135–44.

O'Leary, A. (2011), *Tragedia all'italiana: Italian Cinema and Italian Terrorisms, 1970–2010*, Oxford: Peter Lang.

Olney, I. (2013), *Euro Horror: Classic European Horror Cinema in Contemporary American Culture*, Bloomington: Indiana University Press.

Palmerini, L. M. and Mistretta, G. (1996), *Spaghetti Nightmares: Italian Fantasy-Horror as Seen Through the Eyes of their Protagonists*, Key West, FL: Fantasma Books.

Thrower, S. (1999), *Beyond Terror: The Films of Lucio Fulci*, Godalming: FAB Press.

Urbano, C. (2007), '*Don't Torture a Duckling*', in Schneider, S. J. (ed.), *100 European Horror Films*, London: BFI, pp. 73–4.

Uva, C. (ed.) (2007), *Schermi di Piombo: Il Terrorismo nel Cinema Italiano*, Soveria Mannelli: Rubettino.

11. THE HORROR OF
PROGRESSIVE ROCK:
GOBLIN AND HORROR SOUNDTRACKS

Craig Hatch

Audio is perhaps the most vital component in the construction of horror films; from the child's lullaby in *Profondo rosso/Deep Red* (Dario Argento, 1975), Bernard Herrmann's use of stingers in *Psycho* (Alfred Hitchcock, 1960), to the *musique concrète* of *The Texas Chainsaw Massacre* (Tobe Hooper, 1974), the canon of great horror films are inextricably tied and indebted to their soundtracks. And yet despite the importance of this audio-visual synchronicity, Italian horror soundtracks in particular have endured not only as part of the films they were made to complement, but also independently of them. With Goblin embarking on their first US tour as a band as late as 2013, to being sampled by contemporary electronic and hip hop acts such as Justice and Madlib, the work of Goblin and other composers such as Fabio Frizzi has received a continued level of interest both with and without the context of their accompanying images. But perhaps this independence always existed? While the enduring legacy and influence of Italian horror film music is in itself evidence of how these soundtracks contained a quality that allowed them to also exist as popular music, I would propose that it is this same quality, this stand-alone nature, that makes them notable even at the point of 'viewing'. Drawing influence from popular music rather than filmic conventions, Italian horror soundtracks (following on from experimentations in Euro Crime) not only liberated themselves from the structural confines of visual editing, they imposed a structure of their own. In analysing their sectional construction or 'pop music' approach to film composition I look not only to describe the legacy of their

CRAIG HATCH

popularity *sans* visuals, but more importantly to define how this perceived detachment plays a vital role in shaping the experience of the films themselves.

Horror soundtracks often function on a strict synchronicity with the events unfolding onscreen. In more unkind terms, films within the genre are often accused of 'mickey-mousing' (Malsky, 2008: 111), a practice that relies on well-worn codes and audio reinforcement to synthesise a reaction rather than one that is seen to be achieved 'fairly', that is to say visually (Greene, 2010: 53). *Halloween* (John Carpenter, 1978) used this strictly synchronous method of scoring to great effect, which outside of its iconic, recurring motif habitually relied upon what Alan Howarth (composer for the *Halloween* sequels) refers to as 'a grab bag of stingers, just all these horrible sounds with sharp attacks, that go "eeaaahhhh" which are cut in to the film to reinforce the scares' (quoted in Larson, 1989). A stinger is an often high-pitched, amplified sound or note that is occasionally out of sync with the inherent rhythm of the music, but does relate to an edit or movement on screen in order to force a physical reaction in the viewer. Italian horror films, however, tend to have an aversion to stingers and synchronous reinforcement and opt for an approach that is closer to rhythmic than physical, with the music driving scenes forward in a sectional and rhythmic motion, rarely serving simply as aural punctuation.

When Goblin arrived on the Italian horror scene in 1975 they marked a radical departure from the breezy bossa nova/*musique concrète* fusion of the early *giallo* cycle and set the template for the direction that Italian horror film music would take until the industry collapsed in the mid-1990s. Goblin brought to the horror genre a sound that Dario Argento in particular had been looking for as early as 1971's *4 Mosche di velluto grigio/Four Flies on Grey Velvet*. Deep Purple were originally sought to score the final film in the 'animal trilogy', but after contractual obligations prevented them from doing so Argento referred back to Ennio Morricone, which resulted in a falling out that lasted until 1996. Argento's frustration with 'traditional' film composition and his desire to incorporate rock music raised its head again when he worked with composer Giorgio Gaslini on the score for *Profondo rosso* which resulted in him leaving the production. Recollections of the reason for the split are inconsistent, with Gaslini and members of Goblin citing scheduling and commitment issues (Cozzi, 2005: 123, 140), and Argento sheer dissatisfaction with the work of Gaslini (quoted in Jones, 2012: 65), but the end result was the introduction of Goblin to complete the score and reinterpret the pieces already written for the film.

The film became a commercial and critical success, with the soundtrack in particular remaining in the Italian music charts for over a year. From this point on, Goblin would become intrinsically tied to the films of Dario Argento, it becoming almost impossible to mention one without the other. Goblin's reach, however, was not confined only to Dario Argento's films, or just to Italy, with the various different incarnations of the band providing music for other films such as *Dawn of the Dead* (George A. Romero, 1978), *Patrick* (Richard Franklin, 1978) and *Contamination - Alien arriva sulla Terra/Contamination* (Luigi Cozzi, 1980), as well as collaborations with Stelvio Cipriani and Fabio Frizzi.

While Goblin consider themselves '[t]he original instrumental progressive rock/soundtrack band',[1] the history of progressive rock in film, especially in Italy, is somewhat more complicated, with a few antecedents that with distinction could rightfully make the claim their own. It is always tempting to attribute dramatic shifts in genres or artistic movements to a singular person or group, artists that we can lionise as auteurs and innovators, but the reality is that industries such as filmmaking often move slower than that. The adoption of rock music into horror soundtracks was rather more granular, as well as being more complicated, both in the retelling of how Goblin came to be involved in their first soundtrack for Dario Argento's *Profondo rosso* and how they relate to industry trends at the time. It is, then, important to cover the immediate pre-history of progressive rock in Italian genre soundtracks to provide a clear contextualisation of Goblin's position in film history, as well as explaining Gaslini's departure from *Profondo rosso* and the conflicting stories that have erupted since the film's release.

First of all, it must be acknowledged that Italian horror and *gialli*[2] are *filone*-driven cycles and therefore certain elements in the soundtrack (such as genre and instrumentation) were often driven by commercial pursuits influenced by recent trends and commercial successes both in film and music. The term *filone* refers to the cyclical nature of the Italian film industry and films that are commonly 'in the tradition of' the most recent commercial success rather than adhering to strict genre codes (Koven, 2006: 7). An example of this in terms of score can be evidenced in the genre-wide move away from the relaxed, bossa nova-tinged music prevalent in the first half of the 1970s to the progressive rock soundtracks found in the wake of *Profondo rosso*'s success. Similarly, the kinds of music used in the films (especially in the early 1970s) differ from those that had traditionally been associated with horror. This often creates an anempathetic mood in the films that is frequently commented upon by critics. In a remark that could apply to many *gialli*, Kristopher Spencer in reference to *5 bambole per la luna d'agosto/5 Dolls for an August Moon* (Mario Bava, 1970) commented how:

> Never before has a group of people been knocked off one by one to such an absurdly breezy, fun-loving musical backdrop [. . .] The mood is so light it is tempting to think Umiliani never even saw the film when he delivered the music [. . .] The theme gets reworked over and over again,

and while there isn't a lot of reinvention taking place, it's difficult not to be seduced by it. (Spencer, 2008: 261)

In Italian popular cinema *filone* takes precedence over genre codes and so expectations or assumptions about the country's output or genre linguistics may or may not be confounded. Spencer's comment regarding the level of repetition in the main theme and being seduced by the music is also an example of the anempathetic nature of the music, which often is accompanied by a 'catchiness' that is unusual for the genre.

As a result, Goblin's brand of horror can be contextualised in view of other successes from the period. Although barely remembered today, one of the original experimentations of a horror-rock fusion soundtrack can be found in Jean Rollin's *Les frisson des vampires/The Shiver of the Vampires* (1971) by Acanthus. Although falling more accurately under the banner of guitar-based acid rock than the bass- and keyboard-focused soundtracks by Goblin, there are similarities, from the groaning and screeching vocals found in the title tracks of both *Les frisson des vampires* and *Suspiria* (Dario Argento, 1977) to the constant shifting between the avant-garde and more recognisably 'rock' predictability in their respective structures. However, due to Acanthus disbanding immediately after the release of Rollin's film and Argento's familiarity with the film being unquantifiable, it would be a stretch to imply that this experiment had any impact on Argento's desire to hire a rock band for his future films.

I would argue that instead, the influence came not from other horror films, or even *gialli*, but a small movement that was beginning to build in the Euro Crime genre, specifically under the supervision of Argentinean-Italian composer Luis Bacalov. Although most fondly remembered nowadays for his iconic *Django* (Sergio Corbucci, 1966) soundtrack, in 1971 Bacalov experienced something of a career boost through the unlikeliest of means by collaborating with the burgeoning Italian progressive rock scene. The first of these collaborations was the soundtrack to *La vittima designata/The Designated Victim* (Maurizio Lucidi, 1971) with the rock band, The New Trolls, which was rearranged and released as the LP *Concerto grosso per I New Trolls*. Being the first Italian rock-symphony fusion album, it has since become a classic of Italian progressive rock and won multiple awards upon release, including the *Discografia Internazionale Marchio di Novita*, which recognised the album as a work demonstrating a 'valid and original approach . . . from an artistic or commercial point of view'.[3] The soundtrack was not only an artistic success, but a commercial one and remained in the top ten of the Italian pop charts for eight weeks, an achievement Goblin would go on to replicate four years later.

There are a few distinctions to make, however, regarding the differences between the music heard within the film and the arrangements heard on

Concerto grosso per I New Trolls. While the album *Concerto grosso* is a true collaboration between Bacalov and The New Trolls, the music heard in the film itself is more segregated in its approach, much of which is performed without the participation of The New Trolls and with a traditional orchestra instead. The music of The New Trolls can still be heard in *La vittima designata*, and the band even earned themselves cameos, but outside of a few instances, Luis Bacalov and The New Trolls are heard independently of each other. The most notable example of these differences can be heard in the title credit song performed by The New Trolls, *My Shadow in the Dark*, as sung by Tomas Milian. The versions heard within the film are performed either on a single harpsichord or acoustic guitar accompanying the vocals. On the album, however, the song is performed under the title of 'Adagio', in which the whole band performs alongside Bacalov's orchestra, complete with guitar solos as well as a more traditional orchestral instrumentation. While the film is somewhat unknown today, the album, *Concerto grosso per I New Trolls*, became an enormous success, and is still performed live in its entirety by the band complete with orchestra today. The album also saw two follow-ups by the band, *Concerto grosso no. 2* in 1976, and *Concerto grosso: The Seven Seasons* in 2007. Rather conveniently, both of these 'sequel' albums were released in conjunction with the launch of reunion tours by the band, demonstrating just how much of a resonance the original album had.[4]

ARGENTO'S HISTORY AND SEARCH FOR ROCK

After two very successful soundtracks with Ennio Morricone for *L'uccello dalle piume di cristallo/The Bird with the Crystal Plumage* (Dario Argento, 1970) and *Il gatto a nove code/The Cat o' Nine Tails* (Dario Argento, 1971), Argento found himself becoming more interested in having a rock soundtrack for his next film, *4 Mosche di velluto grigio*. Although it is usually Goblin that are most often associated with Argento when discussing soundtracks, it is important to remember how influential Morricone's approach to the *giallo* was. In comparison to Goblin, Ennio Morricone provided scores that were more avant-garde, borrowing from the unstructured *musique concrète* rather than the hard-hitting rock precision that was to come from Goblin.

Beginning as an audio movement in 1940s Paris, *musique concrète* constituted the manipulation and use of collected 'concrete' sounds made by items that were not specifically created for musical expression. The musicologist responsible for the movement, Pierre Schaeffer, termed the technique *musique concrète* 'because it is constituted from pre-existing elements taken from whatever sound material, be it noise or conventional music, and then composed by working directly with the material' (Schaeffer quoted in Taylor, 2001: 45). This working practice of collecting sounds and composing music with them after the fact meant that *musique concrète* was very often paired with other avant-garde movements in terms of structure simply due to the production process. He stated that:

> It starts from concrete sounds and then moves towards a structure. In contrast, traditional music starts from an abstract musical schema. This is then notated and only expressed in concrete sound as a last stage, when it is performed. (Schaeffer quoted in Hodgkinson, 2001: 34)

The style, Schaeffer insists, is not a genre, but a compositional aesthetic. This leaves the technique open to different methods of employment, and Italian horror films often played with this philosophy by utilising *musique concrète*-related codes not only in their own avant-garde terms, but by incorporating them into more traditional, sectional musical cues.

Although elements of *musique concrète* found their way into Italian cinema initially through the Spaghetti Western, its true unfiltered introduction was in Ennio Morricone's scores for Dario Argento's earliest films. Morricone recalls that his introduction to *musique concrète* began at a concert in Florence.

> ... a man came onto the stage and began in complete silence to take a stepladder and make it creak and squeak. This went on for several minutes and the audience had no idea what it was supposed to mean. But in the silence the squeaking of the ladder became something else, and the philosophical argument of this experiment was that a sound, any sound at all from normal everyday life – isolated from its context and its natural place and isolated by silence – becomes something different that is not part of its real nature. (Morricone quoted in Frayling, 2005: 96–7)

In the same period as his initial audio-visual experimentations with *musique concrète* in Spaghetti Westerns, he joined Franco Evangelisti's music ensemble Il Gruppo di Improvvisazione Nuova Consonanza, a group dedicated to creating 'spontaneous music' with a keen interest in musical structure and the use of uncommon sounds (Beal, 2009: 103). Although he had previously experimented with *musique concrète* in areas of sound design, his work with Nuova Consonanza delved further into experimentation and removed any context of the noises being created. One composition from the group's 1967 release *The Private Sea of Dreams*, titled *Lip Service (Canata)*, uses only sounds emanating from the human mouth and surrounding areas of the face as instrumentation. The composition's focus on throat noise, grunting, cheek slaps and coughing has similarities to the more outrageous cues such as *Sighs* and *Witch* written for *Suspiria* by Goblin ten years later, albeit in a more structured form. Using his experience from working with Nuova Consonanza, Morricone began to use the avant-garde stylings in full force on his work for genre films, beginning in full with Argento's *L'uccello dalle piume di cristallo*. In a recent interview he remarked how he:

> used the avant-garde music when scoring films as an experiment [. . .] I used this music when I wanted to describe a certain kind of trauma, when the situation was very, very difficult or when something horrible had happened. For example, when I started to score for the film director Dario Argento and I went ahead with scoring other films, which are not so well-known or famous.[5]

The other films that he mentions presumably are other *gialli* scores of the period such as *Chi l'ha vista morire?*/*Who Saw Her Die* (Aldo Lado, 1972) and *Gli occhi freddi della paura*/*Cold Eyes of Fear* (Enzo G. Castellari, 1971), which were more experimental than even those he did for Argento. That is not to suggest that these films only used avant-garde compositions, however. In the same interview Morricone states: 'I used tonal music, which you might call melodic music. And I used this style and into this type of music I sneaked in some styles of avant-garde music and this was unnoticed.'[6] The score he wrote for *L'uccello dalle piume di cristallo*, for example, shares as many traits with Pierre Schaeffer's *Etude Noire* as it does with Simon and Garfunkel.

While Morricone's cues are not as in tune with the visuals as American slasher films such as *Friday the 13th* (Sean Cunningham, 1980) or *The Burning* (Tony Maylam, 1981), he still provides what can definitely be considered suspense pieces that are more typical than those put forth by Goblin. The films scored by Morricone also contain many shorter cues than those by Goblin, sometimes constituting five to ten seconds, which is something that is almost entirely absent in *Suspiria* or *Profondo rosso*, in which the music occupies a very definitive space that is far from the percussion mentioned earlier and noticeably has a clear beginning, middle and end. Perhaps as a result of these more abstract suspense cues, Argento reasoned that 'Ennio Morricone always wrote victim music' (quoted in Jones, 2012: 290) and wanted something harsher and more modern for his next film, *4 Mosche di velluto grigio*.

As is made evident by the inclusion of a rock drummer as the central character, as well as Argento's original intention to cast musician James Taylor in the lead role, Argento was seemingly consumed by rock music at the time. Argento originally approached English rock band Deep Purple to contribute the score for the film, but due to co-production obligations surrounding tax breaks from the Italian government that required a quota of Italian professionals as key crew members, Deep Purple lost out in favour of keeping French editor François Bennot (Cozzi, 2005: 137). As a result, Ennio Morricone returned as composer and delivered a score that was in keeping with the tradition of the work he had done previously for Argento. Despite his best efforts, however, Argento was deeply unhappy with the score, considering the rock tracks in particular to be weak, which resulted in a split that would last until *La sindrome di Stendhal/The Stendhal Syndrome* (Dario Argento, 1996).

Enter Goblin

The circumstances surrounding *Profondo rosso*'s soundtrack vary depending on who is recounting the events. Although Goblin are now recognised as the authors of the soundtrack and it is their name that is plastered across the front cover of many re-pressings of the album, it is important to remember that over half of the album was in fact written by Giorgio Gaslini, and even some of the pieces that were performed by Goblin were also composed by him. Argento first collaborated with Gaslini on his sole excursion from the horror/thriller landscape, the historical comedy *Le cinque giornate/The Five Days of Milan* (Dario Argento, 1973), as well as on his television series *La porta sul buio/ Door Into Darkness* (Dario Argento, 1973). On *Profondo rosso*, however, Argento states that he felt as though Gaslini 'didn't understand the spirit of the film' (quoted in Jones, 2012: 65) and wanted an act that could give the modern, urgent atmosphere that he felt his newest *giallo* needed.

Reacting to the insinuation that he was 'removed' from the project due to Argento considering his music old-fashioned, Gaslini remarked:

> I wrote the score for *Deep Red* just the way Argento wanted, after five films which were fully satisfying experiences for both of us [. . .] it's not true to say that Dario didn't know what kind of music I wrote when he called me for *Deep Red*. (Gaslini quoted in Cozzi, 2012: 123)

The most common reason stated for the introduction of Goblin to complete the score and to reinterpret the pieces already written by Gaslini is that he was on tour with his jazz band at the time and was therefore unable to commit to the recording (Jones, 2012: 78). As noted in reference to the relationship between Luis Bacalov, Osanna and The New Trolls, bringing in session musicians or a band in order to act as a counterpoint to a traditional composer was far from unusual at this time in Italian cinema, neither was it as contentious nor as inflammatory as it sounds. In fact, even after the success of *Profondo rosso* and *Suspiria* Goblin would still often act in the role of session musicians for composers such as Fabio Frizzi on *Amore libero/Free Love* (Pier Ludovico Pavoni, 1974) and *Perché si uccidono/Percy is Killed* (Mauro Macario, 1976), and Stelvio Cipriani's scores for *Solamente nero/The Bloodstained Shadow* (Antonio Bido, 1978) and *Un'ombra nell'ombra/Ring of Darkness* (Pier Carpi, 1979).

To lend credence to Argento's version of events, however, and in a move that adds weight to Goblin's claim to being '[t]he original instrumental progressive rock/soundtrack band',[7] there are a few important differences that should be noted between Goblin's *Profondo rosso* soundtrack and the Bacalov/Osanna/ New Trolls collaborations from a few years earlier; the most important of these being that while Goblin were initially introduced to the project to simply perform the music already written by Gaslini, Argento began to have second thoughts regarding the music and asked the rather inexperienced band Goblin not only to rework some of the material but also to create entirely new songs for the film (Simonetti quoted in Jones, 2012: 78).

THE MUSIC

One of the most important factors of Goblin's approach to making music is that it is very sectional in nature and as a result helps to signal set-piece moments in a stronger manner than traditional soundtracks. As Claudio Simonetti states, this approach to scoring in conjunction with the visuals helps to create moments that truly are 'films within films' (quoted in Cozzi, 2012: 143). In Goblin's soundtracks we hear time signatures that we recognise, and in their contributions to the *Profondo rosso* soundtrack in particular many of the sound cues are not traditional motifs at all, in that they do not serve as sub-conscious reminders of other scenes, but are fully formed riffs typical of rock music. This of course is a notable influence from Spaghetti Western soundtracks, the *filone* that the *giallo* was quickly replacing in popularity. Set-piece moments in Italian Westerns are often referred to as being operatic in the way in which narrative subsides to allow for moments that are purely cinematic and musical in nature rather than serving any kind of realism.

In reference to lower-budget Spaghetti Westerns that often played in third-run cinemas, Wagstaff noted how music in Italian cinema was used as a way of ensuring that the audience was paying attention to the scene that was about to unfold, crucial given that Italian audiences in these third-run or *terza visione* cinemas were notoriously inattentive (Wagstaff, 1992: 254). When considering the sheer sonic excess and volume of the music contained within the films this certainly becomes apparent. Once the set piece is signalled by the music the films begin to operate on a purely cinematic level and the narrative coherency of the scene sometimes breaks down in service of the music. The extravagant camera movements, bombastic music and excessive violence become the primary attraction and the narrative is placed on hold for the duration. Although Wagstaff refers more to lower-budget films that played predominantly to rural audiences, it displays a production level awareness of viewing conventions and the importance of sound as well as volume. This purposeful emphasis on aesthetic and aural style over narrative is an aspect of the films that Italian horror directors have often attempted to reassert.

One of the most elaborate examples of the focus on visuals and rhythmic movement in Italian horror can be found in *Tenebre* (Dario Argento, 1982), in which Argento's camera tracks up and over a house all in one three-minute shot choreographed to the main theme written by Goblin members Claudio Simonetti, Massimo Morante and Fabio Pignatelli. As Knee describes:

> Clearly, the craning camera's perspective is not simply that of the killer, nor, given its odd and foregrounded specificity, can it be plainly taken as the omniscient gaze of some narrating agency [. . .] Argento's narrative discourse shifts into a register not so much of sadistic spectacle as of sensory overload, of pure sensual immersion. (Knee, 1996: 222–3)

The narrative effectively pauses for the set piece as we observe his command of the camera and are assaulted by the sheer volume of the soundtrack. The moment is outside of any narrative concern and the music is not in service of the visuals, the visuals are in service of the music, creating a superfluity that calls attention to the spectacle of the moment and the film's disparate elements. Further exacerbating this effect is that in this moment the film's soundtrack is being played on vinyl by one of the film's characters that in a moment of fourth wall violation is subsequently told to 'turn it down!' by another. Due to Argento placing the importance of camera movement and spectacle above narrative in his films it is often remarked that they become 'incomprehensible'. Harper comments how in Italian horror films,

> As time progressed the ideas of plot and script become more and more superfluous, making way for visually impressive set pieces. This tendency towards style over substance occasionally rendered the films incomprehensible, but also produced some incredibly effective cinematic images. (Harper, 2004: 9)

Although it is an exaggeration to claim that the films are incomprehensible, they absolutely operate under their own cinematic language, a language that is cinematic in the purest sense. Although set pieces are commonly mentioned in horror film criticism when referring to murder scenes, as Harper's quote attests to, in Italian horror they are as equally notable for pure cinematic ambition, both in visuals and inherent rhythmical quality. While there is much truth in the age-old adage that the best film soundtrack is one that the audience does not notice, or one that is almost transparent in its manipulation of the audience's expectations, the soundtracks that became prominent in Italian horror in the wake of *Profondo rosso* seem to disprove this rule or at least add a disruption to the adage. However, I would argue that Goblin's music does play to this expectation. While the music is at once instantly noticeable, the beats are fixed to their own time signature and therefore, despite their blunt nature, are less explicit in trying to force an emotion or reaction from the audience.

'DISORDERLY, ELASTIC, IMPROVISED ATMOSPHERE'

Horror is recognised as a very 'physical' genre, in that it contains moments that jolt the audience, and yet jump scares or 'bus scares' are conspicuously absent in Argento's films. The music written for them by Goblin relies far less on short punctual cues designed for a physical reaction and utilises longer pieces of music that rely on predictable pop structures. By the time of *Profondo rosso* Argento desired a more 'disorderly, elastic, improvised atmosphere' (quoted in Cozzi, 2012: 69), which is a good description of the effect that the music had on scenes. This was echoed by bassist Fabio Pignatelli, who remarked that 'a score has to help creating [sic] atmosphere, whilst suspense must generate from the story itself as well as from the director's skills' (quoted in Cozzi, 2012: 135). In the soundtracks by Goblin, the rhythm and structure of the music is markedly detached from the synchronisation points on screen, which helps to give an unmistakable 'feel' to the moments, but is not dictated by them. As mentioned by Simonetti in a recent interview, Goblin simply 'record, 3, 4, 5 minutes of each song'[8] which is then reused on multiple scenes, rather than performing new versions for each moment. As a result, Goblin's music is often locked into its own pop-orientated sectional structure.

This sectional approach to music (which clearly differs from traditional underscoring) raises many questions as to how the visuals and editing of a scene are affected, especially in genres that are typically so underscored. In some sense, giving the music such a distinct sectional construction in its own right breaks the music away somewhat from the form of the film. The peaks and valleys in the waveform are consistent in their structural confines and thus the film, too, is not allowed to climax in the knowledge that the music has several movements left. The visuals are rendered passive and trapped within the confines of the song, only to be allowed release when the final chorus arrives, fades out and the narrative resumes. It is because we as viewers understand basic sectional song structure and sub-consciously recognise that the visuals have entered a purely audio-visual moment rather than one complementary to the narrative. In many ways this approach to scoring a film and the loose-ness in which the visuals react in relation to it mirror the popular music video. There are various 'synch points' still to be found between the music of Goblin and films of Argento, but the equation of power between the audio and visuals is clearly dipped in favour of the music, at least in these set-piece moments.

I do not mean to imply that there are no synch points between the visual component of the film and the audio, but that they instead lay in the edits rather than the actual events onscreen. The music signals not an action but an entire moment. It also has what Chion terms a 'synch point of convergence', in which the music and image end at the same point despite seeming separate in their synchronicity beforehand (1994: 58). This implies that the sound and visual elements of the films are disparate, and yet I would argue that this bookending of a scene instead helps to mark moments specifically as mini-narratives within themselves, which can be taken without reflection of the rest of the plot. Argento, comparing traditional suspense music with Hitchcock as an example of the way in which he uses music, stated that Hitchcock 'uses it as a background, almost like a chamber music concert, which at a certain point comes to the fore, whereas I use it in a much more robust way' (quoted in Mitchell, 2009: 94). Mitchell comments how rather than underscoring, Argento utilises a method of 'sonic excess' and 'aural hysteria' that over-whelms the images rather than commenting on them, an approach that I would argue filters throughout the entirety of Italian horror cinema (ibid.).

Conversely, an American equivalent of the stalk and slash film, *Friday the 13th Part 2* (Steve Miner, 1981), contains barely any examples of sectional song structure (outside of diegetic music heard in a bar), with the vast majority of the soundtrack consisting of either short cues or classically styled composi-tions, all of which give the impression of being through-composed. Through-composed compositions are called such as it is generally assumed that the music is written from beginning to end and focuses on a progression of differ-ent melodies rather than a structure that revisits earlier sections of the music (Wright, 2007: 261). This type of song structure was particularly popular in the nineteenth century with composers of operas or plays who wished to portray a series of ever-developing moods or those who wished to create songs that told stories through their lyrics. This style of underscore composition is inherently dynamic and flexible, and this method of scoring still finds itself in excessive use in American horror films today. Perhaps the most obvious example of this is in the use of 'stingers', an element that is central to the effect of many horror films. Although stingers are applied in the post-production phase, they have an insistence of synchronicity with the visuals, something that Goblin's soundtracks do not seem to have.

Argento's films with Goblin often reject the idea of engaging with common synch points between the visuals and music, and instead prioritise rhythm and poetry of movement over emotional engagement. This prevalence of music and the idea that movement and images should emerge from music rather than the opposite was a common idea in Italian arts. Cinema and theatre critic Sebastiano Arturo Luciani, in a disparaging of various plays in the late 1910s, complained that:

> They have composed their music by trying to comment on the main action, scene by scene, detail by detail, when music, instead, should

determine the action, not just follow it: it could evoke images, not just translate them into sound. It is from the world of sounds that one has to arrive at the one of images. (Luciani quoted in Bertellini, 2002: 49)

American horror films in particular, more often than not, adhere to the kind of underscore that he disparages. They make particular use of dissonance and delayed resolution to create increased tension and unease in their audience. It is not always guaranteed that the resolution will come, but teasing the completion of the phrase is something that is achieved through a song form that has the luxury of being somewhat free of having its own inherent structure (Donnelly, 2005: 90–1). Horror films tend not to contain memorable melodies so as not to draw attention to the artifice of the moment, operating on a purely functional level designed to evoke sub-conscious expectation and physical reaction in the viewer.

Conclusion

By incorporating Goblin's sectional approach to music, the films of Dario Argento work against the notion that music is predisposed to accompany the film's emotional content in accordance with the visuals and instead embrace a different mode of synchronicity. Classical music has expansibility built into its structure and can rely on variable phrase length that offers multiple opportunities for extension, allowing the composer to delay or quicken the closure of a piece when required by the visuals (Altman, 2001: 23). The popular music employed by Goblin, however, is built upon predictability, and the standard four- or eight-bar units and rhythmic closure, as Altman states, 'satisfies audience expectations of return to familiar melodic material' (ibid.: 25). Popular music that is memorable heightens the importance of rhythm and experience through spectacle over emotional connection or a furthering of narrative. The films, as signalled by their sectional music cues, jump from one set piece to another in which the narrative takes a back seat to make way for cinematic expression. Although these set pieces are often associated with murder scenes, it would be wrong to assume that they are only notable for their violence. As Bondanella states, it is the privileging of dramatic camera work, expressive music, set design and editing that mark them out as a true notable feature (Bondanella, 2009: 375). Obviously, the set piece is not just an artistic expression on the part of the director, but also an important element in holding the attention of a general audience.

In Italian horror films the music is incredibly memorable and is very often remarked upon; so much so that fan communities have emerged all over the internet dedicated not to the films but to the scores themselves. Similarly, not one but two remixes of songs from Goblin's score for *Tenebre* feature on Justice's debut release *Cross*, an album which is a certified gold record in the UK – a true sign of the enduring nature and inherent rhythm that these soundtracks have, even outside of their original context. As Newman states, the music comes 'to the fore' in Argento's films in an 'operatic approach which strains the notionally rational frame of the *giallo*' (quoted in Mitchell, 2009: 96). It is generally considered that an audience should not notice music in a horror film, where immersion in the product as a whole is considered vital (Kivy, 2011: 118). Through repetition, melody and the sheer extravagance of the camera movements these components of film language do just the opposite and call purposeful attention to themselves. As with Bacalov and New Troll's score for *La vittima designata*, Goblin's score for *Profondo rosso* reached the top of the music charts in Italy and stayed in the top forty for nearly a year, eventually selling over 3 million copies (Cozzi, 2012: 137). What makes Goblin's achievement that much more remarkable, however, is that they did not have to re-record the music in order to make it a more palatable listen outside of the confines of the film itself. For a film genre where music is traditionally supposed to be 'experienced' and not necessarily heard, the continuing popularity of Goblin's music outside of the films suggests that Goblin not only managed to navigate the boundaries of what constitutes film music and 'pop music', but also managed to create work that successfully inhabits both arenas without contradiction.

NOTES

1. www.goblinofficial.com/main.php [accessed 20 November 2013].
2. Due to the boundaries of the *giallo* being so flexible because of different domestic and international usages, I refer to *gialli* as a *filone* rather than a genre or sub-genre. That isn't to say that the *giallo* cannot be narrowed down to a body of films, or that they do not have horror conventions but rather that the boundaries of the *giallo* were permeable and often worked well in hybrid genre situations. As a result I use the term *giallo* to specify violent Italian thrillers, and Italian horror to categorise the entire output of Italian horror, which while some *gialli* may also come under (specifically those by Dario Argento after 1975) the flexibility of the *filone* will sometimes require its own distinction alongside 'Italian horror'.
3. 'New Italian Prod. Awards To Be Launched', *Billboard*, 4 September 1971, p. 40.
4. The success of this collaboration prompted a follow-up by Bacalov in 1972 with the rock band Osanna, which manifested itself in the soundtrack to Fernando Di Leo's *Milano Calibro 9* (Fernando Di Leo, 1972).
5. John Doran, 'Ennio Morricone Interviewed: Compared to Bach, I'm Practically Unemployed', *The Quietus*, 8 April 2010, www.thequietus.com/articles/04050-ennio-morricone-interview-a-fistful-of-dollars-for-a-few-dollars-more-the-good-the-bad-and-the-ugly-once-upon-a-time-in-the-west-the-thing [accessed 26 August 2012].
6. Ibid.
7. www.goblinofficial.com/main.php [accessed 20 November 2013].

8. Claudio Simonetti, 'A Composition for Carnage: Composer Claudio Simonetti on Tenebrae', Blu Ray Edition of *Tenebrae* (Arrow Video, 2013).

BIBLIOGRAPHY

Altman, R. (2001), 'Cinema and Popular Song: The Lost Tradition', in Robertson Wojcik, P. and Knight, A. (eds), *Soundtrack Available: Essays on Film and Popular Music*, Durham, NC: Duke University Press, pp. 19–30.

Beal, A. C. (2009), 'Music is a Universal Human Right', in Adlington, R. (ed.), *Sound Commitments: Avant-Garde Music and the Sixties*, Oxford: Oxford University Press, pp. 99–120.

Bertellini, G. (2002), 'Dubbing L'Arte Muta: Poetic Layerings around Italian Cinema's Transition to Sound', in Reich, J. and Garofalo, P. (eds), *Re-Viewing Fascism: Italian Cinema, 1922–1943*, Bloomington: Indiana University Press, pp. 30–82.

Bondanella, P. (2009), *A History of Italian Cinema*, New York: Continuum.

Chion, M. (1994), *Audio-Vision: Sound on Screen*, C. Gorbman (trans. and ed.), New York: Columbia University Press.

Cozzi, L. (2012), *Dario Argento: The Making of Deep Red*, Rome: Profondo Rosso.

Cozzi, L. (2005), *Four Flies on Grey Velvet: A Film Directed by Dario Argento*, Rome: Profondo Rosso.

Donnelly, K. J. (2005), *The Spectre of Sound: Music in Film and Television*, London: BFI.

Frayling, C. (2005), *Sergio Leone: Once Upon a Time in Italy*, London: Thames & Hudson.

Greene, R. (2010), *Quentin Tarantino and Philosophy: How to Philosophize with a Pair of Pliers and a Blowtorch*, Chicago: Open Court.

Harper, J. (2004), *Legacy of Blood: A Comprehensive Guide to Slasher Movies*, Manchester: Headpress/Critical Vision.

Hodgkinson, T. (2001), 'An Interview with Pierre Schaeffer', in Rothenberg, D. and Ulvaeus, M. (eds), *The Book of Music and Nature: An Anthology of Sounds, Words, Thoughts*, Connecticut: Wesleyan University Press, pp. 34–44.

Jones, A. (2012), *Dario Argento: The Man, the Myths & the Magic*, Godalming: FAB Press.

Kerswell, J. A. (2010), *Teenage Wasteland: The Slasher Movie Uncut*, London: New Holland.

Knee, A. (1996), 'Gender, Genre, Argento', in Grant, B. K. (ed.), *The Dread of Difference: Gender and the Horror Film*, Austin: University of Texas Press, pp. 213–30.

Koven, M. J. (2006), *La Dolce Morte: Vernacular Cinema and The Italian Giallo Film*, Oxford: Scarecrow Press.

Larson, R. D. (1989), 'Hyper Reality: Alan Howarth's synthesized scores & specialized sound effects', www.alanhowarth.com/press-articles.html.

Malsky, M. (2008), 'Sounds of the City: Alfred Newman's "Street Scene" and Urban Modernity', in Beck, J. and Grajeda, T. (eds), *The Boom: Critical Studies in Film Sound*, Chicago: University of Illinois Press, pp. 105–22.

Mitchell, T. (2009), 'Prog Rock, the Horror Film and Sonic Excess: Dario Argento, Morricone and Goblin', in Hayward, P. (ed.), *Terror Tracks: Music, Sound and Horror Cinema*, London: Equinox Publishing, pp. 88–100.

Spencer, K. (2008), *Film and Television Scores, 1950–1975: A Critical Survey by Genre*, Jefferson, NC: McFarland.

Stein, L. (1979), *Structure and Style: The Study and Analysis of Musical Forms*, Miami: Summy-Birchard.

Taylor, T. (2001), *Strange Sounds: Music, Technology and Culture*, New York: Routledge.

Wagstaff, C. (1992), 'A Forkful of Westerns – Industry Audiences and the Italian Western', in Dyer, R. and Vincendeau, G. (eds), *Popular European Cinema*, London: Routledge, pp. 245–59.

Wright, C. (2007), *Listening to Western Music*, Belmont: Cengage Learning.

12. 'THE ONLY MONSTERS HERE ARE THE FILMMAKERS': ANIMAL CRUELTY AND DEATH IN ITALIAN CANNIBAL FILMS

Mark Bernard

Many contemporary horror filmmakers pride themselves on violating taboos in their films, especially taboos concerning violence. However, there is a line that even many of the most hardened filmmakers refuse to cross: violence against animals. In fact, some horror filmmakers have spoken out against animal abuse. For instance, heavy metal musician-turned-horror filmmaker Rob Zombie, director of *House of 1000 Corpses* (2003), *The Devil's Rejects* (2005) and the remake of *Halloween* (2007), teamed up with the organisation People for the Ethical Treatment of Animals (PETA) in 2007 to record a message for their 'Thanksgiving Hotline', a 'compassionate alternative' to the Butterball Turkey Talk Line that offers tips on turkey preparation. Zombie is a self-described 'ethical vegetarian' and as such his contribution details the cruelty and mistreatment to which turkeys are subjected in Butterball's factory farms (PETA, 2007). In 2009 another horror filmmaker, Eli Roth, director of the *Hostel* films (2006–7), appeared in a promotional spot for PETA. More lighthearted than Zombie's message but no less serious, the promo features Roth being squeezed by a large snake puppet as he says to the camera: 'While violence in the movies is make-believe, sadly violence against animals is all too real . . . So, let's leave the violence where it belongs: on the screen.'

Zombie's and Roth's attitudes towards animal violence differ significantly from those exhibited by Italian exploitation directors such as Umberto Lenzi, Ruggero Deodato and Sergio Martino. These filmmakers had an undeniable influence on contemporary horror filmmakers – especially Roth, who featured Deodato in a cameo in *Hostel: Part II* (2007), provided a video introduction for the 2011 DVD release of Martino's *I corpi presentano tracce di violenza carnale/Torso* (1973), and paid homage to the Italian cannibal sub-genre with his film *The Green Inferno* (2013). However, these Italian directors took an extremely different position on violence towards animals, as several of their films feature graphic footage of real animal torture, mutilation and death. The cycle of cannibal films made by Italian exploitation filmmakers lasted roughly from the early 1970s to the early 1980s and consists largely of what are undoubtedly some of the most controversial films in world cinema, depicting white Westerners confronted in the jungle by indigenous cannibalistic tribes.

Perhaps the most shocking element of these films – even more so than the gore effects and prejudiced depictions of indigenous peoples – is the inclusion of real animal mutilation and death. Writing about the challenges of teaching exploitation movies in the college classroom, Eric Schaefer notes that while the 'sexual and violent content' of most exploitation films is often 'met with a jaded amusement by students' (2007: 94), the 'mistreatment of animals' in films like Deodato's *Cannibal Holocaust* (1980) still has the power to unnerve even the most jaded students. For Schaefer, it is helpful to address these issues 'through an ongoing discussion of disgust' (2007: 94). However, for many, it is understandably difficult to gain the emotional distance necessary to critically evaluate the disgust these films provoke in the spectator. For instance, Louis Paul, in a book devoted to Italian horror directors, dismisses Deodato's *Ultimo mondo cannibale/Last Cannibal World* (1977) as 'a vile piece of garbage' (2005: 113), and he calls *Cannibal Holocaust* 'one of the vilest pieces of celluloid on the planet' (2005: 113). Similarly, writing about Lenzi's *Cannibal ferox* (1981), perhaps the most brutal film of the cycle, Andrew Parkinson states, '[t]he only monsters here are the filmmakers' (2006: 163).

Some commentators, however, argue that these films are powerful indictments of Western ideological and colonial imperialism, admiring the 'deconstructive eagerness' with which cynical films like *Cannibal Holocaust* and *Cannibal ferox* blur the boundary between 'civilised' and 'savage' (Dickinson, 2007: 172). Specifically, *Cannibal Holocaust* has been singled out as a powerful departure from earlier cannibal films because of the ways it erodes the boundaries between 'civilised' Westerners and the 'savage' indigenous peoples and thus 'creates a series of moral ambiguities rarely matched by other examples of paracinematic excess' (Mathijs & Mendik, 2011: 44). With its story of ruthless American filmmakers who kill both animals and natives and stage atrocities for a documentary they are shooting in the Amazon jungle, the film is, for some, a 'comment on the nature of representations of native populations and the media's role in shaping public perceptions of supposedly savage populations' (Hunter, 2009: 266).

At the same time, however, others read these films' cynical worldview as a philosophical dead end, arguing the exploitative nihilism of this sub-genre has been present since its origins. Italian cannibal films grew out of the popular *'mondo'* documentaries made in Italy in the 1960s, like *Mondo cane* (Paolo Cavara, Gualtiero Jacopetti and Franco Prosperi, 1962), *Mondo cane n.2* (Jacopetti and Prosperi, 1963) and *Africa addio/Africa: Blood and Guts* (Jacopetti and Prosperi, 1966). These films consisted of bizarre and sensationalist footage from around the world and anticipated the cannibal film by including footage of 'wildlife . . . tribal rituals and culinary grotes-query' (Hughes, 2011: 289). While many read the cannibal film as a savage deconstruction of the colonial voyeurism of *mondo* movies, others do not see the films as a significant improvement from their predecessors, claiming that the Italian cannibal film merely replaced the 'your culture sucks' mantra of the *mondo* movies with an '"every culture sucks" attitude' (Shipka, 2011: 124). In a review of Deodato's *Ultimo mondo cannibale*, Kim Newman muses that it 'seems strange that scads have been written about this micro-genre, comment-ing on extensive faked gore . . . unforgivable slaughter of wildlife to pad out less thrilling narrative stretches . . . and a mix of cynicism about civilisation (the "we're worse than cannibals" argument) with naïve but offensive racist stereotyping of various Third World populations' (2006: 68). For him, the cannibal sub-genre 'offers a shoddy load of goods', with any point about the barbarity of humans, both 'civilised' and 'primitive', cancelled out by callous animal cruelty (ibid.).

If Newman is correct in asserting that the value of these films is relatively paltry and certainly does not justify the brutal, on-camera slaughter of animals, why have, as Newman puts it, 'scads' been written about these films? Why do audiences continue to watch them, talk about them and write about them? What value can the spectator or critic possibly glean from these films? This chapter grapples with these questions. Acknowledging the sub-genre's origins in the *mondo* documentary filmmaking tradition, this analysis considers how Italian cannibal films blend documentary realism with fictional filmmaking by narratising footage of actual animal slaughter at the service of an imag-ined story. Next, the various ways in which Ruggero Deodato has discussed the issue of animal cruelty provide a case study of how a specific director addresses the use of real animal death in his films. In many instances, Deodato has related the use of real animal death in his films to the topic of food. Along these lines, the chapter concludes by posing the possibility that animal cruelty in Italian cannibal films can profitably be examined through the lens of food studies, considering how the movies and their use of footage of real animal death expose – intentionally or not – the often-hidden brutality behind food procurement and preparation.

THE 'CLOSEST PROXIMITY TO THE FORBIDDEN WORLD OF REAL DEATH':
DOCUMENTARY REALISM, MODALITY AND ANIMAL CRUELTY

For the purposes of this argument, any type of pain, harm or death inflicted on animals – whether by other animals or humans – captured by the camera and used to embellish a fictional film and imbue it with an air of 'reality' is considered animal cruelty. There are various types of footage of real animal brutality, cruelty and death used in Italian cannibal films. Sometimes, footage of animal brutality consists of predators attacking prey or two animals fighting each other to the bloody death. This battle sometimes takes place in the wild, with the animals – ostensibly, at least – in their natural habitant. An example of this type of animal violence appears in *Ultimo mondo cannibale*, which features footage of a snake attacking and consuming a Gila monster. Other times, battles between animals are obviously staged, with a crowd of characters in the film cheering on the fight. Umberto Lenzi's *Il paese del sesso selvaggio/Deep River Savages* (1972), which Jay Slater identifies as 'Italy's first graphic cannibal film' (2006: 44), features two such scenes, one featuring a cobra and mongoose pitted in a fight to the death and another showing a cock-fight. Finally, there are plenty of examples of animal cruelty perpetrated by actors who directly hurt and/or kill animals for the camera. An actor playing a tribesman slits open a goat's throat to commemorate a child's birth in *Il paese del sesso selvaggio*. In *Cannibal Holocaust*, an American documentarian (Luca Barbareschi) kicks a small pig, then shoots and kills it on camera.

While these categories of animal cruelty and death are useful for analysis, at the same time one must remain aware of the fluidity of these categories, as the lines between them are sometimes blurred. Sergio Martino's *La montagna del dio cannibale/The Mountain of the Cannibal God* (1978) provides an example of this ambiguity. The film contains a sequence in which a python grabs a small monkey, crushes the monkey with its body, and slowly begins to consume it. Martino claims that filming this python's attack on the monkey was 'a chance opportunity. It was not planned' (*Mountain of the Cannibal God*, 'Legacy of the cannibal god', 2007). However, a 'frame-by-frame analysis of this scene' suggests that 'an optical effect' was used to hide a 'device . . . apparently used to thrust the monkey into the mouth of the python' (ibid.). This example illustrates that it can often be difficult to discern if animal brutality in these films that takes place 'in the wild' is authentic or is staged for the camera.

Whether the scenes of animal death happen 'naturally' or are staged, the ways Italian cannibal films employ footage of various types of animal brutality, cruelty and slaughter aim to ground the films in some sort of 'reality', to make their narratives more 'realistic' and 'believable'. These appeals to 'reality' go hand-in-hand with the sub-genre's origins in *mondo* documentary traditions. Several Italian cannibal films underscore their 'realism' from the opening frames, as they often include title cards that boast about the film's basis in reality. An example of this type of appeal to documentary realism can be seen in the opening of Lenzi's *Il paese del sesso selvaggio*. The film tells the story of John Bradley (Ivan Rassimov), an Englishman who is taken captive by a primitive tribe in the jungles of Indochina. After enduring many trials from the tribespeople and gaining their trust, Bradley is accepted into the tribe and eventually becomes its leader.

The film's opening resembles a low-budget travelogue film that might be used to promote tourism, showing Bradley arriving via airplane at an exotic locale. Subsequent scenes depict Bradley snapping photos of the locals while drifting down a canal in a boat, walking through a farmers' market, and surveying ancient temples. As Bradley takes a photo of a ritual dance, a title appears that reads: 'In the dense jungle along the often ill defined border between Thailand and Burma, it is still possible to find primitive tribes which have no contact with the outside world.' The title is followed by another:

> This story was filmed on location with one of these tribes, and even though some of the rites and ceremonies shown are perhaps gruesome and repugnant they are portrayed as they are actually carried out. Only the story is imaginary.

These opening titles evince the dance between documentary and fiction that is a staple of the Italian cannibal sub-genre. After insisting upon the real-world setting of the film and the veracity of the events it portrays, the concluding sentence takes a step back, noting that while the setting and rituals are authentic, the story is fabricated. These titles foreshadow how the film's narrative will oscillate between real and simulated violence, between bloody footage of real animal death and gory sequences of faked human death. In a video interview included on a 2004 DVD release, Lenzi describes the film as 'in some way anthropological . . . fictional, but also a documentary' (*Man from Deep River*, 'Interview with director Umberto Lenzi').

The opening titles of Sergio Martino's *La montagna del dio cannibale* follow a trajectory similar to that of *Il paese del sesso selvaggio*, but this time around, scenes of animals brutally battling in the wild underscore the film's blurring of reality and fiction. The film tells the story of Susan Stevenson (Ursula Andress) who travels to New Guinea and hires Edward Foster (Stacy Keach), a professor and explorer, to help her find her scientist husband who has disappeared in the jungle. The film's opening credits conclude with titles that read:

> New Guinea is perhaps the last region on earth which still contains immense unexplored areas, shrouded in mystery, where life has remained at its primordial level. Today, on the dawn of the space age, it seems

unimaginable that only twenty hours' flight from London there still exists such a wild and uncontaminated world. This story bears witness that it does.

These titles suggest that the fiction of this film's narrative paradoxically serves to 'bear witness' to the reality of the merciless nature of this 'wild and uncontaminated world'. The audience may be willing to buy into the film's claims of veracity because they are pummelled during the opening credits with footage of real animal brutality towards other animals in their natural environs. In the first minute of the film, the audience is confronted with footage of a crocodile suddenly and violently clamping down its jaws on a small, furry mammal. Later, the opening credits, which consist almost exclusively of footage of various animals in the jungle, feature a brutal, bloody battle between a crocodile and a large turtle. In an interview, Martino explains that he wanted the images of animal violence to 'have a documentary quality' (*Mountain of the Cannibal God*, 'Legacy of the cannibal god', 2007). In this opening sequence, animals – both living and dying – establish the reality and veracity of a film that can use some verisimilitude, as it features one of the more conventional narratives of Italian cannibal cinema, with mainstream stars like Andress and Keach and a story complete with action, intrigue, romance and a third-act surprise plot twist.

One could claim the inclusion of footage of real animal cruelty and death in these films undergirds their narratives, making them more thrilling, real and unique. Danny Shipka argues that while the killing of animals for these films is reprehensible, the inclusion of this type of footage at least makes Italian cannibal films a type of viewing experience audiences are unlikely to find anywhere else. He writes, '[a]nimal snuff magnifies the fictional construct of the human death, giving audiences their closest proximity to the forbidden world of real death' (2011: 115). The footage of actual animal death enhances the faked deaths of humans in the film, bringing audiences as close to the experience of death as possible. Shipka's theory is also shared by Lloyd Kaufman (the infamous president and co-founder of Troma Entertainment), who penned an essay about Deodato's *Cannibal Holocaust* published in 2006 in which he offers an analysis of the film's editing techniques. Kaufman writes:

> *Cannibal Holocaust* could be shown in film schools as proof of Pudovkin's theory of editing. Pudovkin's theory held that if you took a shot of someone with a neutral expression . . . and cut to a shot of a steak, the viewer would think the person looked hungry . . . In *Cannibal Holocaust*, we see the actors kill and rip apart a giant sea turtle and other animals. Later on, they run across a woman impaled upon a stake (the shot clearly demonstrating that the actress is sitting on a bicycle seat). The

Figure 12.1 *Cannibal Holocaust*: does the power of this image depend on animal cruelty?

audience has already seen actual death on screen, and have been subtly brainwashed into assuming they're now seeing a woman with a stake rammed up her genitalia. The brain has been conditioned to accept that which it's now seeing as real. (2006: 105)

Giving the audience this experience of 'reality' made these films unique and apparently profitable, and this simulation of reality was, as both Skipka and Kaufman argue, dependent on the inclusion of real animal slaughter and cruelty in the film. Thus, it stands to reason that some financiers and producers would insist on inserting animal cruelty and death into the films – whether the directors wanted it there or not – to increase the films' ability to shock and gross out audiences. According to Deodato, this is the situation he faced with *Ultimo mondo cannibale*. Deodato claims that the producer, Giorgio Carlo Rossi, inserted all scenes of animal cruelty and death into the film against his wishes (*Jungle Holocaust*, 'Introduction by Ruggero Deodato', 2001). Rossi was an executive producer on Lenzi's *Il paese del sesso selvaggio*. Perhaps Rossi suspected the success of Lenzi's film was linked to its footage of animal violence and, galvanised by the success of *Il paese del sesso selvaggio*, insisted that Deodato's film include similar scenes of animal cruelty. No matter what Rossi's intentions may have been, a close examination of *Ultimo mondo cannibale* seems to bear out Deodato's claims; the footage of animal violence has a different tonality than the rest of the film, is shot mostly in close-up or extreme close-up, and does not feature any of the principal actors from the film. It is intriguing to speculate how producers and distributors of these films might have insisted that the films contain footage of real animal violence in hopes of luring audiences to cinemas and grindhouses. Equally intriguing is a consideration of the Italian cannibal film's origins in the *mondo* documentary tradition and how footage of actual animal death infuses simulated human death with 'reality'.

Perhaps more productive than both of these approaches, however, is to examine the inclusion of real animal cruelty and death in these films in terms of modality. Geoff King argues that modality is 'a broader way of analysing the manner in which specific elements of [a] film are presented both within and across generic territories' (2007: 47). King's application of the concept of modality as a means of studying cult cinema grows out of Robert Hodge and David Tripp's usage of the term to gauge how films '[situate] messages in relation to an ostensible reality' (quoted in King, 2007: 47). King explains, '[a]ll texts contain modality markers, devices that position them in some way in terms of the kinds of claims they make in relation to an understanding of the real world' (2007: 47). Following this, a documentary 'deploys conventions that make claims to the status of representing the actual events of an identifiable exterior world' (King, 2007: 47). Similarly when watching a 'horror, science fiction or fantasy' film, 'the viewer is encouraged to accept a frame of reference at least partially different from that applied to avowedly more "realistic" fictions' (ibid.: 48). One may be tempted to consider the documentary text with modality markers that place it closer to ostensible reality as being in diametrical opposition to a fantasy film with modality markers that place it in the realm of the obviously imagined, far away from ostensible reality. However, King is quick to note that considering the modality of a film is more of 'a question of *relative* degrees rather than absolute distinctions' (2007: 48). Films exist along a spectrum of modalities, and modalities within a film can also vary, shifting between reality and fantasy.

Italian cannibal films are ripe for this manner of interpretation, as the modalities of these films vary widely. These films skirt across different generic boundaries as they oscillate between documentary traditions and fictional constructs. While considering these films as a mix of genres offers an avenue of inquiry, approaching these films in terms of their mixed modalities seems a better fit for examining their blend of documentary and fiction. As such, looking at the mixed modalities of these films is crucial for contemplating their use of real animal cruelty and death, for the footage of animal death is the most striking means by which the films access 'true reality'. For Sergio Martino, the footage of animals – including animal slaughter – is what, for him, gives *La montagna del dio cannibale* a 'documentary quality'. Likewise, in Kaufman's analysis of *Cannibal Holocaust*, the footage of real animal death is what lends the image of the impaled woman, one of the most iconic of the film, its power.

Figure 12.2   *Cannibal Ferox*: Can this spectacle of suffering compete with real animal death?

As Shipka argues, the ostensive reality of animal death in these films shatters the films' fictional constructs and thrusts audiences into the 'closest proximity to the forbidden world of real death' that a fictional film can offer. Similarly, in his analysis of *Cannibal Holocaust*, Xavier Mendik observes that the 'mixing of real footage ... of animal slaughter' with 'staged fictional inserts' of violence against humans enables the film to '[expose] moral contradictions in the realist frame' (Mathijs & Mendik, 2011: 44). In this case, the shifting modalities of the Italian cannibal film allow not just a vicarious thrill of coming close to the 'proximity of death', but also an opportunity to contemplate both the virtues and the costs of stripping away elements that mark the film as fantasy and moving the film closer to ostensive reality.

Other Italian cannibal films may be less successful in the ways they deploy real footage of animal brutality, cruelty and slaughter to bring their films closer to reality, with the use of real animal death ironically exposing the fictional nature of the documentary-like 'reality' these films try to establish. Jay Slater argues that in *Cannibal ferox*, Lenzi attempts to use shifting modalities to make up for narrative deficiencies and shoddy special effects. According to Slater, the film's copious simulated violence against humans 'loses ... its visual impact and emotional charge' and 'these hardcore mutilation sequences soon become tiresome', causing Lenzi to resort to '[killing] animals for entertainment' (2006: 159). In other words, footage of real animal death steers *Cannibal ferox* towards ostensible reality while the film's 'barely adequate' special effects threaten to place the film in the realm of fantasy. The simulated violence against humans in the film is undoubtedly extreme. One female character (Zora Kerova) has giant hooks shoved through her breasts by the cannibal tribesmen and is hoisted by the hooks several feet above the ground to hang until she bleeds to death. Another character, crazed cocaine dealer and would-be emerald thief Mike Logan (Giovanni Lombardo Radice), suffers triple mutilation: native cannibals castrate him, chop off his hand, and finally lop off the top of his head and eat his brains straight out of his skull.

Despite the extremity of these simulated acts of violence, however, Slater shrugs them off as overly phony, claiming that the film 'springs from one hardcore effect to another that seem much poorer in execution than one would expect from an Italian splatter movie' (2006: 159). Similarly, Andrew Parkinson comments that all the action in the film is overshadowed by 'the memory of seeing an animal dying slowly, painfully and utterly needlessly for the sake of "entertainment"', like when the natives dismember a small alligator and consume its innards onscreen (2006: 163). Slater's and Parkinson's comments suggest that the real death of animals makes the film's simulated violence against humans look all the more fake, unconvincing and forgettable. In his dismissal of the Italian cannibal sub-genre, Kim Newman observes that the special effects in many of these films are 'inept' and made with 'the general get-something-on-the-screen-fast-before-the-trend-passes approach' often used by 'Italian anything-for-a-buck merchants' (2006: 68). Whether or not the footage of real animal death causes the Italian cannibal film to feel closer to ostensible reality or, instead, fantasy, animal cruelty remains central to these films' shifting modalities.

'*YOU* EAT THE ANIMALS!':
CONSIDERING THE ITALIAN CANNIBAL CYCLE AS FOOD FILMS

Without a doubt, the footage of violence against animals in these films has made an indelible impression on audiences, for the issue invariably arises when one discusses these films or when people involved with the production are interviewed. Ruggero Deodato cannot, it seems, avoid the subject and has a varied and complex relationship with the animal cruelty and death in his films. As discussed earlier, in the case of his first cannibal film, *Ultimo mondo cannibale*, Deodato claims that the footage of animal cruelty was added to the film without his knowledge or approval. The situation with Deodato and *Cannibal Holocaust*, however, is more complicated. In this case, the film's cast is undeniably responsible for the carnage seen onscreen. For instance, in the scene in which the documentary crew kills and eats a sea turtle, members of the cast are clearly involved with the death and dismemberment of the turtle. Perhaps most horrific is the film's first instance of animal cruelty in which a character kills a muskrat by jabbing a knife into its throat as the camera captures the animal's painful and protracted death in close-up. In the years following the film's production, Deodato has expressed regret for the slaughter of animals for the camera. When asked in 2005 if he would include animal violence if he were to make the film again, he replied, 'absolutely not' (*Cannibal Holocaust*, 'On camera commentary', 2005). Included in distributor Grindhouse Releasing's 2005 DVD release of *Cannibal Holocaust* is the option to watch an animal cruelty-free version of the film; in 2011, Xavier Mendik reported that Deodato has expressed an interest in producing another re-edit of the film 'to fit better with twenty-first-century sensibilities' (2011: 45), although this re-edit has not surfaced and was not on the film's 2014 Blu-ray release, which included the same animal cruelty-free version from the 2005 DVD. Nevertheless, Deodato often seems acutely aware of how attitudes towards such acts of animal violence have dramatically shifted during the past few decades.

At other times, Deodato has been more defensive when it comes to animal cruelty, and his defensive stance bears consideration. In a 1996 interview, when asked why he chose to inflict violence on animals and film it, Deodato explains, '[t]he rats, wild pigs, crocodiles and turtles were killed by the Indios for food. I simply followed them on their hunts – the equivalent of shooting the butchers at the city slaughterhouse' (Palmerini & Mistretta, 1996: 42). When asked what he thinks about animal rights advocates, Deodato complains, 'I think these people are very inflexible: they make such a fuss about films when so many animals are killed to produce food' (ibid.). On a commentary track recorded for the 2005 DVD release of *Cannibal Holocaust*, his position is similar; when scolded by actor Robert Kerman for the murder of animals, Deodato accusatorily shoots back in his broken English, '*You* eat the animals!' (*Cannibal Holocaust*, 'On camera commentary'). In other words, Deodato defends the death of animals in his films by claiming the animals all ended up being used for food, thus making what he did no different than what a slaughterhouse worker or the owner of a food corporation does every day. By including this footage in his films, he is simply, to borrow a phrase from William Burroughs, showing us exactly what is at the end of every fork.

While the ethics of Deodato's position remain questionable, his comments do point to how films of the cannibal cycle – and the violence against animals in these films – might be productively analysed through the lens of food studies. Deodato's remarks about the animals killed in *Cannibal Holocaust* eventually being used for food aside, scenes of animal slaughter often function within the diegesis as scenes of consumption. In six key films of the cycle – *Il paese del sesso selvaggio*, *Mangiati vivi!/Eaten Alive!* (1980) and *Cannibal ferox* directed by Lenzi; *Ultimo mondo cannibale* and *Cannibal Holocaust* directed by Deodato; and *La montagna del dio cannibale* directed by Martino – there are roughly thirty-eight incidents of violence against animals. Out of these thirty-eight scenes, twenty-two involve the slain animals being consumed onscreen (with the consumption being both simulated and real). Given this high frequency and, of course, the importance of cannibalism to their narratives, perhaps it makes sense to examine these movies as 'food films'.

To be considered a 'food film', a film should, according to Anne L. Bower, position food in a starring role and 'depict characters negotiating questions of identity, power, culture, class, spirituality, or relationship through food' (2004: 5–6). One of the ways Bower tests the boundaries of the genre is to consider whether or not cannibal films are 'food films'. This question leads her to conclude that an 'overreliance on strict genre definitions may be limiting' and that looking at food in films that do not fit comfortably within the 'food film' genre can lead one to realise how 'semiotic uses of food are even more multivalent and powerful than a concentration on "food films" alone would allow us to understand' (2004: 6–7). An analysis of cannibal films from a food studies perspective can enable insightful ideological readings that illuminate those questions of identity, power, culture and class Bower argues are at stake. When grappling with the issue of animal violence in the cannibal films, folklorist Don Yoder's concept of foodways is of particular use. As explained by Lucy Long, foodways 'refer[s] to [the] extended network of activities surrounding the procurement, preservation, preparation, presentation, performance, and consumption of food' (2000: 144). A foundational assumption of foodways methodology is that an analysis of 'food behaviours' can offer insights into the 'beliefs, aesthetics, economics, and politics' of a particular social group (ibid.).

Foodways methodology can shift focus away from the mere act of food consumption and call attention to those aspects of food procurement and preparation that are elided in most films. Food scholar Warren Belasco explains, '[m]ass entertainment [has] glamorized the convenience-consumption ethic [and] mystified – or simply ignored – the details of food production' (1989: 157). Echoing Belasco's observation, film scholars have noted that 'the decidedly unglamorous labor required to procure food, preserve food, and prepare daily meals' is hidden from view in most films, even those focused on food (Baron, Carson & Bernard, 2014: 148). However, these unglamorous stages of foodways emerge, somewhat surprisingly, in the horror film, especially those concerning cannibalism. For instance, the American grindhouse classic *The Texas Chain Saw Massacre* (Tobe Hooper, 1974) '"labors" the food film by focusing on food procurement and the early stages of food preparation and by making . . . the labor that must be expended before a meal is consumed horrifically visible' (Baron, Carson & Bernard, 2014: 149).

The ways a film like *The Texas Chain Saw Massacre* – or any number of other, more mainstream Hollywood productions for that matter – makes visible the early stages of food procurement and preparation are relatively mild compared to the way these processes are exposed in the Italian cannibal film.

In most films focused on cannibalism in which humans are food product, the early, brutal stages of food procurement and preparation emerge allegorically. In other words, the simulated death of humans that are killed and consumed in cannibal films act as a metaphor for 'the ills of a corrupt society' (Baron, Carson & Bernard, 2014: 31). With the inclusion of real animal death, Italian cannibal films largely dispense with metaphor. In a 2001 interview, Massimo Foschi, the lead actor in Deodato's *Ultimo mondo cannibale*, describes the use of real animal slaughter in the film as 'crazy . . . It's not necessary . . . it's not a metaphor . . . [it is] violence for violence' (*Jungle Holocaust*, 'Massimo Fosschi Interview', 2001). If Foschi is indeed correct and there is no metaphor in the inclusion of animal cruelty in these films, the absence of metaphor does not preclude these films from engaging with socio-political issues.

By this token, one might argue Italian cannibal films are part of a larger conversation about ecological issues. Russ Hunter observes that Italian genre films of this era 'approach environmental concerns from a different angle, offering a less metaphoric and more literal ecological position' (2014: 113–14). As such, these films '[contribute] to a form of national discourse that was current in Italy with regards to environmentalism in the late 1970s' (Hunter, 2014: 113). For some, these environmental concerns were tied directly to issues surrounding food. Indeed, in this period, 'polarized views of food that emerged' in the US led to the 'food wars of the 1970s' and 'the U.S. farm crisis of the 1980s' (Baron, Carson & Bernard, 2014: 10; Belasco, 1989: 112). The various debates around the subject of food and the environment could have created a reception context in the US that invited audiences to contemplate the damaging effects of food production, an enterprise founded on the cruel treatment and slaughter of animals with little consideration of environmental impact. For better or worse, cannibal films featuring animal death can force audiences to contend with the labour it takes to create food and the brutal practices that often take place during the food-making process.

When these food practices are cast within narratives so preoccupied with colonialism and imperialism, they are linked directly with struggles over power and identity. Attending to how the films narrativise footage of real animal death can help draw attention from simulated incidents of cannibalism and focus more on how the culinary practices of almost all cultures are predicated on the slaughter of animals. This type of analysis can move scholars past the 'every culture sucks' readings of the films that Daniel Shipka laments. Reading the films from a food studies perspective can also circumvent the 'offensive racist stereotyping of various Third World populations' that Kim Newman argues the films depend on in order to make the tired – and possibly trite – argument that 'we are worse than the cannibals'. Ian Olney observes that when the cannibals revolt against the evil documentary crew and eat them at the conclusion of *Cannibal Holocaust* 'perhaps . . . this narrative twist undercuts

Deodato's postcolonial critique of Western imperialism as inherently canni-balistic, reinscribing the centuries-old trope of the non-white colonial subjects as cannibal' (2013: 202). While the film's use of footage of real animal death is obviously problematic and unethical, it does, at the very least, place white Westerners on the same level as indigenous, 'primitive' tribes in the films, neither better nor worse than the other since both of their meal cycles depend on the slaughter of animals.

This is not to say, however, that white imperialism gets off the hook in these films. The Italian cannibal cycle grew more critical of white imperialist and colonial impulses, a criticism traceable by examining the use of real animal violence in the films. Looking at differences between Lenzi's *Il paese del sesso selvaggio* and *Cannibal ferox* – two films that bookend the Italian cannibal cycle – is useful in tracing their evolving depiction of white cruelty. In the early films, only natives are depicted harming and killing animals. *Il paese del sesso selvaggio* goes to great lengths to *not* show Englishman John Bradley harming an animal. For example, one scene depicts Bradley and the tribesmen hunting and capturing a boar. The film conveniently cuts from the hunt to Bradley's hut as he brings in a slab of the boar for himself and his native wife (Me Me Lai), discreetly deleting any hand Bradley may have had in slaying the animal. A later scene of Bradley benevolently playing with a bear cub is vastly dif-ferent from crazed cocaine dealer Mike Logan violently stabbing a trapped pig to death in *Cannibal ferox*. In analysing cannibal films from a foodways perspective, the critic can move away from an 'every culture sucks' attitude and towards a position that acknowledges how almost all cultures have been constructed upon the brutal and unfair treatment of animals for food. In this context, one is able to address the ways Italian exploitation films '*explicitly* [make] the association between whiteness and death that is only implicitly acknowledged in . . . Anglo American horror films' (Olney, 2013: 186).

Contemporary Anglo-American horror films by directors like Rob Zombie and Eli Roth may frighten and shock audiences, but these directors' work with PETA reminds us that the days of brutality towards animals for filmed entertainment have passed. However, the films made during the Italian can-nibal cycle are still very much with us and continue to spark heated debate among critics and fans. For instance, in May 2014 on the blog *Blood and Guts for Grown Ups*, blogger Saucy Josh posted an op-ed piece titled '"Cannibal Holocaust" Re-Release Should Not Be'. This piece critiques Grindhouse Releasing's upcoming Blu-ray edition of *Cannibal Holocaust*; as an 'animal rights activist' Saucy Josh takes objection to how Grindhouse Releasing 'is, in a very direct way, benefitting from the film's cruelty to animals' (Saucy Josh, 2014). Predictably, Saucy Josh's piece incited a flurry of discussion, with sixty-four responses in the comments section. One commenter writes, '[n]ot watching it isn't going to bring those animals back, now is it?', followed by a smiley face emoticon (Saucy Josh, 2014). While this commenter's statement is, at best, flippant and, at worst, callous, it reminds us of the immutable fact that world cinema and film culture are stuck with these movies. We cannot bring back these slaughtered animals, but we can at least try to find a way to come to terms with – and possibly productively analyse – the footage of their demise.

Bibliography

Baron, C., Carson, D. and Bernard, M. (2014), *Appetites and Anxieties: Food, Film, and the Politics of Representation*, Detroit: Wayne State University Press.

Belasco, W. J. (1989), *Appetite for Change: How the Counterculture took on the Food Industry, 1966–1988*, New York: Pantheon.

Bower, A. L. (2004), 'Watching food: The production of food, film, and values', in Bower, A. L.(ed.), *Reel Food: Essays on Food and Film*, New York: Routledge, pp. 1–13.

Cannibal Holocaust, 'On camera commentary', Hollywood: Grindhouse Releasing, 2005. DVD.

Dickinson, K. (2007), 'Troubling synthesis: The horrific sights and incompatible sounds of video nasties', in Sconce, J. (ed.), *Sleaze Artists: Cinema at the Margins of Taste, Style, and Politics*, Durham, NC: Duke University Press, pp. 167–88.

Hughes, H. (2011), *Cinema Italiano: The Complete Guide from Classics to Cult*, New York: Palgrave Macmillan.

Hunter, R. (2009), '*Cannibal Holocaust*', in Schneider, S. J. (ed.), *101 Horror Movies You Must See Before You Die*, Hauppauge, NY: Barron's, pp. 265–6.

Hunter, R. (2014), 'Nightmare cites: Italian zombie cinema and environmental discourses', in Hunt, L., Lockyer, S. and Williamson, M. (eds), *Screening the Undead: Vampires and Zombies in Film and Television*, London: I. B. Tauris, pp. 112–30.

Jungle Holocaust, 'Introduction by Ruggero Deodato', New York: Media Blasters, 2001. DVD.

Jungle Holocaust, 'Massimo Fosschi Interview', New York: Media Blasters, 2001. DVD.

Kaufman, L. (2006), 'Review: *Cannibal Holocaust*', in Slater, J. (ed.), *Eaten Alive! Italian Cannibal and Zombie Movies*, London: Plexus, pp. 104–6.

King, G. (2007), *Donnie Darko*, London: Wallflower.

Long, L. (2000), 'Holiday meals: Rituals of family tradition', in Meiselman, H. L. (ed.), *Dimensions of the Meal: Science, Culture, Business, and Art of Eating*, Gaithersburg, MD: Aspen, pp. 143–59.

Man from Deep River, 'Interview with director Umberto Lenzi', New York: Media Blasters, 2004. DVD.

Mathijs, E. and Mendik, X. (2011), *100 Cult Films*, New York: Palgrave Macmillan.

Mountain of the Cannibal God, 'Legacy of the cannibal god', West Hollywood: Blue Underground, 2007. DVD.

Newman, K. (2006), 'Review: *Last Cannibal World*', in Slater, J. (ed.), *Eaten Alive! Italian Cannibal and Zombie Movies*, London: Plexus, pp. 68–71.

Olney, I. (2013), *Euro Horror: Classic European Horror Cinema in Contemporary American Culture*, Bloomington: Indiana University Press.

Palmertini, L. M. and Mistretta, G. (1996), *Spaghetti Nightmares: Italian Fantasy Horrors as Seen Through the Eyes of Their Protagonists*, Key West, FL: Fantasma.

Parkinson, A. (2006), 'Review: *Cannibal Ferox*', in Slater, J. (ed.), *Eaten Alive! Italian Cannibal and Zombie Movies*, London: Plexus, pp. 161–3.

Paul, L. (2005), *Italian Horror Film Directors*, Jefferson, NC: McFarland.

PETA (2007), 'Rob Zombie's Thanksgiving message', *PETA*, 15 November, www.peta. org/blog/rob-zombies-thanksgiving-message [last accessed 23 January 2015].

Saucy Josh (2014), 'Opinion: "Cannibal Holocaust" re-release should not be', *Blood and Guts for Grown Ups*, 13 May, www.bloodandgutsforgrownups.wordpress. com/2014/05/13/opinion-cannibal-holocaust-re-release-should-not-be [last accessed 23 January 2015].

Schaefer, E. (2007), 'Exploitation films: Teaching sin in the suburbs', *Cinema Journal*, 47: 1, pp. 94–7.

Shipka, D. (2011), *Perverse Titillation: The Exploitation Cinema of Italy, Spain and France, 1960–1980*, Jefferson, NC: McFarland.

Slater, J. (2006), 'Review: *Cannibal Ferox*', in Slater, J. (ed.), *Eaten Alive! Italian Cannibal and Zombie Movies*, London: Plexus, pp. 159–61.

Slater, J. (2006), 'Review: *Deep River Savages*', in Slater, J. (ed.), *Eaten Alive! Italian Cannibal and Zombie Movies*, London: Plexus, pp. 44–7.

13. ITALIAN HORROR CINEMA AND ITALIAN FILM JOURNALS OF THE 1970s

Paolo Noto

This chapter will focus on the domestic reception of Italian horror cinema in journals and magazines during the 1970s in order to begin a process of understanding the ways in which the genre was valued, discussed and (less commonly) analysed by Italian critics of the period. Although Italian horror in general has been subject to a considerable amount of scholarship, in fact, little has been written (in English, but also in Italian) about the criticism it aroused, and the way it was used by Italian critics to deal with genres and popular cinema. Given the entire history of Italian horror, the decision to focus on the 1970s is not casual and merits some preliminary contextualisation. Compared with the previous decade, which witnessed the blossoming of Bava, Ferroni, Freda and Margheriti's gothic genre, and the subsequent one, which accompanied the work of Dario Argento as a director and a producer of both his and others' films, the brief but intense season of the cannibal movie and the exploitation films of directors like Fulci, Massaccesi and Lenzi, the 1970s were relatively 'empty'. Most notably, there were a handful of titles that attempted to emanate the success of *The Exorcist* (William Friedkin, 1973), the release of an Argento film (*Suspiria*, 1977) and the production of another (*Inferno*, 1980), and little more. Nevertheless, if we consider the period in the light of the developments in Italian criticism at the time, the situation changes radically and in fact the 1970s fast become a crucial case study: it permits us to evaluate how horror as a genre is framed within the conceptual and ideological frameworks of criticism at that time and, moreover, the ways in which discussion of horror impacts on the birth of a critical and academic tradition.

As in the USA and the UK, in Italy the 1970s saw the notion of 'genre' debated with increasingly sophisticated methodologies in the field of film studies, with popular film becoming an object of interest for specialised journals. The reasons that brought about this change, however, were completely different. In the Anglo-American academy, genre was a foundational conceptual tool that was necessary for the 'scientifically' accurate study of popular cinema, and particularly Hollywood (Neale, 1999: 10), as well as for the broad validation of film studies within the British education system (Hutchings, 1995: 60–5). In Italy, on the other hand, the reconsideration of genre film that took place in the same years could not be separated from a reframing of the experience of neorealism. It was only when the legacy of neorealism was brought into question that critics began to take an interest in those forms of cinema that were formerly repressed by that authoritative model (in other words, neorealism as a concrete movement and a benchmark against which to assess single films and to frame the historical development of Italian cinema as a whole). The debate on genres and the popular in Italy had its most notorious and influential episode in the Matarazzo case (Bachman & Calder-Williams, 2012). In that case the cinephiliac – often provocative – revival of the domestic dramas directed by Raffaello Matarazzo in the 1950s (and generally considered until the mid-1970s as examples of lowbrow, conservative escapism) enabled a generation of young critics to come to terms with that historiographical monument that was neorealism and, at the same time, to distinguish themselves from their predecessors and establish new patterns of criticism (Bisoni, 2009). In such a context, a great part of the critical attention dedicated to horror and thriller revolved around the only director perceived from his debut as a potential auteur: Dario Argento. Films like *L'uccello dalle piume di cristallo/The Bird with the Crystal Plumage* (1970) and *Profondo rosso/Deep Red* (1975) played out a variety of tensions in Italian film culture (the representation of national landscape, the clash between domestic and foreign cinematic tradition, the possible existence of native film genres, and so on); this explains why, in this chapter, critiques to these and other Argento works are mentioned more often than those devoted to other films.

In order to depict this context as accurately as possible, the present survey will take into account a variety of publications: not only will I analyse 'serious' and academic journals, but also bulletins issued by associations and amateur filmmakers, fanzines, promotional materials, news reports addressed to the film industry, and the like. Books dedicated to horror that were published in the 1970s will be taken into consideration too. This will allow me to outline the first assumption that is a starting point for my analysis: that the discourse surrounding horror cinema is low-intensity, but nonetheless ubiquitous. One infrequently comes across in-depth analyses of horror films or of horror as an autonomous genre. However, the frequent use of the notion of *fantastico* enables critics and contributors to draw together diverse production cycles, all characterised by narratives that oscillate between different regimes of reality and supernatural elements: science fiction, gothic, thriller and even the *giallo* derived from the first films of Dario Argento. This does not apply solely to Italian cinema, as is illustrated by Steve Neale's definition of 'Horror and Science Fiction' (1999: 92–3). What nevertheless does remain specific to Italian film culture is the recursive (if not obsessive) deployment of neorealism as a categorical, evaluative tool, as well as a criterion for defining what can be properly labelled as *national*.

A NON-NATIONAL GENRE

Beginning a discussion of horror with neorealism might sound specious, yet this is necessary insofar as it was the category called upon by those who initiated the critical and philological re–examination of the genre. Realism provided the co-ordinates for discussions of horror and of other neglected genre categories, allowing them to take shape. Lorenzo Codelli, for example, begins his introduction to *Fant'Italia*, the printed catalogue of the fourteenth *Festival Internazionale del Film di Fantascienza* (held in Trieste in July 1976), with a vivid claim, addressed to unidentified worshippers of neorealism, then 'misbelievers' about non-realist genres:

> This festival, in any case, is not aimed at them – those eminent thurifers of a neo-deceased realism that is eternally theorised, prophetised, banalised, and more poorly publicised . . . than any other stereotype in our asphyxial and provincial non-culture. (Codelli, 1976: 11)

Fant'Italia has long been a point of reference for fans of Italian horror and *cinema fantastico*, providing them with a detailed survey of the films produced between 1957 and 1966, and a critical anthology of reviews, interviews and articles drawn from French film journals, such as *Midi-Minuit Fantastique* and *Photon*. Another milestone in the Italian reception of horror is Teo Mora's *Storia del cinema dell'orrore*, first published in 1978. The author assumes the ambitious task of providing an account of the genre production all over the world (the chapter on Italy is notably followed by one on Filipino cinema). He begins the part dedicated to Italian horror with an accurate description of the process that inspired critics to re-evaluate a whole range of since then overlooked genres:

> For years the Italian cinema acknowledged by critics has been limited to neorealism, to the few national *auteurs* (Antonioni, Fellini, Pasolini, Visconti, and so on) and to the cinema of social *impegno* (*Investigation of*

a Citizen Above Suspicion and the like) [. . .] During the last decade critics have increasingly broadened their scope, thus catching up first with the leading genres of 'popular' cinema [. . .] then expanding their investigation towards the cinema of Fascism [. . .] and the 'popular' cinema of the 1950s. (Mora, 1978: 289)

If Codelli and Mora praise, or take into consideration, the Italian *fantastico* because of its links with the national cinematic culture, others reverse the same argument and claim the non-existence of such links. According to Gualtiero Pironi, for example, the reason behind the poor domestic box-office takings of the '*fantastico*: horror, science fiction, thriller' is the 'lack of an Italian cultural tradition in this field. The horror and science fiction audience considers only English and American films, and is almost always skeptical about our own science fictions' (1977: 730). Accordingly, one film – Avati''s *La casa dalle finestre che ridono/The House With Laughing Windows* (1976) – can be evaluated in two sets of opposite terms, in view of its deliberate attempt to transfer a gothic atmosphere into the unusual setting of the Po Valley. In the Catholic *Rivista del Cinematografo*, Piero Pruzzo writes that the film fails insofar as it 'simply juxtaposes two traditions, or more precisely two sets of spectacular conventions: the Anglo-American horror film and the grotesque, provincial dimension [. . .] in a more decorative and arbitrary setting than one might first notice' (1977: 41). Maurizio Porro of *Cineforum*, another journal with Catholic tendencies, which nevertheless since the early 1970s has featured contributors of diverse political leanings, instead employs the basic argument of landscape as an index of realism to claim that the Italian location makes Avati's film 'fascinating' and 'more credible' (1977: 153).

THE RELUCTANT PRODUCER'S GAME

The panorama of film journals of the 1970s is extremely varied, and certainly not limited to ideologically or aesthetically committed criticism. It also encompasses glossy spin-offs of soft-core magazines (like *New Cinema* spanning from 1970 to 1972, derived from *King*), as well as promotional booklets disguised as periodicals and publications addressed to the film industry. In these publications the boundaries between information, criticism and advertisement are very thin, and one can chance upon bizarre hybrid objects such as an advertorial for Alfonso Brescia's *Ragazza tutta nuda assassinata nel parco/Naked Girl Killed in the Park* (1972) in the 'vetero-Marxist' stronghold of neorealism that was *Cinema Sud* (Luciani, 1972).

These materials comment on the 'dubious' nationality of Italian thrillers and horrors – albeit with completely different purposes to the articles mentioned in the previous paragraphs – and as such can help us to shed some light on the process of 'generification' undergone by these films (Altman, 1999). For example, Italian directors are frequently identified in reference to foreign auteurs: Fulci is labelled as 'the Italian Roger Corman' in a short piece on *Paura nella città dei morti viventi/City of the Living Dead* (1980) in a magazine whose subtitle is 'Rivista mensile dell'industria cinematografica' ('Monthly Cinema Industry Journal') and Margheriti as 'the American of Rome' (Cozzi, 1970b). *Nuovo Cinema Europeo*, another journal directed at international film professionals, also published many of its articles in English; one of these read: 'Dario, the young director dubbed the Italian Hitchcock for his numerous thrillers, has started work on a new film which is shrouded in mystery. In fact, the title is still secret. But we've heard that it's a real horror-story' (1976: 11).

Such references are clearly instrumental in putting the films onto the most suitable shelves of the film market, for the benefit of spectators, theatre owners and distributors. In a film industry characterised by the exploitation of short-lived production cycles aimed at the foreign markets (Wagstaff, 1998) – and within a genre that since the 1960s has enhanced this tendency (Di Chiara, 2010) – it is hardly surprising to find, in the marketing process, explicit claims of non-originality, as well as references to generic standards of other national cinemas, and to previous films of the same director. As *Cinematografia d'oggi* reported in 1972, for example, '[f]ollowing the big success of *The Night Evelyn Came Out of the Grave* [1971], Emilio P. Miraglia has directed a new film, *The Red Queen Kills Seven Times* [1972]. This picture is a *giallo* packed with suspense and features a really prestigious cast.'

When it comes to the only acknowledged auteur of the genre, this strategy of communication becomes even more complicated. Dario Argento is described as a director with a personal style even by those critics who reject his films: they often reproach his presumption of taking inspiration from great foreign directors, though do not deny that he created a new, albeit despicable, trend. The veteran critic Morando Morandini, for example, rounds up all these points in *Cineforum*:

> Italian cinema has learnt from Hollywood at least the lesson of genre [...] The thriller has several followers, but just one champion: Dario Argento, the son of a producer and former film critic, which permits him to state during press conferences that his reference model is Fritz Lang, rather than Hitchcock, without being slapped. (1972: 22–3)

Similar considerations can be found in industrial magazines, too (anonymous 1970b; anonymous, 1971a; anonymous, 1971b). Argento, for his part, verbalises the influences of Lang and Leone in interviews and in promotional material (Cozzi, 1970a), though he also very attentively constructs his own image as a forerunner being pursued by pale imitators. A promotional booklet for *4 mosche di velluto grigio/Four Flies on Grey Velvet* (1971), edited by Luigi Cozzi, is significant from this point of view (Cozzi, 1972). The booklet provides a brief profile of the director, an interview with him, a long synopsis of the film accompanied by many photographs in black and white, information from backstage and details on the two previous films. There is also, however, a long chapter entitled '*Gli imitatori*' ('the imitators'), in which nine films are listed that have allegedly been inspired by the trend inaugurated by Argento, yet which have not matched his results in either artistic terms or box-office success.

The marketing strategy here therefore seems to alter subtly the producer's game described by Rick Altman. The director/producer proudly shows off the elements that define the uniqueness of his work, but at the same time groups together other films that share some narrative and stylistic elements with those of his own – *Una lucertola con la pelle di donna/A Lizard in Woman's Skin* (Lucio Fulci, 1971), *La bestia uccide a sangue freddo/The Beast Kills in Cold Blood* (Fernando Di Leo, 1971), *Una farfalla con le ali insanguinate/ The Bloodstained Butterfly* (Duccio Tessari, 1971), and so on – films which, unlike the original, are doomed to commercial failure. Instead of having the effect of standardising the work of Argento to that of his alleged imitators, this comparison functions as an argument in support of the authority of the director. While the producers, in Altman's framework, are usually not keen to suggest that their films have similarities with others (thus linking them to already existing genres), Argento here also plays 'the critic's game': he does not deny the existence of the genre, but reverses this potential weakness into a strength. In effect, the genre exists because he has created it, therefore making his film different.

GENRE, AUTEURS AND STYLE

The notion of the auteur is far from absent in the debate on genre that animated Anglo-American criticism in the 1970s, a debate that, moreover, was fuelled by the need to 'situate the auteur more systematically (and perhaps more credibly) within the Hollywood set-up' (Hutchings, 1995: 60). One of the most enduring notions, in this sense, is that the auteur plays the role of a genius against the system; that is, an artist able to unhinge – perhaps in subtle and barely perceptible ways – the narrative and representative conventions imposed by the cultural industry. The space for the auteur's manoeuvring is guaranteed by 'the conflict between the movie's pre-text (the script, the source of the adaptation) and its text (all the evidence on the screen and sound track)' (Bourget, 2003: 51). Furthermore, given that genres as discursive structures embody the industry's ideology, the auteur's activity also has a political effect, that to some extent is independent from her/his own personal beliefs. According to Robin Wood, for example, in Alfred Hitchcock's *Shadow of a Doubt* (1943) 'the subversion of ideology within the film is everywhere traceable to Hitchcock's presence, to the skepticism and nihilism that lurk just behind the jocular facade of his public image' (Wood, 2003: 63).

This interpretive framework is also present in the Italian debate, where it moreover affects, albeit to a lesser extent and one mostly devoid of overt ideological connotations, the assessment that some critics give of the horror film. In a review of *5 bambole per la luna d'agosto/Five Dolls for an August Moon* (Mario Bava, 1970) published by *Filmcritica*, for example, Alessandro Cappabianca appreciates the film for its deliberate disregard of the plot and the characters in favour of creating: 'a style beyond what is narrated, beyond the characters, even beyond kitsch and despite kitsch. Standing on the opposite side to the innovators, at a pre-intellectual stage (though doesn't art mean *techne*?), Bava too makes real cinema [*cinema–cinema*]' (1970: 195). *Filmcritica* is the journal in which such a sensitivity to genre film is more common, and indeed it is not by chance that it carried one of the earliest references to Argento as an auteur (Bruno, 1972), as well as one of the few in-depth analyses from this perspective (Della Croce, 1980). The idea, again, is that the director becomes an auteur only if he is able to subvert the codified set of conventions inherited by the genre. In other words, standard tropes of horror films, such as doors opening and thunderclaps, may happen without any narrative justification (and with much unnecessary creaking) as long as 'the cinema of Dario Argento is deliberately crossed by the normative transfiguration of the *eternal laws of cinema*. The most distinct mode of expression, that Dario Argento's cinema has gradually refined, is the rupture of the usual representation of cinematic "reality"' (Della Croce, 1980: 131).

Nevertheless, Argento is more commonly accused of the opposite, that is, of affecting an arty image both in his activity and in his public persona without being able to make his films efficiently work as genuine genre films. In brief, the charge that most critics aimed at him is similar to that made in the same period of Elio Petri (Bisoni, 2011): that of employing a hypertrophic yet basically unmotivated style, with the aggravating circumstance of not knowing (or not correctly applying) the golden rules of the genre. For Guido Fink (1977), the problem with *Suspiria* lies in the recurrence and intensification of its horrific effects, which inevitably leads the director to violate the grammar of a genre that always needs to maintain a minimum level of verisimilitude in its representation.

Comparing *Il gatto a nove code* (1971) with Argento's previous film, Aldo Bernardini argues that 'the tone is considerably lower, due to the coarseness of the detection plot, which doesn't hold water and stumbles upon glaring improbabilities, and to the even more frequent deployment of distasteful, gruesome effects' (Bernardini, 1971). Giacomo Gambetti (1972) rhetorically queried if *4 mosche di velluto grigio* was a 'reversal of the traditional rules of the giallo? A quite explicit statement of who the culprit is, keeping only the "hows" related to his discovery uncertain? In fact, everything remains at the level of a childish B-movie adventure.' In a dual review of *Suspiria* and Brian De Palma's *Carrie* (1976) written by Ermanno Comuzio for *Cineforum*, the Italian director is blamed for having 'a gross idea of *cinema fantastico*, relying entirely on effects and on textual references' (1977: 317). Here De Palma is referred to as a positive model, as he is once again by Piero Sola in *Rivista del Cinematografo*, who argues that, instead of 'revolutionising the mechanisms' of the horror, Argento just 'destroyed them at the root' (1980: 496).

Thus, in the cases discussed above the issue of style as a non-functional element in relation to the narrative (and to the symbolic effects that these films are supposed to achieve) is used either to criticise films and directors or to highlight their ability of elaborating personal traits. It is nevertheless worth noting that the fanzines focusing on horror or *cinema fantastico*, on the other hand, completely reframe the question. In *Proposta SF*, a fanzine dedicated to science fiction narratives, Danilo Arona published a long and pioneering article in which he pinpoints twelve 'recurring topoi of Argento's cinema' (1978: 27). This includes a variety of factors, such as stylistic devices ('the point of view shot', 'a descriptive soundtrack'), narrative registers ('the oneiric dimension'), narrative techniques ('the misleading ending', 'the theme of the painting to which the denouement is related'), thematic issues ('misogyny'), and so on. Teo Mora similarly wrote a piece entitled 'Per una definizione del film di fantasmi' ('For a definition of ghost films') in another short-lived but extremely influential fanzine: *Il falcone maltese*. In it he uses two of Antonio Margheriti's films (*Contronatura/The Unnaturals*, 1969, and *Nella stretta morsa del ragno/Web of the Spider*, 1971) as case studies that reveal the structural elements that inform that specific sub-genre. In his examination, Mora is eager to encompass thematic, visual and ethical components within the notion of style:

> Style is important in the definition of these films [. . .] a delirious baroque taste that finds its expression in overloaded scenic design, in the reddish tones of the cinematography (blood and fire), in the elaborate camera tracking; all elements that turn out to be functional to the themes of these films. (Mora, 1974: 28)

It is evident that these latter articles, in their use of sophisticated tools that draw on structural analysis, are moreover provocative in their intention to treat formerly reviled objects as high culture.

AN ESCAPIST GENRE

While the observations on the relationships between genre and authorship have prevalently focused on the case of Argento, a different critical category ends up being more uniformly applied to horror productions of the time, and especially to those that hold aesthetic or sociological ambitions: the category of escapism. In this case once again, Italian critics prove to be in tune with a way of understanding genre films, and genre generally, which has specific resonance in Anglo-American criticism. This ideological pattern, clearly inspired by the works of Marxist thinkers like Althusser or Horkheimer and Adorno, is reflected, for example, in Judith Hess Wright's assumption that genre films 'relieved the fears aroused by a recognition of social and political conflicts' and 'serve the interests of the ruling class by assisting in the maintenance of the status quo' (1974: 42).

Although not always expressed so effectively, this interpretive framework is used almost obsessively by Italian film journals. Escapism can be viewed in this as affecting the experience of horror film on several levels, which of course overlap each other in practice, but which I will single out for the sake of clarity. First of all, it can be viewed as a problem that is specific to a single film, which either pursues regressive objectives, or, even if designed with the best intentions of societal critique, is not able to achieve its goals because of its flawed ideological and artistic setting. Escapism can otherwise be an effect of the genre as such – as an ideological structure connected to the capitalist mode of production, therefore inevitably doomed to reaffirm the existing power relations (this is the thesis of Hess Wright, at least). Escapism can also be connected to a cinephiliac culture – such as that which emerged in Italy during the 1970s – which, according to its critics, circulates in surreptitious ways a dangerous and regressive concept of art as an autonomous domain by means of notions such as popular and genre.

The first paradigm can be easily found in the reviews published by the Marxist journal *Cinema nuovo*. Led by Guido Aristarco, this journal, notorious for its tireless defence of realism and for the creation of a critical canon that was increasingly concentrated on a small group of major auteurs, devoted constant attention to genre films. They were usually torn to shreds, but almost always analysed with the same serious attitude and the same hermeneutical tools dedicated to the masterpieces of world cinema. In the short review of *L'uccello dalle piume di cristallo*, it is ironically noted that in the film,

> the police are as much efficient as restrained, composed by professionals that modestly and dutifully carry out their job, and will not be late. The detective is perfect: tenacious in the investigation, democratic in his interrogation, clumsy and non-rhetorical during TV interviews, he is also

sympathetic with the murderer, who, after all, is only a lunatic. (anonymous, 1970a)

In longer reviews, however, *Cinema nuovo* contributors often use high-culture references and methodologies taken from the contemporary human sciences in order to disapprove of films belonging to the broad area of the *fantastico*. Giuseppe Peruzzi refers to the critique that Kracauer made of the films of Lang and Murnau in order to assess Corrado Farina's *Hanno cambiato faccia/They Have Changed Their Face* (1971), concluding that 'given these explicitly moralistic and religious terms, the supposed critique of the technological age turns out to be a reactionary discourse, that reinforces long standing prejudices' (1972: 218). The basic narrative premise of many films, that evil is a ubiquitous and pervasive – to some extent invincible – force, is considered regressive per se, allowing the critic to reject any work belonging to the genre. If Peruzzi evoked Kracauer, Franco Prono comments on Giulio Questi's *Arcana* (1972) by borrowing the views of the Italian anthropologist Luigi Lombardi Satriani on folklore as a seemingly popular culture, which was unable to create a real alternative to capitalism (1973). The review of Fulci's *Zombi 2/Zombie Flesh Eaters* (1979) written by Giancarlo Grossini is particularly significant in terms of the critical approach of *Cinema nuovo* to genre films and merits a long quotation:

> Setting the story in American Antilles, from Saint Thomas to the western group of the Virgin Islands, immediately produces in the spectators' minds a total detachment from their own reality, permitting them to believe in what they see only because the 'other world's location is unattainable for the lower-middle class [. . .] In a society like ours, strongly authoritarian in power choices (and not surprisingly lax in terms of displays of violence), there is an attempt to implement a manoeuvre of collective depersonalisation by alienating the public from the real, instead giving shape to depressing thanatological fantasies. Sciascia, in a note contained in *Nero su nero* [1979], says: 'It seems an era of ghosts and monsters is coming. The gloomy supernatural of Chesterton is about to populate the world, to invade it. From the country village [*pagus*] it will reach the metropolis. Inevitably. *El sueño de la razon produce monstruos*'. *Zombi 2* does nothing but reaffirm these reflections: reason falls asleep, monsters and bogey men, employed in repressive infant educational systems, return at the level of adulthood, so as only to sustain, even in the cinema, a puerile state of mind for the average citizen. (Grossini, 1979: 44)

This critical trend can be found not only in Marxist journals like *Cinema nuovo* or *Cinema 60*, in which for example, Francesco Calderone reviews *Arcana* in similar terms to those used by Prono (1972: 56). In *Cineforum*, which also dedicates much space to an analysis of Questi's film (Comuzio et al., 1972: 71–92), Gianluigi Bozza addresses Alberto De Martino's *L'anticristo/ The Antichrist* (1974) as a dangerously escapist film:

> These films contain a series of subcultural models that tend to strengthen certain common sense positions, which in turn serves to legitimise disorder and the problems of the present, projecting the causes into hell. And, if nobody believes in a dumb devil, there is the risk that scientific thought is rejected globally (and not for its ideological use), and that at the same time a mystery idea of madness is accepted, in order to deny the necessity of knowing reality, and therefore of its modification. (1975a: 192)

The pervasiveness of this critical framework is demonstrated by the reviews in the Catholic *Rivista del Cinematografo*. Antonio Mazza, writing about *Arcana*, states that 'many different films are needed to counter the brutal logic of the system' (1972: 502), while Stefan Carlilic accuses *Non si sevizia un paperino/Don't Torture a Duckling* (Lucio Fulci, 1972) of lacking societal and political analysis of Southern Italy's backwardness, and proposes Fleischmann's *Jagdszenen aus Niederbayern/Hunting Scenes from Bavaria* (1969) as a positive model in this regard (1972: 612). And Argento is predictably called into question too, de Torrebruna questioning with *4 mosche di velluto grigio* 'the fact that the culprit is a madman, alien to the norm, reassures viewers inasmuch as they can understand his motivations. Psychoanalysis is thus mystified and exploited in order to please the audience' (de Torrebruna, 1972: 107).

Other critics argue that the responsibility of this escapist tendency is not to be attributed to single films, but to genres that are deliberately designed by capitalistic forces in order to distract the masses and provide substitute pleasures. Bozza links *Profondo rosso* to 'those disaster movies that superholliwood [sic] invented in order to make people forget Saigon and Watergate' (1975b: 179). In *Ombre Rosse*, a leading journal of the extra-parliamentary new left, Paolo Mereghetti writes that the successful films belonging to the 'sado-thrilling', among other genres, 'meet precise requests coming not from an audience whose taste is manipulated, but from capitalism, which needs to survive and to dominate the masses' consciousness' (1972: 82). This leads Mereghetti to consider Argento's signature point-of-view shot, that visually aligns the murderer and viewer's positions, as consistent with the need for dominant culture to let an alienated population give vent to 'the desire to wield power on an object that slips away' (1972: 87). According to others, like Franco La Polla, the escapism of these films, the absence of direct political engagement is the reason for the poor success of the Italian thriller (1976: 119–20).

Finally, beyond specific horror films and genres, the nascent cinephiliac culture was furthermore targeted as a generator of intrinsically escapist forms of cinematic consumption. In 1978, Bergamo's *Centro Studi Cinematografici* organised a workshop dedicated to '*I generi cinematografici nel cinema italiano del dopoguerra*' ('*Film genres in Italian post-war cinema*'). A short but fiery polemic followed in local newspapers, in which the opportunity to talk about genres outside of an academic context is brought into question. According to Sandro Zambetti, then director of *Cineforum*, 'the analysis of genres only disguises, underneath the label of "cultural autonomy", the eternal misunderstanding of the "neutrality of culture", and proposes again as a "new attitude" the return to the old practice of sheltering behind an elitist idea of cinematic specificity"' (Zambetti, 1978: 8). Even franker is Nerio Tebano, a reader of *Cinema nuovo*, who wrote in a letter about the screenings of genre films, organised at the Basilica of Maxentius in Rome by the Communist *assessore* Renato Nicolini, that the ancient monument has become 'the Temple in which the death of a cinema of ideas and social *impegno* is celebrated. [. . .] How ingenuous, today's youth! Haloed by bugaboos, they think they are pursuing the cultural revolution, without realising they are the sitting ducks of capitalism' (Tebano, 1980: 5).

Conclusion

In conclusion, I can only restate my initial assumption: the debate about horror, so long as it is included in the broader category of *fantastico*, is marginal but ubiquitous in the Italian film journals of the 1970s. I have focused on mainstream cinema, but it is worth noting that what we might call a 'horror imagination' seeps also into other areas of film production, such as amateur cinema – as proved by the reviews of some works screened at the Montecatini short film festival (Cine club, 1970: 12) – and experimental cinema (Tiso, 1978).

Critical attention is commonly not focused on the genre as such, whose narrative mechanisms, stylistic devices and social functions are more often taken for granted than analysed, but instead revolves around the works of those directors perceived as exemplar bearers of ideologically regressive or ill-formed messages (Argento, of course, but also Questi, Farina, and even Fulci and De Martino). Less space, which does not mean no space at all, is dedicated to exploitation products. The ideological framework is indifferently employed by Catholic and traditional Marxist journals, and it is through this lens that the observations and assessment of horror films may proceed and be justified. From this point of view, it is revealing that some of the most innovative publications of that period, like *Cinema e cinema* (which bridged the gap between politically engaged and academic criticism, thanks to the works of critics and scholars like Adelio Ferrero, Guido Fink, Franco La Polla and

Leonardo Quaresima) and *Ombre rosse* (whose transformation throughout the 1970s from a *cinephile* journal into a cultural tribune for the new extra-parliamentary left exemplifies the loss of the centrality of cinema in Italian culture) dedicate little or no attention to horror, nor broadly to Italian contemporary genre films.

Disdain does not exclude close textual analysis, which can be found in fanzines like *Proposta SF* and *Il falcone maltese*, but also in the reviews of Grossini for *Cinema nuovo* and Fink for *Bianco e nero*. The difference is that the cinephiliac approach side-lines the aesthetic judgement (which is not removed, but rather implicit in the fact that these films are taken into consideration, and transfigured through a lust for cinema generally, not only for great films), and it moreover obliterates both the direct political readings that are based in content and the ideological concept of genre as a weapon in the service of capitalism. In a context of reception in which the distinction between fandom and academic criticism is definitively less sharp than the British case (Hunter, 2010; Hutchings, 2003), the route for an Italian cult appraisal of Italian horror film in the 1970s is not yet accessible, but has begun to be paved.

BIBLIOGRAPHY

Altman, R. (1999), *Film/Genre*, London: BFI.
Anonymous (1970a), 'L'uccello dalle piume di cristallo', *Cinema nuovo*, 19: 204, p. 138.
Anonymous (1970b), 'Il cinema italiano forza vitale del mercato nazionale', *Cinecorriere – Rivista mensile dell'industria cinematografica*, 33: 9, p. 31.
Anonymous (1970c), '7 luglio Concorso. *Eppure non ne ha colpa* di Lorenzo Poli (Cine Club Padova)', *Cineclub – Federazione italiana dei cineclub*, 8 July 1970, p. 12.
Anonymous (1971a), *Cine spettacolo*, 36: 3–4, p. 32.
Anonymous (1971b), *Cine spettacolo* (1971b), 36: 5–6, p. 4.
Arona, D. (1977), 'Dario Argento', *Proposta SF*, 1: 1, pp. 27–34.
Bachman, E. and Calder Williams, E. (2012), 'Reopening the Matarazzo Case', *Film Quarterly*, 65: 3, pp. 59–65.
Bisoni, C. (2009), *Gli anni affollati*, Rome: Carocci.
Bisoni, C. (2011), *Elio Petri*. Indagine su un cittadino al di sopra di ogni sospetto, Turin: Lindau.
Bourget, J. L. (2003), 'Social Implications in the Hollywood Genres', in Grant, B. K. (ed.), *Film Genre Reader III*, Austin: University of Texas Press, pp. 51–8.
Bozza, G. (1975a), 'L'anticristo', *Cineforum*, 15: 141–2, pp. 191–2.
Bozza, G. (1975b), 'Profondo rosso', *Cineforum*, 15: 145, pp. 178–80.
Bozza, G. (1977), 'Tutti defunti . . . tranne i morti', *Cineforum*, 17: 168, pp. 638–9.
Bruno, E. (1972), 'Quattro mosche', *Filmcritica*, 23: 221, p. 56.
Calderone, F. (1972), 'Arcana', *Cinema 60*, 12: 90, pp. 55–6.
Cappabianca, A. (1970), '5 bambole per la luna d'agosto', *Filmcritica*, 21: 206, pp. 194–5.
Carlilic, S. (1972), 'Non si sevizia un paperino', *Rivista del Cinematografo*, 45: 12, p. 612.
Cinecorriere (1980), 33: 7–8, p. 5.

Cinematografia d'oggi (1972), 8, p. 20.

Codelli, L. (1976), 'Introduzione', in Lippi, G. and Codelli, L. (eds), *Fant'Italia. 1957–1966. Emergenza, apoteosi e riflusso del fantastico nel cinema italiano*, Trieste: Azienda Autonoma di Soggiorno e Turismo – La Cappella Underground, pp. 11–13.

Comuzio, E., Frezzato, A. and Lucato, C. (1972), 'Arcana', *Cineforum*, 12: 114, pp. 71–92.

Comuzio, E. (1977), 'Suspiria e Carrie', *Cineforum*, 17: 164, pp. 316–18.

Cozzi, L. (1970a), 'Dario Argento, il giovane dalle piume di cristallo', *New Cinema*, 9, pp. 15–16.

Cozzi, L. (1970b), 'Antonio Margheriti, l'americano di Roma', *New Cinema*, 12, pp. 112–13.

Cozzi, L. (ed.) (1972), *Quattro mosche di velluto grigio. Il terzo film di Dario Argento*, Milan: Inteuropa.

Della Croce, U. (1980), 'Il "volgare" profuso', *Filmcritica*, 31: 303, pp. 130–3.

de Torrebruna, R. (1972), 'Quattro mosche di velluto grigio', *Rivista del Cinematografo*, 45: 2, pp. 106–7.

Di Chiara, F. (2010), *I tre volti della paura*, Ferrara: UnifePress.

Fink, G. (1977), 'Suspiria', *Bianco e nero*, 38: 1, pp. 106–8.

Gambetti, G. (1972), 'Quattro mosche di velluto grigio', *Bianco e nero*, 33: 7–8, p. 50.

Grossini, G. (1975), 'Il mostro è in tavola . . . Barone Frankenstein', *Cinema nuovo*, 24: 235–6, pp. 267–8.

Grossini, G. (1979), 'Zombi 2', *Cinema nuovo*, 28: 262, pp. 43–4.

Hess Wright, J. (2003), 'Genre Films and the Status Quo', in Grant, B. K. (ed.), *Film Genre Reader III*, Austin: University of Texas Press, pp. 42–50.

Hunter, R. (2010), '"Didn't you used to be Dario Argento? The Cult Reception of Dario Argento', in Hope, W. (ed.), *Italian Film Directors in the New Millennium*, Newcastle: Cambridge Scholars Press, pp. 63–74.

Hutchings, P. (1995), 'Genre theory and criticism', in Hollows, J. and Jancovich, M. (eds), *Approaches to Popular Film*, Manchester: Manchester University Press, pp. 59–78.

Hutchings, P. (2003), 'The Argento Effect', in Jancovich, M., Làzaro-Reboll, A., Stringer, J. and Willis, A. (eds), *Defining Cult Movies: the Cultural Politics of Oppositional Taste*, Manchester: Manchester University Press, pp. 127–41.

La Polla, F. (1976), 'Il genere come sottoprodotto', *Cinema e cinema*, 3: 7–8. pp. 114–20.

Luciani, F. (1972), 'Enigmatismo e "suspense" nuovo filone della produzione italiana', *Cinema Sud*, 14: 55, p. 24.

Mazza, A. (1972), 'Arcana', *Rivista del Cinematografo*, 45: 10, pp. 501–2.

Mereghetti, P. (1972), 'Kitsch all'italiana', *Ombre rosse* n.s., 2, pp. 82–90.

Mora, T. (1974), 'Per una definizione del film di fantasmi', *Il falcone maltese*, 1: 2, pp. 27–9.

Mora, T. (1978), *Storia del cinema dell'orrore*, Vol. 2, Part 2, Rome: Fanucci.

Morandini, M. (1972), 'Il vecchio e il nuovo nella produzione odierna', *Cineforum*, 12: 117, pp. 13–24.

Neale, S. (1999), *Genre and Hollywood*, London and New York: Routledge.

Peruzzi, G. (1972), 'Hanno cambiato faccia', *Cinema nuovo*, 21: 217, pp. 216–18.

Pironi, G. (1977) 'Cinema italiano '77: una stagnazione non solo economica', *Cineforum*, 17: 170, pp. 723–31.

Porro, M. (1977), 'La casa dalle finestre che ridono', *Cineforum*, 17: 162, pp. 153–4.

Prono, F. (1973), 'Arcana', *Cinema nuovo*, 22: 226, pp. 453–4.

Pruzzo, P. (1977), 'La casa dalle finestre che ridono', *Rivista del Cinematografo*, 50: 1–2, pp. 41–2.
Quargnolo, M. (1971), 'Il gatto a nove code. Una Lucertola con la pelle di donna', *CM*, 1: 1, pp. 71–2.
Sola, P. (1980), 'All'inferno e dintorni', *Rivista del Cinematografo*, 53: 8–9, pp. 495–7.
Tebano, N. (1980), 'La conquista del palazzo per l'esercizio del disimpegno', *Cinema nuovo*, 29: 264, p. 5.
Tiso, C. (1978), 'Anche l'estasi: cinefobia, cinefollia, altri fantasmi', *Filmcritica*, 29: 286, pp. 219–27.
Wagstaff, C. (1998), 'Italian genre films in the world market', in Nowell-Smith, G. and Ricci, S. (eds), *Hollywood and Europe. Economics, Cultural, National Identity 1945–1995*, London: BFI, pp. 74–85.
Wood, R. (2003), 'Ideology, Genre, Auteur', in Grant, B. K. (ed.), *Film Genre Reader III*, Austin: University of Texas Press, pp. 60–74.
Zambetti, S. (1978), 'La lettera di Zambetti al *Giornale di Bergamo*', *Centro Studi Cinematografici. Notiziario*, 11: 5, p. 8.

INDEX